K

240199007550
24-1-2000 *

KT-435-831

20 038 91

Transforming Managers

351.
41
(Tra)

WITHDRAWN

WITHDRAWN

Gender, change and society

Series editors: David Morgan, Department of Sociology, University of Manchester, UK and Gail Hawkes, Department of Sociology and Interdisciplinary Studies, Manchester Metropolitan University, UK.

Books in the series include:

Transforming Managers
Gendering Change in the Public Sector

Stephen Whitehead

Keele University

Roy Moodley

Sheffield University

© Stephen Whitehead, Roy Moodley and contributors, 1999

This book is copyright under the Berne Convention.
No reproduction without permission.
All rights reserved.

First published in 1999 by UCL Press

UCL Press Limited
A member of the Taylor & Francis Group
11 New Fetter Lane
London EC4P 4EE
UK

Simultaneously published in the USA and Canada
by Routledge
29 West 35th Street, New York, NY 10001

The name of University College London (UCL) is a registered trade mark used by UCL Press
with the consent of the owner.

British Library Cataloguing-in-Publication Data
A CIP catalogue record for this book is available from the British Library.

Library of Congress Cataloging-in-Publication Data are available

ISBNs: 1–85728–875–0 HB
       1–85728–876–9 PB

UNIVERSITY OF
NORTHUMBRIA AT NEWCASTLE
LIBRARY

ITEM No.	CLASS No.
20 0389 1102	301 · H1 TRA

Typeset by Graphicraft Limited, Hong Kong
Printed by T.J. International, Padstow, UK

In loving memory of Soraya Georgette

Contents

Notes on contributors

Joanna Brewis is Senior Lecturer in Organizational Behaviour at the University of Portsmouth Business School. Her research interests centre mainly on gender, sex and sexuality in organizations. Current projects include women's bodies at work, and time, place and identity in prostitution (the latter with Stephen Linstead of the University of Sunderland). Joanna has published in journals including *Gender, Work and Organization*, *Management Learning* and *Human Relations*.

John Clark works in a business school, where he runs change management and personal development programmes for managers. He is an active governor in a secondary school. His research interests include the use of action inquiry with managers responding to change and the application of Foucault's work to issues of discipline, self and gender in organizational analysis and management development. For his doctoral research he is based at the Centre for Action Research in Professional Practice, Bath University.

Rosemary Deem is Professor of Educational Research, Director of the Social Science Graduate School and a member of the Institute for Women's Studies at Lancaster University. She was head of the Department of Educational Research from 1992 to 1994 and Dean of Social Science from 1994 to 1997. Her research interests include gender, culture and organizations, feminist approaches to research, women's leisure, and educational governance and management. She is currently directing an Economic and Social Research Council funded project entitled " 'New managerialism' and the management of universities", with three Lancaster colleagues.

Jeff Hearn is Professorial Research Fellow in the Faculty of Economic and Social Studies, University of Manchester, UK; Donner Visiting Professor in Sociology with particular reference to Gender Research, Abo Akademi University, Finland; and Visiting Professor II, University of Oslo, Norway. His publications include *"Sex" at "Work"* (with Wendy Parkin, Harvester Wheatsheaf/St. Martin's, 1998; rev. edn 1995) and *The Gender of Oppression* (Wheatsheaf/St. Martin's, 1987) and he has co-edited *The Sexuality of Organization* (Sage, 1989), *Taking Child Abuse Seriously* (Unwin Hyman, 1990), *Men, Masculinities and Social Theory* (Unwin Hyman, 1990), *Violence and Gender Relations* (Sage, 1986), *Men as Managers, Managers as Men* (Sage, 1996) and *Men, Gender Divisions and Welfare* (Routledge, 1998).

Deborah Kerfoot is Lecturer in Organizational Analysis at the School of Business and Economic Studies at the University of Leeds. Her research interests and publications are in the fields of: the sociology and critical study of management, work and organization; empirical research on employment and management practices; post-structuralism; and gender and sexuality in organizations. Having recently worked on an ESRC-funded project on the management of change, she is currently engaging in critical work on total quality management and HRM, in addition to a co-authored book, *Management, Masculinity and Organisation*, under contract with Sage. Deborah Kerfoot is the book review editor for the *Journal of Management Studies* and an associate editor of *Gender, Work and Organization*, both published by Blackwell.

David Knights is Professor of Organizational Analysis in the Department of Management at Keele University. His research interests and publications are in the fields of management strategy and control, the management of information technology, equal opportunity, and theoretical contributions to debates on power, managerialism and subjectivity. He is co-editor of *Gender, Work and Organization*. Recent books include: *Managers Divided: Organizational Politics and IT*, with F. Murray; *Financial Service Institutions and Social Transformation*, co-edited with T. Tinker; and *Resistance and Power in Organizations*, co-edited with J. Jermier and W. Nord.

Stella Maile is a Senior Lecturer and Research Fellow in the Faculty of Economics and Social Science at the University of the West of England (UWE), Bristol. She has gained a PhD in Sociology of Work and Organisation from the University of Bristol, focused upon managerial discourses and local authority restructuring. This developed out of her insight from a variety of employment experiences in both public and private work environments. These research interests are being further developed in relation to an exploration of emerging forms of governance in the global economy. To complement this, Stella is Director of the Corporate and Global Governance Research Group based at UWE.

Diane Meehan is Director of the School of Computing and Mathematical Sciences at Liverpool John Moores University. She entered higher education as an academic in 1986 and completed her PhD as a "mature student" in 1993. Diane moved into management in 1993. While her main research interests are in the field of computing, she is interested in and concerned about the position of women academics in higher education.

Roy Moodley is currently a freelance trainer in "race", psychotherapy and counselling and is also completing a PhD at the University of Sheffield. He was Assistant

Director for Research and Development at Thomas Danby College, Leeds. Research interests include: "race", gender, disability in psychoanalysis, psychotherapy and counselling; black students and staff in further and higher education; "race", culture and ethnicity issues in management.

Jenny Ozga is Professor of Education Policy at Keele University. Before that, she was Dean of the Faculty of Education at the University of the West of England, Bristol, and worked for many years for the Open University. She has also worked for the National Union of Teachers. Her main areas of writing and research are concerned with understanding education policy, and with teachers' work and the historical and contemporary development of state policy for the teaching labour force. As a result of illuminating experience gained in attempting to combine academic work and management, she has become particularly interested in gender issues in management.

Lesley Thom worked for many years as a teacher, lecturer and educational manager, before starting her own business as a trainer and educational consultant. In addition to running courses on women in management, assertiveness, and related issues, she works for the Qualifications and Curriculum Authority and is an Associate Inspector for the Training Standards Council. Lesley is particularly interested in researching the covert and overt barriers to personal and career progress for women and men. She is currently completing a PhD on the subject of gender and educational management.

Lynne Walker is Associate Dean in the Faculty of Education at the University of the West of England, Bristol. She has held a number of management posts in schools, a local education authority and higher education. She has developed her interest in the management of education, particularly gender, sexuality and management, through teaching, consultancy, training activities and writing.

Stephen Whitehead is Lecturer in Postcompulsory Education at Keele University. His research interests and publications concern the critical study of men and masculinities; empirical research into gender and further education management; post-structuralism; and subjectivities, epistemologies and identities in organizations. He is currently researching changing forms of postcompulsory education management.

Foreword

In this collection, which originated in a conference in Leeds, we see the convergence of several areas of concern. The first is, of course, gender and the recognition that the study of and theorizing about gender has changed just as the relations of men and women – in and out of the labour market – have themselves undergone dramatic transformations. One major change is the growing recognition that the term "gender" includes men as well as women, and that this is not simply a question of adding men to the analysis, but of exploring the multiple and complex patterns of inter-relationships between genders in different sites. Another significant development is the increasing willingness to see gender as a process, rather than as a thing or a bundle of relatively fixed characteristics. The increasing use of the term "gendering" to refer to the way in which gendered understandings develop over an increasingly wide range of institutions and practices is an important aspect of this more fluid and dynamic approach.

The other key area represented in this volume is management. This itself has become a dominant discourse within modern society; some bookshops, indeed, have sections labelled "Popular Management". It is seen as an area of specialized expertise and the object of numerous educational institutions, training courses and textbooks, with a growing specialized language and an increasing number of gurus. Yet it has also become a contested discourse, and in some contexts the term "managerialism" is a ready-made term of abuse. Part of the debate around management and man-agerialism has been the question of gender, seeing this not simply in terms of equal opportunities and glass ceilings but also in examining the very terms of the debates and the extent to which the principles and practices of organizations can themselves be understood in gendered terms.

The third element here is to do with the public sector. While, as the editors argue, much of the debate reflected here could readily apply across a wide range of institu-tions, all of the contributors have, at some time or another, worked in the public sector. It does not need to be emphasized that this sector too has undergone con-siderable upheaval and challenge in recent years, and that this sense of turbulence is by no means over. People who work in this sector can be in no doubt that their particular sections – education, social services or health – are heavily implicated in wider economic and social transformations. Within this context, questions of management take on new meanings and new significances. At the same time, increasing recognition is being given to the gendered character of the transformations that are taking place, even where such considerations may sometimes become obscured under apparently neutral labels to do with efficiency or quality.

This volume explores the ways in which gender, management and the public sector interact with each other in this particular period in our history. Perhaps of particular importance here is the emphasis given to the interplays between social and organizational transformations and personal experience. C. Wright Mills' desire to see the development of imaginative linkings between history and biography is manifested in many of the contributions to this important collection. It is hoped that people currently working in the public sector (and beyond) will have the opportunity to read this volume and to take these debates about gender and management further.

David H.J. Morgan
University of Manchester

Acknowledgements

The impetus for this volume came from the conference "Men in Management: Changing Cultures of Education", held in 1995 under the auspices of Thomas Danby FE College, Leeds. We would like to thank all of the contributors to that conference together with those who played a role in its planning, organization and execution, in particular our then work colleagues: Karen Llewellyn, John Allen, Abby Cathcart, Lisa Clarke, Alan Edgar, Peter Fereday, Kevin Hylton, Linda Khammo, Mike Lewis, Vikki Slee, Gordon Wood and Judith Wright. We also thank Sheila Scraton for advice in initiating the conference. We owe a particular debt to the series editor, David Morgan, without whose help this volume would not have materialized. Also, we offer thanks to Caroline Wintersgill and Claire Hart of UCL Press, for their good advice and professional support. The experience of producing this volume has been one of collaboration, and we are grateful to all of the contributors for their efforts in helping the project to fruition; in particular, Jeff Hearn who has been a good friend throughout. Finally, and certainly not least, our very special thanks go to Anissa Talahite and Deborah Kerfoot for supporting us intellectually, emotionally – and patiently!

Leeds
January 1999

CHAPTER ONE

Introduction: locating personal and political transformations

Stephen Whitehead & Roy Moodley

It is increasingly apparent that the end of the twentieth century marks an epoch of change, transformation and discontinuity. What once appeared "solid" has indeed now "melted into air". Whether one perceives this to be merely characteristic of the information society, post-industrialization, late modernity or similar end-of-millennium phenomena, the sense of ending – and new beginning – is acute. And no area of life is immune. In politics pragmatism replaces ideology; religions compete like products on a supermarket shelf; cultural relativism displaces cultural supremacy; heroes and heroines, few as they are, have only their Warhol-inscribed "15 minutes"; and new managerialism asserts its eminence over the charismatic leader. While all are affected by these social shifts, it is, arguably, those in employment, or seeking employment, who feel the cold draught of insecurity most. For whatever certainties and securities organizational life once held are now long gone. Organizational change has become ceaseless, unpredictable and remorseless, especially in the so-called "public services". No one is immune from "downsizing", no one is safe; certainly few feel safe. Thus it is one of the great ironies of the age that modern management has achieved something of a cult status at a time when social phenomena – and individuals – appear increasingly amorphous, complex and unfathomable. For men and women are not only grappling with organizational transformation; their very identity as gendered beings is also subject to question and scrutiny. What it means to be a man or a woman has never been less distinct nor more fluid. As traditional gender codes flounder in the face of social movement, new and multiple ways of being male or female have surfaced, an experience that some find exciting, and others disturbing. For of all the rocks on which we build a "core identity", gender and sexuality can appear the most solid, the most fixed, the most secure. Moreover, gender identity is, for many, reinforced by the gendered constitution of organizational life itself; the codes and orthodoxies of the workplace providing, albeit tentatively, the opportunity to fashion our identities in the public sphere – to "confirm" who we are. Organizationally, we may be managers, cleaners, secretaries or technicians, but when we walk into a room what do others see? Is it not the gender of the subject,

1

and the colour if you happen to be black, that marks you out, that labels, categorizes and distinguishes – all before a word is spoken or a deed is done? Thus the turn of the millennium is not only a time of social transformation; for many it is simultaneously a time of profound personal disruption.

As critical gender theorists have long noted, to be a woman or a man is to be a culturally embodied signifier of a collective identity, to exist in a gendered landscape in which notions of femininity and masculinity appear static – and often invisible. Yet it is also apparent that notions of gender are under constant revision; they shift, albeit slowly, but shift nonetheless. But what, if any, is the drive, the reasoning, the logic, behind these transformations? And how do individuals experience these movements? Masculinity and femininity may be spatially and temporally located tools in identity work, but are they tools that we choose in any rational or reasoned way? Moreover, despite the impermanence of being, the dominance of men and masculinism in organizations appears to be particularly resistant to change of either a micro- or macro-variety. Indeed, as this volume stresses, there is as yet little evidence to support the notion of a post-feminist era, certainly in so far as management is concerned. Given this, how are individual women and men working through these political and personal tensions? What sense do individuals make of this managerial and organizational landscape?

These are the key questions that inform this volume. In the process, an important debate is engaged concerning gender, change, dominance, resistance and management: in short, the critical study of the often random, generally unpredictable, yet political (gender) transformations that occur in public-sector management and, importantly, how individuals experience, "manage" and in part determine these movements. Although empirically based in the public sector, the writings speak to all institutional sites and, indeed, beyond the institutional setting.

It is, we consider, an apposite moment to construct such a study, given the rapidity of change in managerial practices and in the lives of those men and women who are managers. As many commentators have observed, the end of the twentieth century appears to be, "feels", a time of deep-rooted insecurity, if not chaos: the demise of grand narratives, the "end of order", a time of risk (Lyotard 1984, Giddens 1991, Bauman 1992, Beck 1992, Fukuyama 1997). Correspondingly, it is an era in which managers, most of whom are men, search ever more desperately for systems of control; mechanisms, often covert, that "promise" conclusiveness and closure. This lust for certainty is as much a personal quest for assurance – and identity – as it is an organizational objective. For like the casino gambler, managers are increasingly forced to place their reputations and futures against the unknown and unquantifiable; to carry the risk. Thus the search for the verifiable and the infallible becomes both endless and yet necessary. This inevitably futile quest requires that managers invest much time, energy and effort in the pursuit of objective absolute "truths". Witness, for example, the increasing use of graphological and psychometrical profiling of applicants and employees; the endless search for "total quality management"; the now ubiquitous, yet oxymoronic, human resource management; and the often banal manifestations of evangelical corporate culture visited on unsuspecting employees. Not surprisingly, across both public and private sectors, these "modern management

2

techniques" have been promoted as the panacea for the chaos and insecurity that lurks behind managerial rhetoric and managers' expressions of self-belief. Companies, individuals and indeed academia itself have been quick to note the opportunities here. Management consultancy is now a growth area, and academics are increasingly prepared (at a price) to lend an air of professional credibility to the latest jargon or orthodoxy of modern management. Indeed, there are now many academics lucratively employed in devising and promoting "solutions" to the insoluble problems of management and organization. Yet despite recourse to both bizarre and sophisticated managerial practices, permanence and certainty remain ever elusive. Employee resistance continues to manifest itself in the most unpredictable and subversive ways, even (especially?) in the most avidly managerialist cultures.

But what are the consequences and effects of new managerialist practices on individuals? Does not the quest for total control damage many, both inside and outside the organization? In Chapter 4, Lesley Thom suggests that the emergent masculinist managerial culture that is now apparent in secondary education has had an adverse effect on women's opportunities for advancement. Similarly, Diane Meehan (Ch. 3) highlights the various ways in which a (male-dominated) organizational culture acts as a powerful variable and influence on women managers' behaviour. But neither are men managers protected from the practices that they invest in so heavily. As Deborah Kerfoot discusses in Chapter 11, one effect of this avid instrumentalism is to encourage many men managers to avoid or displace emotional intimacy, fearing its disruptive consequences for them as masculine/managerial subjects, an action which only further problematizes their relationship to others.

But why is the fact of change, unpredictability and contingency so problematic for managers and many men? Is it, as Stella Maile (Ch. 9) suggests, because many men managers find change, especially in relation to shifting gender relationships, so threatening, confusing and indeed incompatible with who they are as managers and men? For what is a man, or manager, if not someone in control; a gendered subject "at ease" with himself in his paternalistic perception of women and others? Recognizing this, it is little surprise that the descriptor "arena" fits so comfortably with organizational life; the internal and external competitiveness, combat and calculation all engaged in, to some degree, by the organizational subject. But, paradoxically, it is increasingly evident that this combative approach to organizational life is underpinned for many men managers by a constant and deep-rooted fear of failure – as men and as managers (Deborah Kerfoot and David Knights, Ch. 12). To reiterate, when women and men enter the organizational arena they enter not as neutral individuals but as prior gendered beings; actors in a social and political arena grounded only in its incessant unpredictability.

The chapters in this book are not, however, merely accounts of change, for they are themselves the products of change and personal transformation: the outcomes of political and social upheavals that make a nonsense of any notion of neat and tidy public and private separations, linearity, or fixed, categorical compartmentalizations. Consequently, each chapter marks change, not just in the particular theory or sector of work being researched and described, but also in the writers themselves. It is impossible, indeed inappropriate, to explicate these individual movements precisely, although some – for example, John Clark's account (Ch. 10) of being a man/manager during a period of organizational conflict – are recounted in some depth. What is evident is that none of the contributors to this volume writes as a disembodied individual. How could they? Their very purpose in writing is to offer a personal/political position or standpoint, born of and sculptured by the often random, yet powerful, experiences of being a woman or man in diverse organizational, social and cultural settings. Consequently, in every chapter there is something of the writer, a residual element which, it is hoped, will reach out to and resonate with the reader – the most important part of this particular intersubjective configuration. It is worth, then, reflecting on this book's genealogy and our part in that, for in so doing are revealed some of the macrostructural factors and the intersubjective moments that in complex combination constitute the social web in which we all exist.

Influences and movements

In May 1995, an undistinguished, medium-sized further education (FE) college in Leeds held an international conference titled, "Men in Management: Changing Cultures of Education". At a time when the FE sector was experiencing major shifts in work culture and ethos, a small number of people in one FE college created space for the articulation of an alternative discourse; the critical relationship between men, masculinities, organizational culture and education management. Many of the chapters in this volume were originally papers presented at that conference, and most of this book's contributors had some involvement as speakers, presenters or seminar coordinators. Despite extensive advertising across the education sector, the conference, not surprisingly perhaps, attracted few men managers. Nevertheless, on reflection, we like to think that it was a successful event. It was certainly enjoyable and informative. And clearly, as organizers, the conference was important for us personally, politically and professionally. Yet there was another significance, for unbeknown to us at the time it marked our swan-song from FE. In the autumn of 1995 we both took voluntary redundancy from that FE college, uncertain as to the future but undoubtedly relieved to be out of the Kafkaesque nightmare into which the sector was, by then, fast degenerating. Does this sound bitter? Well, to be fair there is an element of that. Certainly, like many in FE, we found the radical transformations in organizational culture following incorporation in April 1993[1] profoundly disturbing and often depressing, if not threatening and stressful. Yet it had not always been so. Our experience of FE from entering the profession in the late 1980s was of working in a public-sector site which continued to receive some sense of legitimacy from a liberal, humanistic discourse; framed by notions of student empowerment, access for all and educational opportunity. Archaic or simplistic as it may sound ten years on, like many in FE over the years we wanted to put something back into the community, and working in post-compulsory education provided us with a sense of purpose, as well as some significant material comfort. What the students gained is of course for them to say, but – as is so often the case in education – they had, as now, little concrete opportunity to influence events. For to be sure, pre-incorporated FE was no golden age. As one of us has written elsewhere (Whitehead 1999b), the sector was always riven with gender differentials, petty power struggles and vested interests. To be precise, FE was very much like the public sector generally: heavily bureaucratic, unresponsive, at times frustratingly arrogant and self-important, and this despite being characterized by the notion of public accountability and grounded in a public-service ethos. No, it was certainly no golden age. So, you may rightly (cynically?) ask, "What exactly has changed?"

Well, surprisingly, quite a lot. Many of the characteristics that signalled the transformations occurring in education and the public sector generally during the 1980s and 1990s – specifically their relationship to gender dynamics – will be discussed in the following chapters. It is useful though, at this juncture, to identify certain macrostructural influences, for these have had a profound, arguably chaotic, impact on public services in this, and most other European/American/Australasian countries, during the past two decades. These influences or forces include the now ubiquitous, New Right, market-managed ideology (Ball 1990, Tomlinson 1993, Farnham and Horton 1996); new managerialisms imported (not necessarily intact) from the private sector (Pollitt 1993, Warner and Crosthwaite 1995); the variant conditions that mark post-industrialization and post-Fordism (Harvey 1991, Kumar 1995); postmodernity (Bauman 1992, Usher and Edwards 1994); middle England's culture of contentment (Galbraith 1992); shifting patterns of work and leisure (Hewitt 1993, Rojek 1995); an increasing polarization of poverty and wealth (Hutton 1995); new privileged knowledges (Lyotard 1984); new privileged work skills (Reich 1991, Handy 1994); and, of course, significant shifts in traditional notions of masculinity and femininity. These movements and influences were, and remain, interconnected, indeed often interreliant. However, rather than perceiving them as the predetermined or pre-ordained outcomes of some larger instrumental rational process, we are much more comfortable in locating them as prominent parts of the pot-pourri configuring the late twentieth century: mostly unplanned, quite unpredictable in their effects and tenuous rather than consistent.

Whether one considers the origins and characteristics of these transforming forces to be primarily ideological or discursive (or both), there is no denying their power. Nobody in paid employment, indeed nobody at all, is exempt from their impact. There is no hiding place: neither wealth nor poverty, nor education or ignorance, will provide a safe haven. And that is an important point, for while, as critical enquirers, we might talk with some confidence of macrostructural forces, the precise impact that these have had at the level of the individual – indeed, how individuals do themselves constitute them – is of course more difficult to discern: a tantalisingly elusive moment of transformation.

As middle-aged, middle-class, educated men, albeit one black and one white, we felt the impact of these transforming forces no less than other persons. And one cannot prepare for this. To reiterate, protection is limited. Inevitably, however, for us, some aspects appeared to be more influential than others. For the sake of brevity, we will refer to just two, both interconnected and both clearly relevant to this volume: feminism and managerialism.

5

The felt impact of feminism

When we entered education management in the late 1980s, neither of us could be described as (pro)feminists. In our different ways we each had a critical perspective on, for example, organizational life, political processes, equal opportunities and so on, but we remained very much the "invisible gendered subject" (Whitehead 1998). Partly, this was born of our different backgrounds – very different backgrounds. Roy, a black South African, was an activist against the repressive regime in the 1970s, with a personal/political awareness born out of direct experience of apartheid, racism and cultural imperialism. Stephen was the issue of white upper-working-class parents, shopkeepers, for whom university was considered a second-best option to "making your own way in the world" (a euphemism for self-employment): thus each, in his own way, came to "know his place" in social and cultural hierarchies into which he was born. During our first four decades, we learnt, assimilated, progressed and developed, along the way exercising and experimenting with our sexuality, our emotions – and our identities. Careers, marriages, children, relationships, build-ups and break-ups – the very stuff of life ensued: nothing particularly unique, in fact.

For us, as for many men, it was a journey that both opened and closed doors, for one cannot wash away one's colour; one cannot totally exorcise a cultural and social history. Indeed, why would one wish to? Are not these aspects the very material of our "self" construction, the theatrical costumes that adorn our Goffmanesque display of self? But what of gender – that unseen yet omnipresent sense of self? Suddenly this is more problematic, for to shift one's subjective position and to take on the mantle of oppressor is not so straightforward. It is one thing to be a working-class Marxist or to be a anti-racist black person. But to be a man and a profeminist? Michael Kimmel captures the dilemma quite succinctly:

> When I look in the mirror . . . I see a human being – a white middle-class male – gender is invisible to me because that is where I am privileged. I am the norm. I believe most men do not know they have a gender. (Kimmel, cited in Middleton 1992: 11)

As Middleton observes, the notion of the male self-reflexive subject is problematic because "men don't see what they are seeing when they see themselves" (ibid.: 11): a gender-invisible state assisted by many men's apparent propensity for compartmentalizing emotions, feelings and, moreover, public and private experiences (see Seidler 1997).

So how did we come to "see ourselves"? What influences wrought this particular and profound change? The detail is possibly another story for another occasion, for this is not a process that is ever final, or indeed holistic. Certainly, we would concur with Middleton that any attempt by men at reconstituting their male subjectivity is difficult, emotional, ego-laden and can only ever be partial. Indeed, as Roy Moodley (Ch. 13) observes, is not male (inter)subjectivity often nothing more or less than the attempt to reorder the inherent fragility of masculinity behind the "mask" of dominant gendered discourse?

Yet it is also important to recognize that some change did occur. This is not to suggest that in Hegelian terms we came to self-knowledge, but that rather, as discursive subjects, we became inculcated by alternative discourses, which each of us in his own way has (largely unknowingly) reshaped and reconstituted. Feminist thought did impact, did influence and did change our perceptions – and our lives. Women, events, writings and other men, including each other, moved us and in the process made us profoundly, indeed uncomfortably, aware of the gender differentials and inequalities that, to varying degrees, constitute "reality" for all subjects – ourselves included.

In locating ourselves as such, it is not our intention to suggest that moving to a profeminist standpoint is straightforward. As Morgan (1992) and Hearn (1993) note, there are many tensions and ambiguities for men in feminism (see also Hall 1990), not least of which is: how does a man "step outside" that which "he is"? Becoming a profeminist was never (and never can be?) "embarked on" as a rational or instrumental process. Nor does it promise much material advantage. On the contrary, once our perceptions of the organization, and us as managers in it, became more deeply rooted in a critical understanding of men and masculinity, so we found it increasingly difficult to engage in the new FE work culture. For although, as Jeff Hearn notes in Chapter 8, it is possible to be a profeminist and a manager, this particular combination of subject positions is, we consider, difficult to sustain in today's FE. The tensions that arise from these contradictory positions are acute, more so for women feminist academic managers, a point explored in depth by Rosemary Deem in Chapter 5. Certainly, our experience was that in a few short years we went from being pioneers in the organization to being escapees and, for a time at least, refugees. In stating this, we are neither presenting nor offering some privileged personal/political position, nor claiming a moral superiority. We are not the first men to be influenced by feminists and feminism, and certainly not the first middle-class men academics to write about this experience (see, for example, Tolson 1977, Jackson 1990, Stoltenberg 1990, Hearn 1992, Morgan 1992, Rutherford 1992, Seidler 1997).

The point that we wish to stress is that this volume exists only in relation to the variant, unique experiences of each contributor – there being no clear separation between subject and object; nor, for that matter, between structure and agency. Similarly, neither are the connections between men, women, gender identities and the local and macro-politics of organizational life discrete. As Jo Brewis (Ch. 6) stresses, the embodied experience of being a gendered subject is crucial to understanding how work relations, and feminine identities, are transformed, reconstituted and sustained.

As this book aims to demonstrate, the gendered and sexualized interrelationships of organizational life, while powerful, remain fluid, contingent and under constant renegotiation by (partially) knowing subjects. Although the volume has its own unique history, one informed and framed by feminism and subsequently by a critical understanding of men and masculinities, the process was largely random and unplanned. We did not sit down and decide to edit such a volume: it grew out of our experience of the changing world of FE and the various discursive formations which were prominent in our lives during the early 1990s. It was not a managed transformation. We are still very much in it, as are all the contributors. We are not claiming prior knowledge, nor the autonomy of the rational, reasoned individual. Indeed, we suggest such an individual to be illusory, grounded only in the masculine/feminine dialectic of modernism (for elaboration, see Seidler 1994).

There is, then, some irony in reflecting back on the past decade and perceiving, subjectively, the dynamic configuration of different, sometimes conflicting, discourses and seeing ourselves, no less than other subjects, caught (still) in this vortex; not managing it, but merely responding and very occasionally being proactive. For it is this configuration that the contributors aim to pin down, and subsequently critically address; that is, the unique, complex and dynamic shifts in both management and organizational culture that have come to characterize the public sector during the past decade. Importantly, this period of significant transformation has occurred at an historic moment in shifts in women's subjectivities and gender awareness generally. These parallel discursive movements deserve to be blended and closely examined, for although they may appear to be unrelated at first sight, they are not. However, to enable any critical examination to occur it is necessary to utilize appropriate theoretical tools and, paradoxically, it is feminist scholarship that in this instance provides them. For at the very moment that the public sector has experienced often harsh, political, cultural and gendered transformations, alternative discourses have come to prominence; perspectives that critically locate this transformation by recognizing the personal and political diversity of gendered experience in organizational life.

Feminism and critiques of management and organizational life

Feminism and feminist writing has been around for many decades, with feminist scholarship now encompassing numerous strands. The foundations of this "movement" have beginnings in the eighteenth-century scholarship of Mary Wollstonecraft, the nineteenth-century writing of John Stuart Mill, and the mid-twentieth-century work of Simone de Beauvoir and Betty Freidan. However, it has been the final third of this century that has seen the discourses of feminism emerge to power and prominence, arguably transforming – certainly influencing – the *Zeitgeist* of the late or postmodern era. Since the early 1970s, feminist theories have proliferated; coming to encompass, for example, the radical feminism of Andrea Dworkin; the Marxist feminism of Michell Barrett; the socialist feminism of Heidi Hartmann; the psychoanalytical feminism exemplified by Nancy Chodorow; and the more recent postmodern, poststructuralist feminism reflected in the writings of Judith Butler (for elaboration, see Chafetz 1988, Tong 1994).

The sheer energy of this scholarship, coupled with its personal/political implications, has had profound consequences in all corners of the globe, although the impact on Western epistemological forms has been especially significant. For feminism has emerged as, arguably, the most subversive and influential expression of critical thinking this century, challenging not just malestream sociology (see O'Brien 1981, see also Morgan 1981), but coming to transform the everyday practices and expectations of countless women, and – albeit often by default – many men. It is a process of change that is far from exhausted: indeed for many, particularly men, it is just beginning. Given form and direction by critical academic enquiry, the wider impact of feminism has been, then, to privilege feminist/womanist epistemologies and ontologies, ways of thinking and being that create spaces for women's diverse identities and experiences while subverting masculinist ideology.[2]

One direct consequence of this burgeoning feminist enquiry has been to leave uncritiqued few sites previously solely occupied by male perspectives and values, the study of management and organizational life being no exception. Some of the first feminist explorations into these gendered arenas were those undertaken by Acker and Van Houten (1974), Kanter (1977) and Wolfe (1977). Kanter's work especially has stood the test of time in relation to shifts in critical organizational theory. In particular, her theory of "proportionality"[3] remains both topical and highly relevant for understanding the masculinization of organizational culture (see Cheng 1996). These works, and others (see also Mills and Tancred 1992), began the process of exposing the previously hidden, symbiotically gendered relationships, existing in, indeed arguably sustaining, the public sphere of paid employment. Mirroring the various theoretical trajectories that occurred across feminist scholarship more generally, critical studies into the gendered character of organizational life proliferated through the 1980s and 1990s. Examples include the Marxist feminist analysis undertaken by Walby (1988), and emphasizing the oppressive conditions of a patriarchal/capitalist order; the liberal feminist concern for "breaking through into the man's world of work" (see, for example, Flanders 1994); a radical feminist interpretation of male dominance and equal opportunities in industry and commerce (Cockburn 1983, 1991); the application of feminist poststructuralist theory to organizational analysis (Calás and Smircich 1991); and a feminist metaphorical exploration of the "symbolic order" of organizations (Gherardi 1995).[4]

This feminist scholarship has served to illuminate and explicate the "man" in manager; a connection that, by virtue of being seen as given, has facilitated and sustained both men's numerical dominance in management and the masculinist culture that is embedded in most organizations (for an overview, see Collinson and Hearn 1996). In exposing this once invisible interrelationship, theoretical and empirical investigations by both feminist and profeminist writers have developed important insights into the affairs of men as managers. Examples include: men, organizations and sexuality (Hearn and Parkin 1987); men and emotions in the organizational arena (Fineman 1993); shifting discourses of masculinity and managerialisms (Kerfoot and Knights 1993, Collinson and Hearn 1996); the changing masculinisms/managements of postwar British manufacturing industry (Roper 1994); organizational culture and formations of hegemonic masculinity (Cheng 1996); masculinity, management and identity work (Collinson 1992); and the globalization of an entrepreneurial masculinist work culture (Connell 1993, 1995).

While much of the above literature has rightly focused, directly or indirectly, on the gendered conditions that prevail across the private sector, less direct attention has been given to transformations in the public sector. An example here is education. While extensive critical insights have been developed into the social, cultural, economic and class arrangements that inform educational opportunity and experience, only relatively recently has the critical eye of academia turned its attention to education and the new managerialism now privileged across the sector. Even those texts engaged in such a task often fail fully to acknowledge the explicitly gendered conditions under which education managements now exist, thrive and proliferate (see, for example, Usher and Edwards 1994, Miller 1995, Smyth 1995). Yet, as Jenny Ozga and Lynne Walker emphasize in this volume (Ch. 7), education is now seen as pivotal to personal, social, political and economic transformations, especially at this particular juncture in the post-Fordist, postmodern age. A consequence of this focus has, they argue, been to reinforce, not reduce, men's dominance within this arguably most influential of discursive arenas.

Education is, then, highly pertinent in any critical examination of the public sector, being – as Jeff Hearn notes in Chapter 8 – both a vehicle for (gendered) ideologies, discourses and knowledges, and constituted and invented by those very same dynamics. In recognition of this, many of the chapters in this volume focus their critical attention on the rapidly changing scene of education management – and, importantly, on the men and women who constitute this influential grouping.

However, education is not the only public-sector site to have experienced the effects of the macro-structural forces described earlier, in particular the neo-liberalist philosophy of the New Right and attendant managerialist practices (Pollitt 1993, Clarke and Newman 1997). The civil service, the Post Office, the NHS, local government and the various police forces have all, in different ways, been subjected to new models of management, new patterns of working, an intensification of labour and new organizational ethics, as various governments, institutions and individuals have attempted to "manage" their way through the random, often chaotic, changes that have seemingly enveloped all subjects/organizations at this time. These are transformatory influences from which no public-sector site is immune; not even, as Stephen Whitehead describes in Chapter 2, one of the most powerful bastions of reactionary masculinist organizational culture – the House of Commons. Nevertheless, while the general effects of these dramatic movements on the public sector have been well documented elsewhere (for an overview, see Farnham and Horton 1993, 1996) as with education, their gendered constitution has received less attention.[5]

To reiterate, in making explicit some of the gendered characteristics that are apparent in public-sector management, this book's contributors speak not from some distant elusive, all knowing position, but as subjects very much bound up in – and partly constituted by – the very conditions and discourses that they seek to examine and critique. These women and men all work in the public sector, a significant majority as managers themselves. Consequently, the contributors bring to their writing both extensive personal experience of public-sector managerialisms and a personal/political standpoint/position, one framed and coloured by various discourses and perspectives. This volume is presented, then, not merely as an account of macro-transformations and changes in a particular organizational setting, but threaded through with personal narratives – sometimes discrete, occasionally overt. We make this point in order again to emphasize the diverse and contingent character of political and personal transformations, and the complex often confusing interrelationship of macro-influences and intersubjective responses.

10

The collection

The volume is divided into two parts. The first, *Women in the Management Arena*, is concerned with critically exploring transformations, resistances and shifts that occur in a number of public-sector management sites and, importantly, women managers' responses to these movements. Stephen Whitehead opens this part with his examination of the Houses of Parliament. Based on recently completed interviews with new women Labour MPs, Stephen considers the possibilities for a gendered cultural transformation in Parliament following the marked increase in women MPs after the 1997 general election. Following this, Diane Meehan explores the relationship between equal opportunities, gender and organizational culture in higher education (HE) management. In so doing, Diane draws on her own experience as a manager in a "new university". One of Diane's themes, the ways in which (gendered) systems and perspectives militate against women's career progression, is subsequently taken up by Lesley Thom. Similarly combining a personal and theoretical perspective, Lesley examines how women's under-representation in secondary education man-agement is simultaneously a condition and consequence of overt and covert gendered processes and barriers, despite the equal opportunities rhetoric now apparent in educational institutions. Moving to an exploration of the interactions of power and resistance in HE management, Rosemary Deem (Ch. 5) examines the various ways in which feminist women academic managers challenge, reinforce or reconstitute gendered organizational cultures. Informed by the narratives of women managers from various public-sector sites, Jo Brewis (Ch. 6) proceeds to utilize a poststructuralist understanding of identity, self and the body. In so doing, Jo illuminates some of the diverse ways in which women receive and negotiate their embodiment as gendered and sexualized subjects in the new managerialist culture outlined in previous chapters. Continuing the focus on sexualities and resistances in organizational life, Jenny Ozga and Lynne Walker (Ch. 7) conclude this part by exploring the various ways in which the patriarchal power paradigm is being reasserted in education organ-izations. Describing this as a re-formation of masculinist/managerialist behaviour, a central aim of their chapter is to encourage counter-hegemonic (feminist) practices in the face of dominant public-sector managerialism.

The second part, *Unmasking Men and Management*, is concerned with illuminating and interrogating men managers' various and contrasting responses to organizational restructuring, new managerialist discourses and the transformations in gender rela-tionships that are now apparent in public-sector sites. Opening this part, Jeff Hearn charts the shifts in ideology and practice that have occurred in HE over recent decades. In so doing, Jeff draws on his own experiences as a profeminist man/manager in the "old university" sector, at the same time exploring the possibilities and ambiguities for equal opportunities in the current ideological climate of universities. Turning attention to local authority managerialisms, Stella Maile examines the personal and professional impact of organizational restructuring on men Health and Environ-ment managers. Drawing on a number of in-depth interviews, Stella's account reveals the tensions and confusion felt by many of these men as they see traditional gender relationships, across both the public and private spheres, undergo profound transformation. Continuing with the theme of disrupted, entrenched and resisted masculine formations, John Clark combines action research and Foucauldian analysis to help understand the ways in which men (and women) experience and respond to organizational conflict and organizational change. Based on his own experiences in university management, John considers the possibilities and difficulties that face men's attempts at self-reflexivity and "care of the self". In a further contribution to a poststructuralist account of the masculine/managerial subject, Deborah Kerfoot (Ch. 11) explores the tensions between men, managerialism and organizational forms of intimacy. In the process, Deborah problematizes the masculine (managerial) subject's need to invest in instrumental intimacy as a synthetic human engagement primarily concerned with control. The concept of the masculine subject is further developed, empirically and theoretically, in Chapter 12, by Deborah Kerfoot and David Knights. Drawing on research recently undertaken in one "old university", they provide a highly charged yet intimate case study, one which serves to expose not only the emotional dimension of managerialist (inter)subjectivities but, moreover, the inherent fragility of the masculine/managerial subject as it seeks (momentarily) to sustain identity through the pursuit of power and control over self and others. Drawing on his own experiences in FE management, Roy Moodley concludes this volume with a psychoanalytical/sociological exploration of the concept of masculinity through the metaphor of the mask. Recognizing that managerialist forms of masculinity are neither secure nor fully sustainable, Roy suggests that dominant ideas about men and masculinities can be unmasked in the disrupted, sometimes pathological, spaces that are now apparent in contemporary public-sector managerialism.

Notes

1. There is an increasing critical academic focus on the changing culture of further education (FE) since incorporation in April 1993. This was the moment at which all colleges in England and Wales became independent corporations, released from local education authority control. See Avis et al. (1996), Whitehead (1996, 1999a, 1999b), Ainley and Bailey (1997) and Kerfoot and Whitehead (1998a, b), for elaboration.
2. See Brittan (1989) for elaboration of the concept of masculinism. The continuing debates that surround feminist epistemology and ontology are informed by, amongst others, Harding (1991) and Stanley and Wise (1993). See also Holmwood (1995) and McLennon (1995).
3. Kanter bases her notion of "proportionality" on an assumption that should sufficient women – a critical mass – emerge into senior positions, then the organizational culture is likely to shift in their favour. See Collinson and Hearn (1995) for a contemporary re-evaluation of Kanter's work.
4. For a comprehensive overview of the literature on women in organizations, see Tanton (1994), Marshall (1995) and Ledwith and Colgan (1996).
5. An exception to this rule is the work by Itzin and Newman (1995), which provides a valuable contribution to the debates that surround gender and the changing cultures of public-sector organizations. See also Ozga (1993) and Limerick and Lingard (1995) for detailed critical examinations of gender and changing cultures of educational management.

References

Acker, J. and Van Houten, D.R. (1974) "Differential recruitment and control: the sex structuring of organisations", *Administrative Science Quarterly*, **19**, 2, pp. 152–63

Ainley, P. and Bailey, B. (1997) *The Business of Learning* London: Cassell

Avis, J., Bloomer, M., Esland, G., Gleeson, D. and Hodkinson, P. (1996) *Knowledge and Nationhood* London: Cassell

Ball, S.J. (ed.) (1990) *Foucault and Education* London: Routledge

Bauman, Z. (1992) *Intimations of Postmodernity* London: Routledge

Beck, U. (1992) *Risk Society* London: Sage

Brittan, A. (1989) *Masculinity and Power* Oxford: Blackwell

Butler, J. (1990) *Gender Trouble* New York: Routledge

Calás, M. and Smircich, L. (1991) "Voicing seduction to silence leadership", *Organization Studies*, **4**, pp. 567–602

Chafetz, J.S. (1988) *Feminist Sociology* Itasca, Ill.: Peacock

Cheng, C. (ed.) (1996) *Masculinities in Organizations* London: Sage

Clarke, J. and Newman, J. (1997) *The Managerial State* London: Sage

Cockburn, C. (1983) *Brothers: Male Dominance and Technological Change* London: Pluto Press

Cockburn, C. (1991) *In the Way of Women* London: Macmillan

Collinson, D.L. (1992) *Managing the Shopfloor: Subjectivity, Masculinity and Workplace Culture* Berlin: de Gruyter

Collinson, D.L. and Hearn, J. (1994) "Naming men as men: implications for work, organization and management", *Gender, Work and Organization*, **1**, 1, pp. 2–22

Collinson, D.L. and Hearn, J. (1995) "Men managing leadership?: 'Men and women of the corporation' revisited", in *International Review of Women and Leadership*, **1**, 2, pp. 1–24

Collinson, D.L. and Hearn, J. (eds) (1996) *Men as Managers, Managers as Men* London: Sage

Connell, R.W. (1993) "The big picture: masculinities in recent world history", *Theory and Society*, **22**, pp. 597–623

Connell, R.W. (1995) *Masculinities* Oxford: Polity/Blackwell

Farnham, D. and Horton, S. (1993) *Managing the New Public Services* London: Macmillan

Farnham, D. and Horton, S. (eds) (1996) *Managing People in the Public Services* London: Macmillan

Fineman, S. (ed.) (1993) *Emotion in Organizations* London: Sage

Flanders, M.L. (1994) *Breakthrough* London: Paul Chapman

Fukuyama, F. (1997) *The End of Order* London: The Social Market Foundation

Galbraith, J.K. (1992) *The Culture of Contentment* London: Sinclair Stevenson

Gherardi, S. (1995) *Gender, Symbolism and Organizational Cultures* London: Sage

Giddens, A. (1991) *Modernity and Self-identity* Cambridge: Polity Press

Hall, M.A. (1990) "How should we theorize gender in the context of sport?", in Messner, M.A. and Sabo, D.S. (eds) *Sport, Men and the Gender Order* Champaign, Ill: Human Kinetics

Handy, C. (1994) *The Empty Raincoat* London: Hutchinson

Harding, S. (1991) *Whose Science? Whose Knowledge?* Milton Keynes: Open University Press

Harvey, D. (1991) *The Condition of Postmodernity* Oxford: Blackwell

Hearn, J. (1992) *Men in the Public Eye* London: Routledge

Hearn, J. (1993) "Researching men and masculinities: some sociological issues and possibilities", *Australian and New Zealand Journal of Sociology*, November

Hearn, J. and Parkin, W. (1987) *Sex at Work* Brighton: Wheatsheaf

Hewitt, P. (1993) *About Time* London: Rivers Oram Press

Holmwood, J. (1995) "Feminism and epistemology: What kind of successor science?" *Sociology*, **29**, 3, pp. 411–28

Hutton, W. (1995) *The State We're In* London: Vintage

Itzin, C. and Newman, J. (eds) (1995) *Gender, Culture and Organizational Change* London: Routledge

Jackson, D. (1990) *Unmasking Masculinity* London: Unwin Hyman

Kanter, R.M. (1977) *Men and Women of the Corporation* New York: Basic Books

Kerfoot, D. and Knights, D. (1993) "Management, masculinity and manipulation: from paternalism to corporate strategy in financial services in Britain", *Journal of Management Studies*, **30**, 4, pp. 659–79

Kerfoot, D. and Whitehead, S. (1998a) "'Boys own' stuff: masculinity and the management of further education", *Sociological Review*, **46**, 3, 436–57

Kerfoot, D. and Whitehead, S. (1998b) "Inhuman resource management: the case of further education", paper given to the *16th Annual International Labour Process Conference*, Manchester School of Management, 7–9 April 1998

Kumar, K. (1995) *From Post-industrial to Post-modern Society* Oxford: Blackwell

Ledwith, S. and Colgan, F. (eds) (1996) *Women in Organisations* London: Macmillan

Limerick, B. and Lingard, B. (eds) (1995) *Gender and Changing Educational Management* Rydalmere, NSW: Hodder Education

Lyotard, J.F. (1984) *The Post-modern Condition: a Report on Knowledge* Manchester: Manchester University Press

McLennon, G. (1995) "Feminism, epistemology and postmodernism: reflections on current ambivalence", *Sociology*, **29**, 3, pp. 391–409

Marshall, J. (1995) "Gender and management: a critical review of research", *British Journal of Management Studies*, **6**, pp. 53–62

Middleton, P. (1992) *The Inward Gaze* London: Routledge

Miller, H.D.R. (1995) *The Management of Change in Universities* Buckingham: Open University Press

Mills, A.J. and Tancred, P. (eds) (1992) *Gendering Organizational Analysis* London: Sage

Morgan, D.H.J. (1981) "Men, masculinity and the process of sociological enquiry", in Roberts, H. (ed.) *Doing Feminist Research* London: Routledge and Kegan Paul

Morgan, D.H.J. (1992) *Discovering Men* London: Routledge

O'Brien, M. (1981) *The Politics of Reproduction* London: Routledge and Kegan Paul

Ozga, J. (1993) *Women in Educational Management* Milton Keynes: Open University Press

Pollitt, C. (1993) *Managerialism and the Public Services* (2nd edn) Oxford: Blackwell

Reich, R. (1991) *The Work of Nations* New York: Knopf

Rojek, C. (1995) *Decentring Leisure* London: Sage

Roper, M. (1994) *Masculinity and the British Organisational Man since 1945* Oxford: Oxford University Press

Rutherford, J. (1992) *Men's Silences* London: Routledge

Seidler, V.J. (1994) *Unreasonable Men* London: Routledge

Seidler, V.J. (1997) *Man Enough: Embodying Masculinities* London: Sage

Smyth, J. (ed.) (1995) *Academic Work* Milton Keynes: Open University Press

Stanley, L. and Wise, S. (1993) *Breaking Out Again* London: Routledge

Stoltenberg, J. (1990) *Refusing To Be a Man* Glasgow: Fontana/Collins

Tanton, M. (ed.) (1994) *Women in Management* London: Routledge

Tolson, A. (1977) *The Limits of Masculinity* London: Tavistock

Tomlinson, J. (1993) *The Control of Education* London: Cassell

Tong, R. (1994) *Feminist Thought* London: Routledge

Usher, R. and Edwards, R. (1994) *Postmodernism and Education* London: Routledge

Walby, S. (1988) *Patriarchy at Work* Cambridge: Polity Press

Warner, D. and Crosthwaite, E. (eds) (1995) *Human Resource Management in Higher and Further Education* Buckingham: Open University Press

Whitehead, S. (1996) "Men managers and the shifting discourses of post-compulsory education", *Research in Post-Compulsory Education*, **1**, 2, pp. 151–68

Whitehead, S. (1998) "The invisible gendered subject: men in education management", paper given to the *Higher Education Close Up Conference*, University of Central Lancashire, 6–8 July 1998

Whitehead, S. (1999a) "Contingent masculinities: disruptions to 'man'agerialist identity", in Roseneil, S. and Seymour, J. (eds) *Practising Identities: Power and Resistance* London: Macmillan

Whitehead, S. (1999b) "From paternalism to entrepreneuralism: the experience of men managers in UK postcompulsory education", *Discourse: Studies in the Cultural Politics of Education*, **20**, 1, in press

Wolfe, J. (1977) "Women in organisations", in Clegg, S. and Dunkerely, D. (eds) *Issues in Organisations* London: Routledge and Kegan Paul

PART I
Women in the management arena

CHAPTER TWO

New women, new Labour?
Gendered transformations in the House

Stephen Whitehead

Introduction

Of all public-sector sites, the House of Commons has to be the most singularly influential and yet most overlooked by critical theorists. It is an invisibility that has served to obscure not only Parliament's culture but, crucially, the contesting forms of gender relations which constitute it. In part, this is because it is easy to forget that our Members of Parliament are paid employees in a public-sector organization and, as such, are no less accountable and open to scrutiny than those employed in more accessible public-service sites such as education, the NHS, the Post Office and so on. One aim of this chapter is to redress something of this imbalance and relative invisibility. In so doing, the intention is to illuminate one of the arguably most dramatic changes to have occurred in the "Mother of Parliaments" during its long and illustrious history; that is, the sudden almost totally unexpected influx of women into its "hallowed chambers" as a result of the 1997 general election.

To put this event in perspective, it should be remembered that one of the most crucial and ferocious struggles for democratic rights to occur in this country took place early this century; the fight for women's political enfranchisement. This cause was not officially won until 1928, and there are many women, and men, alive today who will have memories of that time and who have lived to witness the events of 1 May 1997, when 120 women were elected to the House of Commons; 101 Labour, 13 Conservatives, three Liberal Democrats, two Scottish Nationalists and Betty Boothroyd, the Speaker of the House. The significance of the events of 1 May is also reflected in the fact that there are now more first-time Labour women MPs (64) than the total number of women of all parties elected in 1992. While the process of change in this regard has at times been inextricably slow, the precise moment of transformation in the gendered constitution of parliament has been quite dramatic.

Not surprisingly, this "democratic revolution" has attracted much media attention, with extensive newspaper coverage, a specially commissioned radio programme, "Women in the House" (BBC Radio 4 1997), and a television documentary entitled

19

"Westminster Women", which drew on research by the Fawcett Society[1] into women MPs' attitudes and perspectives (see also McDougall 1998). Moreover, there has been much speculation by feminists as to whether or not these women do represent some partial fulfilment of their political aims, including the weakening of male power and dominance in political life (Walter 1998b), or whether they are merely "window dressing" in an otherwise intransigently maleist environment (Longrigg 1997).

Somewhat inevitably, not all the media speculation, focus and interest has been either informed, academic or benign. For example, following election, the 101 women Labour MPs were quickly labelled "Blair's Babes"; they were subjected to, at times, quite intimate scrutiny of dress and attire; one woman MP found her comments about her sexuality, assumed to be off the record, festooned over the tabloid papers; they were accused of "whingeing" when some complained of the blatant sexist abuse and comments directed at them by certain male Tory MPs; and Angela Eagle MP "came out" as a lesbian, in what was rumoured to be a pre-emptive action against otherwise "unmanaged" exposure in the tabloids. However, arguably the most cutting comments to date have not been from the tabloids, but from other women and those men similarly concerned at the fact that only one of the new intake of women Labour MPs, Ann Cryer, rebelled against the proposed cuts to lone parent benefit when the House voted on this issue on 10 December 1997. It was at this precise moment that the new women Labour MPs were seen by many to be lacking political conviction; too concerned with "breaking their own glass ceiling" (Williams 1997), rather than acting to improve the lot of women generally.

Much of the interest, and at times ensuing hope, optimism, anger and disillusionment, arises from the sheer weight of expectation placed on these women's shoulders. This is not in itself surprising given, first, the particular gender order and associated dominant discourses and ideologies still engrained in UK society and, secondly, the extremely reactionary environment that is the House of Commons. Apart from a small number of notable and creditable exceptions (Clare Short and Barbara Castle are two that come to mind), parliament has not witnessed many MPs, of either gender, who assert their feminism or profeminism through what is in the final analysis the most visible and possibly most important channel – the parliamentary voting system.

The question of political change is, then, central to the numerical gender shift that is currently apparent in parliament and is outlined above (for a discussion, see also McDougall 1998). But other questions are pertinent here, particularly in respect of the micro- and macro-issues now signalled as result of these women's influx into the House of Commons. For example, is it possible to detect the beginnings of a cultural shift in parliamentary processes away from a macho, "yaboo" posturing by politicians towards something more representatively feminine? How are these women reacting to the dominant masculine culture in parliament? Are they merely "window dressing" or do they represent the beginnings of a transformation in the gendered constitution of the House? In addressing these questions, this chapter draws on the narratives of six new women Labour MPs, interviewed during the autumn and winter of 1997–8.

The women MPs: backgrounds and research issues

Eleven women Labour MPs were approached for interview. Three declined, and two agreed on condition that the interviews were undertaken over the telephone. These two were not followed up, as I was concerned to delve somewhat deeper into their identities and motives than would have been possible through that medium. By late summer, when most of the initial approaches were made, the new women Labour MPs were already becoming increasingly reticent about giving interviews, especially to certain journals and newspapers. As they were finding to their cost, much of the media interest was focused less on their policies and more on their appearance and personal lives.

Five of the women interviewed represent constituencies in the North of England and one in the Midlands. Although new MPs, five have extensive experience of local politics as councillors, and two of these have been in politics since their mid-teens. The six women are representative of the new Labour cohort of 64 in terms of age, experience, ethnicity, education and family circumstances (see Fawcett Society Report 1997): one is single and in her 30s; and five are married, four with school-aged children and in their early 40s, and one with children in post-compulsory education and in her early 50s. All bar one of the women are university educated and all are white.

The nature of these women's profession created two difficulties for me in terms of the research. The first was access. It was often extremely difficult to obtain a response from these individuals, not for any evasive reasons, but simply as a consequence of their frantic, high-pressure lifestyle; constantly moving from Northern constituency to parliament and back again. Secondly, as one would expect, these are individuals who are quite well versed in the machinations of the media, and as such are confident and competent in their professional presentation of self. As a result, I found it necessary at times to be more directive during the interview, in terms of keeping to my thematic areas, than I would otherwise have been. The alternative would have meant recording several hours of articulate, smooth, political discourse, little of which would have helped me in acquiring a deeper understanding of these women; their lives, motivations and perspectives.

As mentioned, the pattern of work in which these women MPs are engaged is quite demanding. A typical week begins with a train journey to London early on Monday morning, followed by four days of parliamentary business, often until late in the evening. Nights are spent in hotels or flats in London. Friday signals a return to the constituency for visits, meetings, etc., surgery on Saturday, and, hopefully, Sunday with the family. Clearly, it is not a pattern that lends itself to family life, and I was struck by the time and emotional demands on these women, particularly those with partners and children. The peculiar demands on their families appear to have resulted in a role reversal in terms of a traditional sexual division of labour; in the case of four of the married women, their partners take a major share of the domestic workload and childcare. Moreover, these husbands, who are themselves working full-time, appear prepared to adopt the role of "traditional wife" – holding together the private sphere, and having multiple roles – while their partner does "great things" in the public sphere. One MP has achieved a slightly different balance wherein she employs her husband as a full-time secretary and parliamentary assistant. Consequently, there is here a blurring of the public/private divide and associated roles.

Like many ambitious people who are striving for success in a competitive work culture, all of these women display a remarkable degree of intensity in relation to their political ambitions, being extremely task-orientated, focused and driven. Political life, as the three MPs below describe it, appears to be particularly seductive and self-centred:

> Politics takes over and dominates your life. It shapes the rest of your life and time with the family . . . politics imposes tremendous sacrifices in people's families. The sacrifice is mainly made by our partners and children.
>
> My life is dominated by political activity. Over the years I have become more focused on achieving my aims, more directed at getting results . . . I am very self-contained, very goal orientated . . . I find it hard to relax, to switch off . . . I don't feel pressure, my friends call me the carrier of stress. I don't let go, I make sure what I am seeking to achieve happens . . . But I'm conscious that in pursuing politics in the way I have done I haven't spent time with the family. It's not like having a job, it's different, it's all-demanding, all-absorbing.
>
> Being an MP is quite hard work, it's really time consuming. You have to be a little odd to do it. I don't think there's many normal people in parliament.

It is clear from these typical responses that women MPs are investing much time and energy in their careers, to an extent that significantly cuts into the private sphere. In many respects, their lives and relationships are atypical of what are commonly understood to be the patterns of womanhood, as indeed experienced by most of their women constituents. Where, then, does the personal/political place itself in relation to their gender identity and, importantly, their capacity and desire to act as organizational and social change agents?

Cultural shifts?

Apart from the difficulties described above, the other problematic in this research was the fact that the very revolutionary aspect of these women's election precludes the possibility of there being an historical, organizationally specific point of reference from which to measure their attitudes and progress other than that referred to earlier. Consequently, much of the speculation as to how these women may or may not impact on the culture of British politics has used Scandinavian countries as a model. In their search for a more inclusive and consensual political culture, countries such as Sweden, Finland and Norway have, for many years, embraced gender equality and equity across the social and political spectrum. Consequently, women are well represented at every level of politics, and over a third of all Scandinavian

MPs are women. The point is often put that one result of this gender balance in Scandinavian politics is a more consensual approach, in which negotiation takes precedence over "macho posturing" ("Women in the House", BBC Radio 4, 24 November 1997). Certainly, according to the women I interviewed, the culture of the House leans more to the "macho" than the consensual. As one MP remarked:

> The macho, schoolboy's way of doing things leaves a lot to be desired. At times parliament just sounds like a real rabble – you can't believe the levels of heckling. I do think that has to change. The danger is that if you're not careful, you can get sucked into it.

This latter point, concerning the danger of being "sucked in" to a particular set of dominant organizational practices, alerts us to the problematics involved in any attempt to predict cultural transformation on the basis of a numerical gendered shift, not least because organizational "gender regimes" (Connell 1990), can prove remarkably intransigent and adaptive (see also Hollway 1984, Kerfoot and Knights 1993). Yet, not surprisingly, much hope has been invested by feminists in the centrality of the "numbers game" to equal opportunities. Kanter (1977) for example, is noted for her theory of proportionality; the belief that if women achieve a given numerical level of representation in an organization (Kanter suggested a "critical mass" of about 30 per cent), then not only are they much less likely to conform to the dominant "organizational logic" (Acker 1990) but they will, in time, come to reconstitute the gendered culture of that organization in their favour. In this respect, then, there is still some way to go, for the number of women MPs, at 120, represents less than 20 per cent of the 645 MPs in parliament. However, the difficulty with this thesis also lies in its essentialistic, categorical overtones, for it presumes a "sameness" amongst women and, concomitantly, a unity of purpose and political intent (for a discussion, see Collinson and Hearn 1995; see also Ledwith and Colgan 1996). As many feminists now argue, such unity of purpose is not necessarily an inevitable outcome of being a woman amongst other, albeit politically aware, women (for a discussion, see Nicholson 1990).

Despite concerns with the "critical mass" thesis, one would not wish to be too disparaging of the importance of numbers, nor of the efficacy of mechanistic and instrumental approaches to equal opportunities. Indeed, without such approaches being employed by the Labour Party there would now be many fewer women MPs, for 35 of the 64 new women Labour MPs came through the all-women shortlist system, deployed for the first, and possibly last, time in the 1992 election.[2] Each of the MPs interviewed for this research achieved their candidature through this system. Of concern, then, is the fact that, at the time of writing, the Labour Party has yet to declare a mechanism for encouraging women into parliament in the next election although, as several of the women MPs pointed out, the pressures against women candidates remain acute, not least the gender stereotypes held by many party activists and trade union members (for a discussion, see Mann 1991, Cunnison and Stageman 1993). Similarly, in early 1998 the Conservative Party leadership was forced to abandon its plans for positive action to increase the number of Tory women

MPs, after resistance from party activists. Recognizing that many of the 64 women Labour MPs are in marginal seats, there is a danger then that the current figure of 120 could be a peak, with fewer women, across all parties, achieving candidature in the future.

In trying to ascertain the potential for a substantive gendered cultural shift in parliament, it is also important to note the sheer suddenness of the increase in women MPs. These women have not been assimilated over time into the dominant organizational culture of parliament – they were catapulted into it on 1 May 1997. Consequently, while their progress up the career ladder will, to a large extent, be determined by their ability to "read" organizational politics (for a discussion, see Arroba and James 1987), they are of sufficient number to constitute an alternative potentially very different, yet influential, cultural grouping, one that comes to constitute itself largely outside of the prevailing dominant gendered and organizational discourses. Similarly, neither is it the case that they will feel that they are isolated "travellers in a male world" (Marshall 1984), to the extent that previous women MPs have ("Women in the House", BBC Radio 4, November 1997). Yet a male world it is. At every level – from its peculiar traditions, civil service ethos, spatial design, fraternalism, languages, clubs, values and everyday work practices, to the numerical dominance of men as backbenchers, whips and ministers[3] – the prevailing culture and underpinning ideology is masculinist (for elaboration, see Brittan 1989; see also Cheng 1996). It remains a culture in which the masculine subject is privileged (for elaboration, see Kerfoot and Whitehead 1998a, b), and where competition, aggression, manipulation and adversarial practices are understood as constitutive of "the way we do things around here" (Deal and Kennedy 1982). While all of the women to whom I spoke recognized these characteristics as being dominant in parliament, not all, however, were uncomfortable with this. Representative of this perspective were the four women quoted below, each of whom was disinclined to perceive these practices as indicative of a male-dominated culture:

> No, I don't feel it to be a male-dominated culture, I feel quite at home there. Some people take to it and some don't. I know some of my colleagues feel that it's male-dominated but I don't. It's not a problem . . . It's an archaic organization. Its problems stem from its traditions, this is a class problem not a gender problem. Because of the culture of the past the MPs happened to be mostly male. That is its problem rather than a gender one.
>
> I don't get obsessed with ideas of male domination – I just get on with the job, it's not an issue. Certainly some stances are unnecessarily oppressive but I see many women who enjoy adversarial debate.
>
> I don't spend time worrying about gender, I get on with it.
>
> It's not male domination in parliament – it's the bloody public school.

While not discounting the centrality and influence of class and especially public-school culture in this context, one is compelled to reflect that if (some) women Labour MPs are unwilling to acknowledge the particular gender regime that prevails in an organization such as the House of Commons, then where would they acknowledge it? Like many men in organizational life (see Kerfoot and Whitehead 1998b), the women MPs quoted above appear to consider themselves somehow able to "hack it", in the process positioning themselves as being stronger and more robust than others. The rough and tumble, and the bruising nature of the competitive and individualistic culture apparently presents no problem to some of these women. On the contrary, they appear to enjoy it. Consequently, it is not the organizational culture that comes to be seen as the problem and in need of change but, rather, that more "sensitive" souls are best advised to stay away from it. Those MPs who cannot "adapt" are subsequently seen as unsuited to what one woman MP described as "rough politics". Consequently, it is understood that "weaker members" will fall by the wayside, victims of a Darwinian scramble for prominence if not survival. As one MP reflected:

> A number of people (women Labour MPs) got elected who didn't expect to. A lot had a false impression of political life. Some will adapt and some won't.

This particular MP chose to position herself as one of those better equipped to "mix it in an aggressive male world", having, as she put it:

> . . . survived in the Liverpool Labour Party through the 70s and 80s when Militant were at their peak.

Certainly most people, if asked, would likely not suggest a political career for the "faint hearted", and one can admire a degree of toughness and resilience in the face of adversity. But there is a danger here of coming to habitualize conflict over consensus, thereby reinforcing the very "yaboo politics" which have contributed to undermining public empathy with politicians and political processes. As the interviews unfolded, it became more apparent that the boorish behaviour of certain groups of men politicians borders on a viciousness which seems, to me, hard to justify as party politics (see Gorman and Kirby 1993, Perkins 1997). One MP remarked:

> We know that the Tory opposition are targeting those new women MPs they consider to be a soft touch. They seem to be determined to systematically demoralize selected individuals rather than go for us as a whole.

There does appear to be a deep animosity and anger directed at many of these women MPs by some men politicians in all parties, not just the Tory opposition. Several of the women spoke of the various forms of abuse – physical, emotional and verbal – which they and other women have had to endure since becoming MPs. This includes being groped, being called "whores" and "slags", and being subjected to other forms of sexual intimidation by men, including those in their own party. However, for many of these women none of this is particularly new. One woman recalled her experiences at the hands of her trade union "colleagues" during her early days in local politics:

25

Without encouragement it is extremely difficult to motivate yourself to carry on. Even in the early stages [of my career] I experienced abuse and discrimination. I remember taking on the role of women's officer for the constituency when a whole group of men from the trade union decided to turn up at this one meeting, when they'd never been before, just to vote against having a women's officer. They booed and hissed throughout the meeting but I was finally elected. It was a very unpleasant experience.

While some of the women were silent on male dominance in parliament, none were so when discussing wider society, each articulating a deep appreciation of the gendered difficulties and structures facing many of their women constituents. For example, they were clearly aware of issues pertaining to multiple roles, childcare provision, work practices, single parenting, intensification of labour, and sexual and gender stereotyping. Yet despite this awareness of wider gender issues, some women Labour MPs do appear oblivious to the masculinist culture which has, over centuries, come to shape and define the social field of the House of Commons.

In trying to understand this apparent contradiction, various explanations emerge. First, in wishing to present themselves as able, competent androgynous politicians, they possibly feel it necessary to displace gender issues on to the "Other". These women are not denying that gender is important in other women's lives; they are denying that it is important in theirs. Secondly – and this is linked to the above point – their reticence is a form of defence; by not publicly acknowledging the fact of male dominance (to a man interviewer especially) they seek to maintain the space and opportunity for their own continued advancement as women MPs. Consequently, male dominance assumes a status as the power that dare not be spoken of; for to do so, at least as some of these women see it, is to reify the constraints on their own possibilities as women. As one MP put it:

The minute you say you've special needs, then that shows a weakness.

Research undertaken into women managers' experiences reveals the extent and depth of pressures on them, pressures which, it is argued, conspire to produce "non-threatening" postures in women. Research by Gilligan (1982), for example, indicates that women (managers) cannot be seen to be subversive; that is, speaking with a "different voice" to the mainstream discourse (see also Marshall 1995). When women respond by "being one of the boys" (Tanton 1992), it can be understood, then, as an understandable desire not to be isolated and therefore vulnerable (see also Tanton 1994). Alternatively, these MPs, like many women in organizations, could be seen to be lacking a "fully developed women's consciousness" (Marshall 1984); still "in transition" in terms of their gender awareness, constrained as it is, within an ideologically "robust patriarchal hegemony" (Ledwith and Colgan 1996: 26). Less sympathetically, and more personally, these MPs have been accused of a level of gender ignorance akin to false consciousness; ideologically unsound and seduced by the lure of (personal) power (Longrigg 1997, Williams 1997).

However, it can also be argued that these women MPs are, in Foucauldian (Foucault 1977, 1980, 1982) terms, both recognizing and exercising power. Wishing not to "show weakness" to men reveals a subliminal recognition of the masculinist culture that prevails in the House, their attempts to subvert and resist this gender regime requiring that they engage in "wise behaviour" (White et al. 1992), a strategy that necessitates heightened political sensitivity.

The danger with any deterministic assumptions of organizational change and personal action lies in their presumption of a self-reflexive agency (see, for example, Giddens 1991) – that is, a rational, centred (organizational) subject, capable of being discursively selective; choosing to exist and operate outside of dominant organizational discourses, while still maintaining their organizational identity and membership (Smircich 1983, Kondo 1990). This point encapsulates the tension that faces any possibility of a gendered cultural transformation of parliament: whether these women MPs can constitute and exert a counter-hegemony before they are themselves seduced by a masculinist way of being which, through inculcation of their subjectivity, merely reinforces the gendered and peculiar internal logic of the organization (see also Faith 1994). As one woman acknowledged, the stakes are high, not only for the future "way of doing things" in parliament, but also in terms of the very identities of these women:

There is a unique opportunity now to change the culture, but if we (women MPs) fall into men's ways of doing things [in parliament], if we never break that, then nothing is achieved. Then we just end up behaving like men. That's a danger.

Women restricted to patrolling the margins?

On balance, then, is it unreasonable to expect these new women MPs to be significant change agents in politics? How influential are they? How different are they from men politicians? Informed by recently concluded fieldwork, this chapter has suggested that the new cohort of women Labour MPs are positioned little differently in terms of their relationship to gendered organizational culture than, say, women managers in education, the NHS, or any other public-sector site. For the accounts that these few women MPs give, while partial, do resonate with other research into women's experiences of organizational life; in particular, the schizogenic (Gherardi 1995) sense of being simultaneously in and yet external to, the dominant organizational culture. In this respect, these women MPs appear to be outsiders; required to display fealty yet condemned to patrol the cultural margins of the organization. Having taken their legitimate place in parliament, they remain "intruders in a hostile culture" (Marshall 1984, Gherardi 1995). For while the House of Commons may indeed be a unique and historically significant institution, it is sadly familiar in respect of the gendered practices and discourses from which it is constituted. To deny that it is male-dominated seems, then, to fly in the face of all the evidence;

both quantitatively and qualitatively. Yet it is also possible to see why some of these women MPs, having fought and striven to reach these political heights, do feel uncomfortable in declaring any "special need". Yet, ironically, their own party has seen fit to recognize that women have "special needs"; the government giving one cabinet minister responsibility for women's issues, while also setting up a Ministry for Women.

But surely it is not only special needs which are at issue here; it is quite simply decent behaviour, together with a respect for one's colleagues – whichever side of the political fence they are on. Furthermore, it should be remembered that the abuses being practised by some men MPs on some women MPs have been condemned in law through the very Acts and policies voted into being by parliament itself.[4] Unfortunately, the prevailing adversarial culture of aggressive, manipulative and vicious competition is so entrenched across all of political life that it appears that only those individuals prepared to immerse themselves in it, or tolerate it, can expect to prosper. Does this, then, preclude any possibility of change, not only in the highly gendered nature of the House but also, for example, in respect of the anti-family work practices which predominate? For is it not ironic that as politicians across all parties continue to preach "family values", they themselves remain so single-mindedly engaged in a work culture which is self-evidently anti-family, if not anti-woman?[5]

Concluding on change

In assessing the possibilities for women Labour MPs ushering in a less "yaboo politics", a more consensual, negotiating stance, contradictory indicators emerge. Pessimistically, one can describe the House of Commons and, moreover, UK political culture, as determinedly masculinist; an arena wherein the masculine subject remains privileged and men numerically dominate.[6] Underpinning this gender regime are the traditions of parliament and, not least, the class divisions reflected in the elitism of public-school culture. Breaking down these walls of privilege will not be easy, although it is fair to say that all of the women interviewed for this study did see this as an important objective of their political careers. While Kanter's (1977) notion of critical mass is relevant here, other research into women's experiences in organizations reveals the complexities and subtleties of male privilege and, importantly, the capacity for organizationally informed masculinities to shift in the face of external pressures and cultural movements, but crucially without men experiencing loss of privilege (see, for example, Kerfoot and Knights 1993, Whitehead 1999). Furthermore, there is no guarantee that the current figure of 120 women MPs is assured for future parliaments. The degree of resistance shown by many men politicians across all parties to any special mechanism for facilitating women's entry into parliament indicates the hurdles that face prospective women candidates.

Compounding the problem of these women MPs' marginalization is also the fact that, as women, they are never outside the gendered gaze. Whatever their political positions might be, women MPs, like women in most organizations, are constantly subjected to scrutiny as sexual objects and female bodies; symbolically and materially positioned in opposition to men and masculinity. While some will experience varying degrees of success in managing this, they can never afford slippage, for the prevailing, but unwritten, "rules of conduct" remain different for them than for men politicians. As some of the women wryly remarked to me, it will be interesting to see how the public and media react to the first "sexual scandal" to erupt around a woman MP. Certainly, the notion of "cross-party affairs" will assume a new meaning.

On a more optimistic note, changes are clearly evident with regard to the sexual constitution of the House. There are now a number of openly gay women and men MPs, none of whom appear to have experienced much adverse reaction in terms of their open sexual orientation from either the public or the media or from their parliamentary colleagues (see also McDougall 1998). In this respect at least, the House appears to be more representative of wider social mores; if, as some commentators note, it still "slouches behind" the rest of the country in making the "psychological shift to democracy" (Barnett 1997). Certainly, since the May 1997 general election, politicians across all parties now appear to be prepared to speak more openly of the "sexual rights of gay men and women", apparently without fear of, or regard for, a political backlash: witness, for example, Michael Portillo's fringe speech at the 1997 Conservative Party conference.

There are also signs of some shifts in the way in which women politicians choose to approach political processes. While Margaret Thatcher sits uneasily as both a feminist icon for some (Walter 1998a) and the epitome of anti-feminism for others ("Women in the House", BBC Radio 4, 1997), few can deny that her approach to politics was less than inclusive in its style. A very different approach is that undertaken by, for example, Mo Mowlam, the current Secretary of State for Northern Ireland. Her decision in January 1998 – a crucially difficult and sensitive period – to go into the Maze prison in Northern Ireland and talk to prisoners convicted of violent terrorist acts, could never be dismissed as "macho posturing". This attempt, successful as it turned out, to emphasize dialogue over posture, was extremely brave, both personally and politically. It sits in sharp contrast to the words and deeds of a succession of previous (men) Northern Ireland Secretaries.

The final change indicator concerns the histories of these women. In many respects, they are atypical of most of the women residing in their constituencies. Rather than a disadvantage, I suggest this to be positive. For, as one woman remarked, MPs are "not normal", but yet neither is the House of Commons. These new women Labour MPs are different from most women; not only in respect of their jobs, but also in terms of the division of labour in their private lives. They are archetypically multiple women (see Kerfoot and Whitehead 1998c). While being as focused, work-oriented and directive as any men politicians, the new cohort of women MPs are living out quite different roles, not least as wives and mothers. As a consequence, their positioning within the gender category of women not only requires them to be skilled negotiators of multiple public and private roles but also adept at negotiating the political and *gendered* machinations of parliamentary life. There is no reason to assume that they are unskilled actors in this regard. The very fact of their presence in parliament is testament to some fairly well-honed political skill and foresight.

Likewise, there is little evidence to dismiss them as over-ambitious careerists, interested only in breaking through their own particular glass ceiling. On the contrary, there is some evidence to suggest that these women could be harbingers of a less confrontational and more inclusive politics, not least within their own party. Negotiation, inclusion, tolerance and dialogue are skills that they have had to learn and polish throughout their political, and personal, lives. One would expect them to utilize these learnt aptitudes to good effect in parliament. At the very least, their highly visible location in the House, one of the last bastions of unquestioned male privilege, is I suggest, interestingly subversive. These women, by their very presence, place under tension the dominant masculinist codes, assumptions and ways of being which have, over centuries, come to constitute and symbolize political and parliamentary processes. As in any organization, change will be slow. I suspect, however, that the gendered transformation of the House has only just begun.

Notes

1. The Fawcett Society campaigns for equality between women and men in the UK. The results of their extensive survey of women MPs informed the "Westminster Women" programme for London Weekend Television, screened during January 1998.
2. In 1996, two men prospective Labour Party general election candidates took the party to the European Court in order to challenge the all-women shortlist system. The case was declared in their favour and the Labour Party subsequently abandoned the system. Apparently influenced by this ruling, in February 1998 Lord Irvine, the Lord Chancellor, blocked plans submitted by the Scottish Secretary, Donald Dewar, aimed at guaranteeing an equal number of men and women in the new Scottish Parliament.
3. Many of the women interviewed indicated the Whip's office to be one of the most powerful offices in parliament. There are currently three women Labour Party Whips.
4. In October 1997 the Government announced that it would take action against those Tory backbench MPs found to be sexually harassing women Labour MPs.
5. The new Scottish parliament appears markedly different from its London "mother": 9–5 hours; electronic voting; email/video conferencing; no "honourable" members; less "confrontational" design and, hopefully, more women MPs.
6. *Public Bodies 1997* (see Cabinet Office 1997). This annual audit indicates that women are still heavily outnumbered by men in Whitehall ministries, in particular the Departments of Defence, Agriculture, Treasury, Environment and Trade and Industry, the Foreign Office and the Cabinet Office. Of 17 ministries scrutinized, only one – the Scottish Office – has anything approaching an equal balance, with 53 per cent/47 per cent in favour of men.

References

Acker, J. (1990) "Hierarchies, jobs, bodies: a theory of gendered organizations", *Gender and Society*, **4**, 2, pp. 139–58

Arroba, T. and James, K. (1987) "Are politics palatable to women managers: how women can make wise moves at work?" *Women in Management Review*, **3**, 3, pp. 123–30

BBC Radio 4 (1997) "Women in the House", 27 October – 24 November 1997

Barnett, A. (1997) "Slouching towards New Britain", *The Guardian*, 20 December, p. 19

Brittan, A. (1989) *Masculinity and Power* Oxford: Blackwell

Cabinet Office/Office of Public Services (1997) *Public Bodies 1997* London: HMSO

Cheng, C. (ed.) (1996) *Masculinities in Organizations* Thousand Oaks, Cal.: Sage

Collinson, D.L. and Hearn, J. (1995) "Men managing leadership? Men and women of the corporation revisited", *International Review of Women and Leadership*, **1**, 2, pp. 1–24

Connell, R.W. (1990) "The state, gender and sexual politics: theory and appraisal", *Theory and Society*, **19**, 507–44

Cunnison, S. and Stageman, J. (1993) *Feminizing the Unions* Aldershot: Avebury

Deal, T. and Kennedy, A. (1982) *Corporate Cultures: the Rites and Rituals of Corporate Life* Harmondsworth: Penguin

Faith, K. (1994) "Resistance: lessons from Foucault and feminism", in Radtke, H.L. and Stam, H.J. (eds) *Power/Gender* London: Sage

Fawcett Society Report (1997) *Fawcett Survey of Women MPs* London: Fawcett Society

Foucault, M. (1977) *Discipline and Punish: the Birth of the Prison* London: Allen Lane

Foucault, M. (1980) *Power/Knowledge: Selected Writings and Interviews 1972–77*, Gordon, C. (ed.) Brighton: Harvester

Foucault, M. (1982) "The subject and power", in Dreyfus, H. and Rabinow, P. (eds) *Michel Foucault: Beyond Structuralism and Hermeneutics* Brighton: Harvester

Gherardi, S. (1995) *Gender, Symbolism and Organizational Cultures* London: Sage

Giddens, A. (1991) *Modernity and Self-identity* Cambridge: Polity Press

Gilligan, C. (1982) *In a Different Voice* Cambridge, Mass.: Harvard University Press

Gorman, T. and Kirby, H. (1993) *The Bastards* London: Pan

Hollway, W. (1984) "Fitting work: psychological assessment in organisations", in Henriques, J. et al. (eds) *Changing the Subject: Psychology, Social Regulations and Subjectivity* London: Methuen, pp. 26–59

Kanter, R.M. (1977) *Men and Women of the Corporation* New York: Basic Books

Kerfoot, D. and Knights, D. (1993) "Management, masculinity and manipulation: from paternalism to corporate strategy in financial services in Britain", *Journal of Management Studies*, **30**, 4, 659–79

Kerfoot, D. and Whitehead, S. (1998a) "Masculinity, new managerial discourses and the problematics of intimacy in organization", paper presented at the Gender, Work and Organization Conference, UMIST, Manchester, 9–10 January 1998

Kerfoot, D. and Whitehead, S. (1998b) " 'Boys own' stuff: masculinity and the management of further education", *The Sociological Review*, **46**, 3, 436–57

Kerfoot, D. and Whitehead, S. (1998c) Engendering Labour: women cleaning up the House?, unpublished paper

Kondo, D.K. (1990) *Crafting Selves* Chicago: University of Chicago Press

Ledwith, S. and Colgan, F. (eds) (1996) *Women in Organisations: Changing Gender Politics* Basingstoke: Macmillan

Longrigg, C. (1997) "So where is big sister?", *The Guardian*, 17 December

McDougall, L. (1998) *Westminster Women* London: Vintage

Mann, K. (1991) *The Making of the English "Underclass"? The Social Divisions of Welfare and Labour* Milton Keynes: Open University Press

Marshall, J. (1984) *Women Managers: Travellers in a Male World* Chichester: John Wiley

Marshall, J. (1995) *Women Managers Moving On* London: Routledge

Nicholson, L.J. (ed.) (1990) *Feminism/Postmodernism* London: Routledge

Perkins, A. (1997) "Chamber of horrors", *The Guardian*, 9 October 1997

Smircich, L. (1983) "Concepts of culture and organizational analysis", *Administrative Science Quarterly*, **28**, 3, pp. 339–58

Tanton, M. (1992) "Developing authenticity in management development programmes", *Women in Management Review*, **4**, pp. 20–26.

Tanton, M. (ed.) (1994) *Women in Management* London: Routledge

Walter, N. (1998a) *The New Feminism* London: Little, Brown

Walter, N. (1998b) "If faith falters, be charitable and hope", *The Observer*, 4 January 1998

White, B., Cox, C. and Cooper, C. (1992) *Women's Career Development: a Study of High Flyers* Oxford: Blackwell

Whitehead, S. (1999) "From paternalism to entrepreneurialism: the experience of men managers in UK postcompulsory education", *Discourse: Studies in the Cultural Politics of Education*, **20**, 1, in press

Williams, S. (1997) "Doing the dirty work", *The Guardian*, 15 December 1997

CHAPTER THREE

The under-representation of women managers in higher education: Are there issues other than style?

Diane Meehan

Introduction

This chapter starts from the premise that women academics continue to be under-represented in UK higher education (HE), particularly at senior levels. In examining why this is so, the chapter draws on both empirical research and personal experience of HE management. The key themes examined are gender and management and the culture and processes within organizations, particularly higher education. The gender imbalance amongst academic staff in HE has been well documented elsewhere, but following the introduction this position is brought up to date and briefly compared to other business sectors. Moreover, in order to make progress towards equity we need to identify why there are not more women managers in HE. Thus I proceed to review some of the literature on female versus male management styles.

In attempting to explain the absence or under-representation of women in management positions, research has focused on the differences (or otherwise) between male and female managers, raising issues of gender both in terms of biological difference (where sex relates to actual differences between males and females) and learned difference or socialization (where gender starts from the basis of biological difference in order to assign social difference; Powell 1988). In fact, there are various ways of considering the issues that surround gender and management. Person-centred theory, for example, looks at factors seen as *internal* to women and attributes them to causes such as gender-differentiated socialization patterns; different early ways of constructing reality and early gender identify formation (Hood and Koberg 1994). Hence, in terms of gender and management, person-centred theory examines the issues from three perspectives: first, male and female managers as the same, secondly, male and female managers as different (and women managers as "better"), and finally, from a "complementary contributions" (Adler and Izraeli 1988) point of view which, while still recognizing "difference", does not consider men or women as fundamentally "better", but just better at certain management tasks. This perspective

33

suggests that organizations need to value both men and women's contributions as managers.

One of the issues raised in the above "styles" debate is that of transformational management (participative, power and information sharing, enhancing the self-worth of others; Rosener 1990) in contrast to transactional management (based on a more traditional, "command and control" style, and relying heavily on a system of rewards and punishments; Rosener 1990) and whether the former is inherently a "female" management style or one which is increasingly recognized as a preferred management style. It is also interesting to explore whether the core definitions of "management" are changing, a question addressed in the conclusion.

In contrast to person-centred theory, situation-centred theory looks at factors *external* to women and explains women's lack of progress in management as being due to lack of opportunity and power (Hood and Koberg 1994). This perspective also suggests that managers in general adopt a range of styles according to the demands of the situation (Freeman 1990). This point also relates to Kanter's (1977) view that it is organizational structures, not biology, that shape the behaviour of women in organizations. Kanter identifies the major factors for the non-progression of women as being their position within the opportunities structure of organizations, the amount of power that they exert and the number of women at the top. Critical mass is an issue here, Kanter's (1977) view being that 25 per cent was a critical mass below which it was difficult to effect (gender) change.

In terms of critical gender theories, it is also important to note the growing body of research around men, masculinities and management (for example, Collinson and Hearn 1994, 1996). This scholarship recognizes the inappropriateness of men continuing to accept the "traditional" notions of management of, and by, men and suggests the critical re-evaluation of management theory and practice together with the inclusion of gender issues. Collinson and Hearn (1994: 18) urge an examination of:

> ... conditions, processes and consequences through which the power and status of men and masculinities are reproduced within organisational and managerial practice.

Thus it is not sufficient for challenges to the status quo just to come from women; for the position of women in organizations to change, then the position of men must change as well. While this work is not central to this chapter, other chapters within this book take it as their central theme.

While the research on female versus male management styles identifies critical issues of style, and how diversity should or could be valued, it does not really help to explain why more women academics are not progressing to higher scales. The premise that a woman's style of management is based solely on biological difference or socialization patterns ignores other potential influences. For example, do women who display the "male" characteristics of management style simply learn these (for example, through "role models" or stereotypes) or do they adapt their style according to the organizational culture? If the culture is results- rather than process-oriented, may not all managers adapt styles to conform? As Marshall (1995a) notes, women may face the requirement to adopt a preferred (dominant) management style, one which conforms more with the culture, or they may opt out of the promotion race altogether. This point requires us to examine the "framework" within which this all takes place, i.e. the organization and its culture.

There are various views of culture. Typically, culture is described as a set of shared beliefs, values or meanings – "how we do things around here" (Smircich 1983). Hence it is argued that it is within a culture that individuals acquire their norms for behaviour, belief systems and an understanding of reality. Krefting and Frost (1985: 155) suggest that as members of an established culture view it as an objective reality, rather than a social construction, it may thus "become a set of blinkers, limiting the alternatives that individuals perceive". Smircich (1985) suggests that an anthropological view of culture, as webs of meaning organized in terms of symbols and representations, provides us with an alternative (better) means of studying and understanding organizational processes. She argues that "to study culture means to study social significance – how things, events and interactions come to be meaningful . . ." (Smircich 1985: 63), and links this with the possibility of a new view of managing "for multiple realities, rather than managing in spite of multiple realities" (Smircich 1985: 71).

Increasingly, the study of culture has become concerned with gender and gendered relationships within organizations, including – from a feminist perspective – authority and power, division of labour and sexuality. Looking at the gendered cultures of organizations provides us with a better framework for understanding the position of women managers in HE. Hence this chapter considers the role of organizational culture as another variable that reinforces the place of women in organizations. Within this debate, I also consider equal opportunities – seemingly well established within HE (part of the culture?). However, while it may apparently be high up on the agenda, it is not always clear what has been achieved (see, for example, Duke 1997) and whether that agenda goes far enough in terms of practice.

It is also suggested here that there are other barriers in HE which serve to exclude women. This chapter goes on to identify some of these barriers and to raise issues which appear to need further research. For example, the new managerialism and general accountability in many universities has resulted in some systems (such as performance appraisal) which, while apparently operating openly and fairly, may in fact further disadvantage women academics (Thomas 1996). The chapter concludes by considering what might be done to ensure that the position of women in HE continues to improve; for example, by changing and challenging the culture and structures within HE.

The current position of women in higher education

As Hearn (Ch. 8, this volume) argues, HE has always been a white, male-dominated, hierarchical environmental in which male norms abound. Women have had to fight for entry as students and academics (see also Kennedy 1995) and for recognition that their academic qualifications and potential are as credible as those of their male colleagues. As Kennedy (1995: 16), observes:

[We might be inclined] . . . to believe that the academic world is one immune to prejudice – a world of genuine equal opportunity, where free expression and liberal values ensure that pure brilliance objectively recognised gains its rewards.

However, Kennedy and others (see, for example, West and Lyon 1995), and of course many women academics working in HE, recognize that the true picture is far removed from this. Statistics show that the proportion of undergraduate female students in HE has increased from 25 per cent in the mid-1960s to over 50 per cent in the 1990s, with recent figures (HESA 1997), showing that about 52 per cent of all undergraduates are female, with the situation slightly reversed at postgraduate level, where about 46 per cent of students are female, although fewer women study at the postgraduate research level. This increase is said to be the result of improved academic performance by female school leavers and a consequence of the broadening of HE, particularly in terms of the curriculum offered (West and Lyon 1995).

However, across the various subjects in HE there is still a gender imbalance, with women students largely ignoring, for example, engineering and technology, and some aspects of science. Again, statistics show that the number of women in academic positions has also increased. In the early 1990s the number of female academic staff in HE was about 20 per cent of the full-time academic staff complement (DES 1992), while now, towards the end of the 1990s, out of a total of over 111 000 full-time academic staff in UK HE institutions, about 29 per cent are women (HESA 1997). However, Bagilhole (1994) suggests that even these figures (small as they are!) may be misleading, as they include staff on research-only contracts. Looking at current figures (HESA 1997), out of over 111 000 full-time academic staff, some 78 000 are classed as wholly institutionally financed, while 33 000 are financed by "other sources" and of this latter category 65 per cent are women (which would include staff on research-only contracts). Hence the proportion of wholly financed, full-time women academic staff in HE is now about 25 per cent and therefore still out of keeping with what might be reasonably expected as we move towards the year 2000.

The proportion of women in senior positions seems to remain even more inequitably small. Kennedy (1995: 15) quotes the historian Janet Sondheimer as saying that "professorial chairs apparently, were designed to accommodate only masculine frames". For example, there has been a slight year-on-year increase of women professors – i.e. at 5 per cent in 1995 (Kennedy 1995, who at that time was comparing it with the US figure of 16 per cent) – with figures now showing 9 per cent of professors in UK HE being female (HESA 1997). These figures help to confirm that the "top jobs" in UK HE are still largely the domain of men, while women remain clustered in lower positions, on temporary or part-time contracts (West and Lyon 1995).

Of course, people will always point to the exceptions and remind you of the vice-chancellor who is a woman, or the fact that the number of women vice-chancellors has increased (albeit still an extremely small number). This approach is best summed up by a remark made to me during a discussion in a lecture about women managers in a male-dominated domain: "We've got one and she is very good!" Until recently, the statistics for education, and in particular HE, painted a similar, if not slightly more negative picture than that in many other occupations. While, overall in the UK, women make up almost half of the workforce (Davidson and Cooper 1992, Eckersley 1992), estimates of their visibility in management positions vary depending on level of position; e.g. 20 per cent in overall management positions, 1 per cent in top management positions (Eckersley 1992), and from 4 per cent (Hanna 1991) to 10 per cent (Eckersley 1992) in senior management positions.

More recent figures (see, for example, Bassett 1997), suggest a significant (as much as 60 per cent) rise in the number of women managers in the past four years. These findings from an Institute of Management survey should, however, be treated with cautious optimism, showing as they do that the percentage of women directors (at board level) has increased to 4.5 per cent from 3.3 per cent the previous year, and that the percentage of women executives has risen from 12.3 per cent to 15.2 per cent over the same time period. Also, the report confirms that there is still an imbalance across functions and sectors, with women occupying one in three marketing management and one in two personnel management posts. This compares with, for example, the 4 per cent of all managers in manufacturing, production, research and development, purchasing and contracting.

Despite this increase in the number of women in management positions, there are still many more women in low-paid, lowly positions, clustering in traditional female occupations such as clerical/secretarial and caring, the service industries and school teaching, particularly primary school teaching (Davidson and Cooper 1992). Moreover, part-time work is one of the most rapidly expanding areas of employment opportunity and women make up over 80 per cent of this market. In addition, recent figures (DTI 1997), show that in each of eight occupational groups – managers and administrators, associated professional and technical, clerical and secretarial, craft and related, personal and protective, sales, plant and machine operatives, and other – the average UK female weekly earnings are consistently less than those of their male counterparts.

Women academics also cluster in traditional female disciplines such as social sciences, business studies, humanities and education, and where represented in any number in science, it is in biology and health sciences rather than physics or chemistry. There is still a notable absence of women academics in engineering, mathematics, computer science and science departments. In fact, in some such departments there are no women academics at all. As West and Lyon (1995: 53) put it, ". . . engineering remains the strongest outpost of male dominance. Women there comprise a mere 5 per cent of academic staff." The picture in other disciplines may not be as clear, particularly where "hard" and "soft" approaches in some subjects (Kennedy 1995) tend to cloud the issues. For example, while I was participating in a workshop on women in computing in 1994, it came as no surprise to hear some heads of computing departments confirming that they had no women staff within their departments. This was mainly in the pre-1992, "old" university sector, where computer science ("hard" approach), was more likely to be taught than computer studies or business information systems ("soft" approach). Some heads claimed that they would like to employ women academic staff if only they applied for the jobs!

This statement could imply that women do not want or are not qualified for jobs, rather than seeking the opportunity to improve the participation of women during the recruitment and selection process. There is well documented research on ways in which this can be achieved, for example, from where the advertisement is placed to make it more accessible to women, or the way in which it is written to encourage women to apply, through to how the subsequent selection and appointment procedures are carried out and by whom, including having women on selection panels (see Lesley Thom, Ch. 4, this volume; Davies 1992, Burton 1993). Burton (1993: 288) argues: "with respect to recruitment, a shortlist which continues to represent an imbalance should be unacceptable to equal opportunities employers". Ruijs (1993) identifies several reasons why it is crucial that there are more women in educational management; namely, justice (or entitlement), the effect on the socialization of future generations and the positive effect on the quality of education (Shakeshaft 1987).

Female versus male management styles

There is currently much discussion about sameness in respect of equal opportunities – women in management positions display the same or similar characteristics to men in management positions – versus difference; i.e. what are the characteristics of women managers which make them different from men? Both debates provide not insignificant arguments to support the premise of sameness or difference. Nevertheless, some authors reject the polarized nature of these debates, arguing that it not only masks the real issues, but that it stands in the way of change (see, for example, Bacchi 1990). Similarly, Cockburn (1991) argues that women can be the same and different from each other as well as different from men.[1]

Women managers as "same"

Marshall's (1984, 1995b) research supported the view that women are very similar to men in management style and where there are differences these are likely to make women better managers; for example, if they have better interpersonal skills. Lawless (1991), discusses a study concerning nine female and six male managers, which again found more similarities than differences. Powell (1988) found that women and men in management jobs do not differ according to the stereotypes. He argues that while there are real differences in society, home and school, these differences become less visible in the workplace. Earlier work also supported this view, revealing few significant differences between male and female managers (Donnell and Hall 1980, Dobbins and Platz 1986).

The research has also shown that both women and men display characteristics which would be considered necessary for effective management, e.g. competitiveness, co-operation and leadership ability (for example, Stevens and Denisi 1980); motivation to manage (Miner 1977); and desire to achieve success (Wood and Greenfield 1976). The "sameness" debate also raises criticism of women who appear more male than their male counterparts. Authors identify the "queen bee" or iron maiden syndrome; women in positions of authority who surround themselves by men (the classic example being Margaret Thatcher) and who do little to further the cause of women colleagues. These women are also seen as likely to adopt masculine styles of management and male norms. It is of concern and irritation to many women that women who succeed often "betray" those who would follow. This is sometimes a seemingly deliberate betrayal, recognizable through statements such as: "I got here because of my own ability. What is the problem for other women?"; "I've never found gender an issue"; "I do not want to be involved in or identified with women's issues" (see also Whitehead, Ch. 2, this volume).

In many ways, women cannot win. They are criticized for adopting the masculine model of management, but they are also likely to be criticized for displaying an overtly feminine approach, which may be perceived as weakness by others or, in its extreme form, as betrayal of other women. It is difficult to know what is more irritating to other women: a woman manager operating within the masculine model or one who flutters her eyelashes. As Kanter (1977: 123) states:

> Women are measured by two yardsticks – how as women they carried out the management role, and how as managers they lived up to the images of womanhood.

White (1995: 200) comments that:

> . . . it appears to be very difficult to bridge the gap between being a woman and being a worker; and even more difficult to move into the top of organisations.

This point also perhaps helps to explain why some women are apparently leaving at the top, an issue of growing concern (Marshall 1995a).

Wong et al. (1985) report that women with "feminine identities" achieve less in their careers and were less likely to attribute success to their own ability compared with women who had "masculine identities". It is also suggested that women may distance themselves from gender stereotypes through, for example, assertive behaviour and masculine dress (Larwood 1991). This adoption of masculine management models may also be a coping behaviour and one which women may perceive as necessary in order to survive and progress within male-dominated hierarchies. Interestingly, although the "queen bee" is discussed as an issue, the "king bee" (or its equivalent) is not discussed. Yet there are also male managers who feel more comfortable (perhaps less threatened?) by female colleagues and who surround themselves with colleagues of the opposite gender.

Women managers as "different"

The "difference" debate attempts to isolate those characteristics and skills which women bring with them to their roles as managers. It is a debate that has been criticized because, while it attempts to identify differences between genders, it treats both men and women as otherwise homogeneous groups, thus failing to recognize differences such as ethnic background, social class, sexual orientation and so on.

While recognizing that I have treated women as a "group" and talked generally about women, this is not an attempt to ignore the heterogeneous nature of that group within which black women, women with disabilities, lesbian women and women not from middle-class backgrounds are even more under-represented in management positions than white, middle-class, heterosexual women, with no disabilities. There is a considerable amount of research undertaken which "unpicks" the variety of issues within this gender debate (see, for example, Hall 1989, Boylan 1991, Corrin 1994, Henry 1994, Mathews 1994). Nor, as stated in the introduction to this chapter, is this an attempt to ignore the growing debate on men, masculinities and management (Collinson and Hearn 1994, 1996), where the need for men to challenge traditional management "ideals" comes to the fore.

Various authors have contributed to the "difference" debate (for example, Rosener 1990, Davidson and Ferrario 1992). It is often suggested that male managers are rational, analytical, strategic, decision-oriented, tough and aggressive (instrumental traits). Notably, such characteristics correspond to the "labels" which most modern business organizations like to assume, and this would now include an HE environment. Women, on the other hand, are perceived to display "softer" characteristics and are hence assumed to be weak(er), emotional, poorer at decision-making and analysis, and to display typical female characteristics such as caring and nurturing (expressive traits).

The "difference" debate is also applied to education. In a study of school principals in the Netherlands, Ruijs (1993) found that women principals were rated more highly on traits such as flexibility, insight into team functioning, economic use of time, tutoring co-operation and willingness to change. In contrast, male principals were rated highly on traits such as authority, ambition, self-confidence and a business-like approach. Rosener (1990) focuses on contrasting leadership styles. She suggests that women managers are "transformational", a style of leadership that encourages participation, shares power and information, and enhances the self-worth of others. It has also been suggested that women's communication stresses relationships and interactions and that, in general, women are more polite and collaboration-oriented (see, for example, Gardner et al. 1994).

Rosener also suggests that men tend towards a "transactional" style of leadership which is based on a more traditional, "command and control" style, relying heavily on a system of rewards and punishments. This compares with a structuring leadership style (see, for example, Marshall 1984) and demonstrates more concern for getting the task done than for the people performing the task. It has also been argued (Blake and Mouton 1964) that an optimum style of leadership would combine a degree of concern for both people and production, i.e. "team and democratic management". A study by Davidson and Ferrario (1992) showed that women managers are more likely to demonstrate this "team management" style than their male counterparts.

Helgesen (1990) believes that the values or principles that women bring to leadership roles are a vital part of that role, rather than a weakness. She concludes that women managers have a unique perspective which makes them better managers; in particular, a greater concern for relationships, disdain for complex rules and structures, and an emphasis on process rather than product or task. Helgesen's ideas have in turn been criticized as too simplistic and "sexist" (Nichols 1993); namely, reinforcing stereotypes by again attributing feminine management styles to women, thereby devaluing their contribution.

It is further argued within the research that the basis of the differences displayed by women and men in management positions is both biological and learned (socialization). Hence women managers adopt "transformational" styles, for example, because of shared experiences and previous career paths.

Reinforcing gender stereotyping

There is also an argument that in debating sameness or difference one is reinforcing stereotypes, gender stereotypes being a major source of discrimination (Powell 1988). Eagly (1987) asserts that gender stereotypes come from women taking on caring and supportive roles such as nurturing and home-making; unlike men, who take on agentic roles that require them to adopt aggressive and controlling behaviour.

Sometimes it is difficult to believe that "old" stereotypes still exist and continue to be perpetuated. Kennedy (1995) remarks on a study which was carried out to explain why, when school leavers entering Oxford and Cambridge enter with similar A-level results, more men than women gain first-class honours degrees. One explanation which came out of the study was that men have larger/better brains than women! Kennedy (1995) also points to the rarely articulated stereotype within academia that women academics are not as clever as their male colleagues. It is also surprising how many males still perceive women to be less committed to their jobs, weaker, off work more frequently and so on. One former male colleague used to call some women colleagues' absences "broken eyelash syndrome". The implication was that they had stayed off work for little or no apparent reason. Yet it is my experience that it is often male colleagues who have to go home early or stay off to look after children, and who cannot go away on the overseas trip because of family responsibilities. In fact, I have ended up undertaking various overseas trips solely because of this. While much of this is commendable, it is too easy for colleagues to believe that we have the new caring man, but that a woman in the same position is not dedicated to the job! Where tokenism occurs, stereotypes are even more visibly reinforced. Tokens may be classified according to stereotypes even when their behaviour is not consistent with that stereotype (Gutek and Morasch 1992). Kanter (1977) found that women become more highly aware of their gender when they are tokens.

These gender stereotypes affect women both in and outside of HE. In a previous position, I had effectively been managing a department after the former incumbent left. When the post was advertised, I applied – imagining that as I had been able to demonstrate that I could do the job and had been spurred on by supportive colleagues, I would have a good chance of being shortlisted (at least). When I wasn't shortlisted I went to ask a very senior manager why, particularly as a male colleague with very limited management experience had been shortlisted for the post. The senior academic explained to me it was nothing to do with capability – he was sure that I could do the job – but my qualifications were not "up to scratch". For example, I had done a part-time degree in a polytechnic, whereas my colleague had a much better degree from an "old", more prestigious university. He likened the situation to his own family: his son had gone to "a good university" to do engineering and had taken up a good job on graduation, but his daughter had entered a typically female job in caring. However, he assured me that he still loved his daughter very much (a classic example of patriarchy, as well as reinforcing the (dated) sexual division of labour)!

Personal experience

As a woman manager, I would advocate self-evaluation in respect of gender roles, expectations and organizational culture, although this might prove to be a painful experience. As Thomas (1996: 144) suggests:

> Women do reflect on their experience and their existence within organisations and this is the root to change.

I have asked myself the question: "Have I chosen to adopt a masculine stance or have I been true to my gender?" Well, I have been called aggressive (by a male colleague whom I challenged in a meeting), tough, as well as inarticulate (when dumfounded by a particular display of male aggression in a meeting in an external organization, i.e. not one in which I was working, where I was the only woman participant) – although, I hasten to add, I have also been called many positive things as well! In addition, I do not fit the stereotypical pattern of being a woman manager with no family and/or no partner. I am both married and have a child.

Whatever the style, I will not compromise my basic stance: for example, I don't believe in aggression and I never shout at colleagues. I want to be thought of as a good manager, not a female or male-like manager. In some ways, this may be seen as the principles and values that women bring with them to the management role (Helgesen 1990). But I would argue that many men work within similar frameworks as well (of course, holding on to the framework may sometimes be difficult because of the cultures in which we work, and no-one is perfect). I also recognize that I present a less than perfect role model, working as I do within the "long-hours" culture.

Other issues

Culture as a variable

The above research on gender and management throws little light on the position of women in HE and leaves the question "Why so few senior women managers in HE?" largely unanswered. By taking up the issue of culture and, in particular, by looking at organizations as gendered cultures, we are immediately acknowledging:

... the difficulties of change as the focus is on the multiple layers of discourse that permeate every aspect of the organisations and which work to subordinate women. (Thomas 1996: 144)

As I discussed above, do women who display the "male" characteristics of management simply learn them or do they adapt their style according to the organizational culture? Women may face the need either to adapt a preferred management style to one which conforms more with the culture or to opt out of the promotion race. It has been argued that success for women is not always measured in terms of promotion "up the ladder" and that women may have different (better) sets of values (McIntyre 1994). It is difficult to know what this then says about women who do want to reach the top: Are we adding a new layer of guilt for women who wish to succeed? In any case, the idea that women do not want promotion and are not ambitious is not borne out by other research (see, for example, Metcalfe 1989).

Higher education and its culture

Various categories and types of organizational culture have been identified. For example, Maddock and Parkin's (1995) typology of gender cultures includes the Gentleman's Club (old-fashioned, polite, paternalistic); the Barrack Yard (military, bullying); the Locker Room (excluding women, allowing men to build relationships on shared assumptions); the Gender-blind (the allusion that everyone is white, able-bodied and male, denying reality and difference); Paying Lip-service and the Feminist Pretenders (with equal opportunities policies but little change); and the Smart Macho (emphasis on corporate performance).

Newman's (1995) categorization of cultures is particularly useful when applied to HE, i.e.:

- Traditional – hierarchical and based on traditional male/female roles and divisions of labour. Men manage, women provide secretarial support. (Common in older, more traditional HE establishments)
- Competitive – macho culture based on competition and results, where there is a notional equivalence between male and female roles. Women however must compete on the same terms as men and may not be seen as, for example, "tough enough". (Some elements of a competitive culture are now visible in HE.)
- Managerialism (transformational) culture – based on mission and vision, with emphasis on customer service and supposedly "softer" values. This "new" managerialism is a feature of many new universities.

In the past 5–10 years, due to the rapidly changing environment in HE, short-termism has emerged as a response to the ever-changing pressures and demands of external agencies. Frequent restructuring, particularly in the new universities, has meant that many managerial jobs have been short-term, the incumbents of those positions being pressured to show quick results. Consequently, many would argue that HE has become less people-oriented, despite the rhetoric of "softer values" and team working (see Ozga and Walker, Ch. 7, this volume).

Higher education and equal opportunities

All HE institutes claim to be equal opportunities employers. Most have reasonably well developed equal opportunities policies and many would see such policies as part of the culture. However, despite this, equality of opportunity for women academics (and other under-represented groups) has clearly not been secured. Equal opportunities polices are also held up by employers to indicate "We have no problem here!" It can also sometimes be difficult for women who are promoted to shed the image of "token woman", someone whose promotion was down to forward-thinking equal opportunities policies. (Perhaps they were just the best person for the job!)

Duke's (1997) account of managing equal opportunities as a senior manager in HE is indicative of the issues which still need to be addressed. In an era of research competitiveness and outputs, establishing a culture more oriented to teaching (which Duke argues is more actively supported by women than men) is difficult. He notes that:

> The strategies and tactics required for promoting a 'teaching culture', for equal opportunity, for the community university and for staff development have much in common. They are loosely linked at the softer, more caring end of the spectrum in what seems to be an increasingly tough, competitive (male?) world. . . . (Duke 1997: 56)

The implication is that equal opportunity policies may be "set aside" when they conflict with other (more important or immediate) objectives. The apparent lack of success of equal opportunities policies in HE may also be explained by Newman's (1995) levels of change approach. She identifies three levels within an organization at which action may be needed in order to effect cultural change:

- the symbolic level which signals what is important and valued in the organization
- the layer of organizational practices – the norms of behaviour embedded in the systems and structures – and
- the layer of values – the deeply held attitudes and beliefs prevailing in the organization

Newman argues that a change at one level, e.g. the symbolic level, can never be effective unless linked to changes in the other layers. Hence the introduction of an equal opportunities policy (a new set of symbols) will not effect cultural change unless it is linked to substantive changes in behaviours, practices, and structures and systems. Interestingly, some organizations are moving away from equal opportunity policy to a managing diversity approach (see, for example, Liff 1993). This fits with Smircich's (1985) view of managing for multiple realities. However, it is possibly too soon adequately to assess the major effects of this approach.

Hidden barriers

The current culture in HE is not only male-dominated but imposes often hidden barriers. Some of these hidden barriers may in fact be deliberate, e.g. disaffiliation tactics (McAllister and Tripoli 1989) in which individuals are specifically chosen for exclusion from information and hence power (power in itself is a much wider debate which is not addressed here – it is also an issue within the men, masculinities and management debate). Simpson et al. (1987) show that women are denied access to networks, while the absence in many organizations of women mentors is also problematic (for example, Noe 1988).

Other barriers may be more subtle. In the new managerialist culture of HE, accountability, as evidenced by systems of performance appraisal, is key. Such systems can, however, work both for and against women (Thomas 1996). Within her study, Thomas found that some women academics used appraisal to their advantage (in terms of recognition and promotion), while others felt severely and further disadvantaged by this tool. Thomas (1996: 152) argues that appraisal is a "disciplinary tool", which has served to define "a highly gendered model of the new academic". Her research indicates that, in order to gain a voice, some women academics conformed to the model of long hours and research outputs and, for this group of women, appraisal confirmed performance. However, for other women, appraisal confirmed "failure", and their "achievements" (often centred around teaching and pastoral care) were discounted.

While Thomas (1996: 153) notes that appraisal could be used to ensure that HE is more receptive to women's needs and experiences thus changing the culture, she concludes that:

> ... the experience of appraisal for most women in this case is that it has failed to challenge the masculine-based norms and values of the institution.

Women's domestic responsibilities also pose a potential problem/barrier HE culture currently values long hours as a sign of commitment. To counter this, Cockburn (1991) suggests that there is a need to redefine values and, in particular, to introduce an economic policy which makes a 30 hour week the norm for all. Hewitt (1993) also posits a new model of work, where only a small minority of people would work a "normal working day or week", and more flexible working practices would become the norm.

It is recognized that women often have a very different career path to men, combining periods of full-time work with part-time employment, temporary employment and full-time child care. Again "valuing diversity" should allow possibly alternative skills earned in this way to be valued. We have for years, particularly in new university environments, attempted to measure "things" (largely undefined) which allow us to assess the potential of students, usually mature, who do not have formal traditional qualifications. However, this is not done on a large scale in HE at academic staff level.

Conclusion

Where does this leave us? Well, clearly, the issue of gendered management style and the debates around sameness versus difference do little to explain the under-representation of women in management positions. However, some key issues do emerge from the above examination of the extensive research undertaken by feminists into gender inequality in organizations:

(a) The issue of structures (as per Kanter 1977) and the location of women within them leads us to look at the organizational systems which help to reinforce the current position of women in HE. An example would be performance appraisal systems operated within a work culture which fails to recognize and appreciate the contingency of many women's career paths.

(b) With regard to the concept of management, it appears that the traditional view of management is changing, many organizations, particularly in the private sector, now recognizing the need for a more person-oriented approach to management (Kettley and Strebler 1997). Thus the transformational (female traits) as opposed to the transactional (male traits) manager is being favoured (see Kerfoot and Knights, Ch. 12, this volume). However, while it may at first seem positive that traditional notions of management are changing, it is unlikely that this will ultimately change the position of women managers, particularly in the public sector, given the entrenched numerical dominance of men at senior levels. Moreover, there is a danger that this simplistic dichotomizing of male/female only serves to further reinforce gender stereotypes.

(c) The issue of culture remains an interesting one to explore. Within organizations one cultural group may be more powerful and dominate another, and certainly in HE one would have to argue that male culture (masculinism) remains prominent. As Mumby (1988) argues, domination occurs when the rules of organizational rationality are structured to favour certain vested interests and to militate against others. As this chapter has discussed, despite the multiple realities of organizational cultures, women will need to be in management positions before they can significantly influence management cultures.

(d) Finally, there is the vexed question of adaptation. Hood and Koberg (1994) describe the process of adaptation in which the newcomer is integrated into the culture, in the process acquiring an increasing level of compatibility with the new environment.[2] They further describe adaptation as having two parts: acculturation and assimilation. Acculturation brings about a change in the non-dominant individual or group's behaviour to that of the dominant group. Hence acculturation would see the woman academic *adapt* to the style of the male-dominated organization in order to gain approval and possibly promotion (as in Thomas's 1996 study), in the process mimicking masculine forms of behaviour.

Assimilation is the *acceptance* of the non-dominant group into the dominant group's environment; clubs, cliques, etc. Thus women academics may be allowed into the common room or invited to the pub on Friday afternoon! According to Hood and

Koberg (1994), acculturation and assimilation are not mutually exclusive and one can facilitate the other. However, it is important to note that acculturation does not guarantee assimilation.

Clearly, if HE is ever to fulfil its current equal opportunity rhetoric as practice and actuality, then neither acculturation or assimilation is the answer. Much more emphasis must be placed on changing the culture rather than the style. And this means men changing rather than women adapting. The recognition that biology is not destiny (nor traits) gives us hope.

Notes

1. It should be noted that much of the literature on management talks in an asymmetrical way about managers and women managers, and immediately underlines a potential difference. Few people talk about male managers.
2. See Kerfoot and Knights (1993) for discussion of acculturation and assimilation, notably in respect of men's relationship to privileged gender and organizational discourses.

References

Adler, N.J. and Izraeli, D. (eds) (1988) *Women in Management Worldwide* New York: M.E. Sharpe

Bacchi, C.L. (1990) *Same Difference* London: Allen and Unwin

Bagilhole, B. (1994) "Being different is a very difficult row to hoe: survival strategies of women academics". See Davies et al. (1994), pp. 15–28

Bassett, P. (1997) "Sharp increase in number of women executives in UK, *The Times*, June

Blake, R.R. and Mouton, J.S (1964) *The Managerial Grid: Key Orientations for Achieving Production Through People* Houston: Gulf

Boylan, E. (1991) *Women and Disability* London: Zed Books

Burton, T. (1993) "Management, 'race' and 'gender': an unlikely alliance?", *British Educational Research Journal*, **19**, 3, pp. 275–90

Cockburn, C. (1991) *In the Way of Women: Men's Resistance to Sex Equality in Organisations* London: Macmillan

Collinson, D. and Hearn, J. (1994) "Naming men as men: implications for work, organization and management", *Journal of Gender, Work and Organization*, **1**, 1, pp. 2–22

Collinson, D. and Hearn, J. (1996) *Men as Managers, Managers as Men: Critical Perspectives on Men, Masculinities and Managements* London: Sage

Corrin, C. (1994) "Fighting back or biting back? Lesbians in higher education". See Davies et al. (1994), pp. 58–74

Davidson, M.J. and Cooper, C.L. (1992) *Shattering the Glass Ceiling – the Woman Manager* London: Paul Chapman

Davidson, M.J. and Ferrario, M. (1992) "A comparative study of gender and management style", *Target Management Development Review*, **5**, 1, pp. 13–17

Davies, L. (1992) *Women and Men in Educational Management: an International Enquiry, IIEP Research Report 95* Paris: International Institute for Educational Planning

Davies, S., Lubelska, C. and Quinn, J. (eds) (1994) *Changing the Subject: Women in Higher Education* London: Taylor & Francis

Department of Education and Science (DES) (1992) *Statistics of Education: Teachers in Service, England and Wales* London: HMSO

Department of Trade and Industry (DTI) (1997) *Competitiveness UK: Our Partnership with Business* DTI, November

Dobbins, G.H. and Platz, S.J. (1986) "Sex differences in leadership: how real are they?", *Academy of Management Review*, **11**, 1, pp. 118–27

Donnell, S.M. and Hall, J. (1980) "Men and women as managers: a significant case of no significant differences", *Organizational Dynamics*, **8**, 1, pp. 60–77

Duke, C. (1997) "Equal opportunity versus elitism? Culture change in a new 'old university'", *Journal of Gender, Work and Organization*, **4**, 1, pp. 47–57

Eagly, A.H. (1987) *Sex Differences in Social Behavior: a Social-Role Interpretation.* Hillsdale, NJ: Erlbaum

Eckersley, A. (1992) *Women in Business Now* London: Macmillan

Freeman, S.J.M. (1990) *Managing Lives: Corporate Women and Social Change* Amherst: University of Massachusetts

Frost, P.J. (1985) *Organizational Cultures* London: Sage

Gardner, W.L., Peluchette, J.V.E. and Clineball, S.K. (1994) "An impression management perspective of gender diversity", *Management Communication Quarterly*, **8**, 2, pp. 115–64

Gutek, B.A. and Morasch, B. (1992) "Sex-ratios, sex-role spillover and sexual harassment of women at work", *Journal of Social Issues*, **38**, 4, pp. 55–74

Hall, M. (1989) "Private experiences in the public domain: lesbians in organisations", in Hearn, J., Sheppard, L., Tansed-Sharif, P. and Burrell, G. (eds), *The Sexuality of Organization* London: Sage, pp. 125–38

Hanna, L. (1991) "Just the job?", *The Guardian*, 22 October, p. 20

Helgesen, S. (1990) *The Female Advantage: Womens' Ways of Leadership* New York: Doubleday

Henry, M. (1994) "Ivory towers and ebony women: experiences of black women in higher education". See Davies et al. (1994), pp. 42–74

Hewitt, P. (1993) *About Time: the Revolution in Work and Family Life* London: IPPR/Rivers Oram Press

Higher Education Statistics Agency (HESA) (1997) *Resources in Higher Education 1995/6* Cheltenham: HESA

Hood, J.N. and Koberg, C.S. (1994) "Patterns of differential assimilation and acculturation in business organisations", *Human Relations*, **47**, 2, pp. 159–81

Itzin, C. and Newman, J. (eds) (1995) *Gender, Culture and Organizational Change: Putting Theory into Practice* London: Routledge

Kanter, R.M. (1977) *Men and Women of the Corporation* New York: Basic Books

Kennedy, H. (1995) "Issues of gender", *Times Higher Education Supplement*, 3 November, pp. 15–16

Kerfoot, D. and Knights, D. (1993) "Management, masculinity and manipulation: from paternalism to corporate strategy in financial services in Britain", *Journal of Management Studies*, **30**, 4, pp. 659–79

Kettley, P. and Strebler, M. (1997) *Changing Roles for Senior Managers, Institute of Employment Studies Report 327*, University of Sussex

Krefting, L.A. and Frost, P.J. (1985) "Untangling webs, surfing waves and wildcatting". See Frost (1985), pp. 155–68

Larwood, L. (1991) "Start with a rational group of people – gender effects of impression management in organisations", in Giacolone, R.A. and Rosenfield, P. (eds) *Applied Impression Management: how Image-making Affects Managerial Decisions*, London: Sage, pp. 177–94

Lawless, L. (1991) "The ascent of woman", *Business Magazine*, July

Liff, S. (1993) "From equality to diversity", in *Organisations, Gender and Power: Papers from an IRRU Workshop* Warwick Papers in Industrial Relations, no. 48

McAllister, D. and Tripoli, A. (1989) "Disaffiliation and socialisation: people processing in organisations", *Academy of Management Journal*

McIntyre, A. (1994) "Sex makes a difference", *Institute of Public Affairs Review*, **47**, 2, pp. 17–20

Maddock, S. and Parkin, D. (1995) "A gender typology of organisational culture". See Itzin and Newman (1995), pp. 68–80

Marshall, J. (1984) *Women Managers, Travellers in a Male World* Chichester: John Wiley

Marshall, J. (1995a) *Women Managers Moving On: Exploring Career and Life Choices* London: Routledge

Marshall, J. (1995b) "Gender and management: a critical review of the research", *British Journal of Management*, **6**, pp. 53–66

Mathews, J. (1994) "Empowering disabled women in higher education". See Davies et al. (1994), pp. 138–46

Metcalfe, A.B. (1989) "What motivates managers: an investigation by gender and sector of employment", *Public Administration*, **67**, pp. 95–108

Miner, J.B. (1977) "Motivational potential for upgrading minority and female managers", *Journal of Applied Psychology*, **62**, pp. 691–7

Mumby, D.K. (1988) *Communication and Power in Organisations: Discourse, Ideology and Domination* New York: Ablex

Newman, J. (1995) "Gender and cultural change". See Itzin and Newman (1995), pp. 11–29

Nichols, N.A. (1993) "Whatever happened to Rosie the riveter?", *Harvard Business Review*, July/August, pp. 54–62

Noe, R.A. (1988) "Women and mentoring: a review and research agenda", *Academy of Management Journal*, **13**, 1, pp. 65–78

Powell, G.N. (1988) *Women and Men in Management* Newbury Park, Cal.: Sage

Rosener, J.B. (1990) "Ways women lead", *Harvard Business Review*, November, pp. 119–25

Ruijs, A. (1993) "Women managers in education – a worldwide progress report", *Coombe Lodge Report*, **23**, 7/8, pp. 570–610

Shakeshaft, C. (1987) *Women in Educational Administration* London: Sage

Simpson, S., McCarrey, M. and Edwards, H.P. (1987) "Relationship of supervisors' sex role stereotypes to performance evaluation of male and female subordinates in non-traditional jobs", *Canadian Journal of Administrative Sciences*, **4**, 10, pp. 15–30

Smircich, L. (1983) "Concepts of culture and organisational analysis", *Administrative Science Quarterly*, **8**, pp. 339–58

Smircich, L. (1985) "Is the concept of culture a paradigm for understanding organisations and ourselves?" See Frost (1985), pp. 55–70

Stevens, G.E. and Denisi, A. (1980) "Women as managers: attitudes and attributions for performance by men and women", *Academy of Management Journal*, **23**, pp. 355–61

Thomas, R. (1996) "Gendered cultures and performance appraisal: the experience of women academics", *Journal of Gender, Work and Organization*, **3**, 3, pp. 143–55

West, J. and Lyon, K. (1995) "The trouble with equal opportunities: the case of women academics", *Gender and Education*, **7**, 1, pp. 51–68

White, J. (1995) "Leading in their own ways: women chief executives in local government". See Itzin and Newman (1995), pp. 193–210

Wong, P.T.P., Kettlewell, G. and Sproule, C.F. (1985) "On the importance of being masculine: sex role, attribution and women's career achievement", *Sex Roles*, **12**, pp. 757–69

Wood, M.M. and Greenfield, S.T. (1976) "Women managers and fear of success", *Sex Roles*, **2**, pp. 365–87

CHAPTER FOUR

Rhetoric versus reality: why women tend not to apply for senior positions in secondary education

Lesley Thom

This chapter is based on research undertaken for a larger project concerned with women in the higher levels of educational management – or, more accurately, their comparative absence. In examining this issue, I intend to move away from the "deficit" model, which, although it takes many forms, tends to arrive at the same conclusion – that under-representation is the fault of women themselves; of their lack of ambition; of their inability to combine domestic with professional responsibilities; in short, their deficiency in one respect or another (for examples, and critiques of this, see, amongst others, Evetts 1987, Zimmer 1988, Grant 1989, Acker 1994). In contrast, it is my contention that despite equal opportunities rhetoric, there remains in place a series of covert processes and barriers which are implicit in the way in which the selection system is currently operated and presented by head teachers, and which deny many women the necessary experience to succeed in the promotion race. My research also suggests that the new, more masculinist managerial culture currently present in secondary education has altered the nature of the opportunities for advancement within the profession, and that this change has had a more adverse affect on women than on men.

The impetus for this study came a number of years ago, when I was involved in running a gender awareness training programme for one particular local authority. During a development meeting, I asked a group of secondary school head teachers why women were so obviously under-represented in their senior management teams. Their answer was unanimous, and delivered with rueful smiles all round – "Women don't get promoted, because women don't apply." National surveys (for example, NUT 1980, 1989), carried out at various stages during the 1980s, and backed up by my own more recent research, support the assertions of these head teachers. When it comes to applying for promotion to the higher levels of management, men continue to outnumber women by at least two to one; for many posts, the imbalance is probably greater still.

This "failure" on the part of women fully to engage with the promotion process is, on the face of it, hard to explain except in terms of a lack of ambition. Teaching, after all, would seem to be one of the more accessible employment arenas for female practitioners. For a start (and this serves only to highlight the male dominance within management teams), women are in the majority within the profession. During the academic year 1989–90, they numbered 243 000, as against 147 000 male colleagues (Fidler et al. 1993). Although this figure pertains to all sectors, the proportion being even higher in secondary schools, women's presence in teaching is both visible and well established. Conditions of service, in particular holiday entitlement and allowances relating to maternity/paternity, suggest that teaching should be one of the easier professions to combine with the domestic responsibilities which many women carry. The presence of strong unions, avowing a commitment to equal opportunities, is another positive factor. Moreover, the promotion system within education is clearly structured and (apparently) readily accessible to those with the appropriate qualifications and experience. Open, competitive and formal in nature, education should be able to avoid some of the difficulties identified by Collinson et al. (1990) in their study of sex discrimination in recruitment across five employment sectors. They concluded that formalization was an important first step when it came to increasing selector accountability and rendering practices more visible.

Collinson et al. also noted that formal and bureaucratic systems, while by no means flawless, were less likely to lead to role segregation, sex discrimination and stereotyping than the informal, "word of mouth" practices that they observed at frequent stages during their field research. Teaching has this formality; in addition, it offers a range of opportunities within a pluralistic structure which allows for changes both of employer and job role – many of them advertised with the assurance that applications from women, along with other "minority" groups, will be particularly welcomed.

Given this positive reinforcement, it might seem almost perverse of women not to apply for promotion in droves! The fact that they tend not to is, of course, potentially very convenient for those who feel comfortable with the male-dominated status quo. After all, if women resolutely keep themselves out of the promotion race by failing to apply for senior posts, what option is there for head teachers, except to shrug ruefully and carry on appointing men!?

While the facts about women's absence in management were impossible to refute, my own experience and observations made the deficit model, in all its forms, appear unsatisfactory as the only reason for women's under-representation. Having worked both in secondary schools and further education, I knew of many female colleagues – married, and in various stages of motherhood – who were confident, capable and ambitious. It seemed, therefore, that to concentrate on the motives (and usually the shortcomings) of women was to take a rather narrow view. In looking at the behaviour and motivation of women with regard to promotion, it felt more appropriate to focus not on women and their "failure", but on the structures which are in place, on the attitudes and perceptions of those who define and operate those structures, and on the way these are understood by those lower down the system. These were the concerns and issues which inspired the research project that this chapter now addresses.

The research project: methodological issues

The aim of the research was to establish a picture of the feelings, assumptions and types of behaviour which characterize the system of selection within a local authority, and the way in which women and men subjectively experience and engage in the process of planning and furthering their careers. The study was focused on a single local authority, and involved semi-structured interviews with ten head teachers, and 10 teachers at varying levels within the school hierarchy, backed up by a larger-scale questionnaire survey to which 84 staff responded.

The authority targeted for the research was selected because it offered a degree of social, economic and ethnic diversity which would, it was felt, add depth and variety to the study. In practical terms, it was an area which was both physically accessible and geographically familiar to me, having worked there as a teacher some years previously. Indeed, it was my experience as a gender awareness trainer in this authority which had originally sparked my interest in womens' career development.

Head teachers were seen as a key starting point for the research, partly because of their pivotal role within the school structure – Burgess (1993: 24) describes them as "critical reality definers . . . central to an understanding of school organisation" – and also because of their importance as gatekeepers, able to provide or withhold access to staff lower down the school. All the secondary head teachers in the area were, therefore, sent a letter which outlined the nature of the study and asked if they would consent to be interviewed. After a variety of follow-up approaches, just under 50 per cent of the available target group agreed. They numbered ten in total: nine men, and one woman.

Much thought was given to the framing of the interview schedule. I was anxious to ensure that my own convictions regarding equality of opportunity affected the collection of data, and its subsequent analysis, as little as possible, and that the responses I got from my subjects were as spontaneous and unrehearsed as they could be. I knew that many professionals, head teachers amongst them, are skilled in the language of equal opportunities, and suspected that if my questions were specifically gender-based I would simply be told what people thought I wanted to hear! I made a conscious decision, therefore, to couch the research project in strictly gender-neutral terms as an investigation into the recruitment and selection process in education; to begin with questions about practice and procedure, and to see if matters relating to gender emerged spontaneously. Where this did not happen, and a prompt was necessary, this was given in terms relating to equal opportunities across the board. Language or questions which might be construed as "feminist" in tone were stringently avoided. As I had hoped, most respondents (ten head teachers interviewed, nine men and one woman; 84 questionnaires returned, 42 women and 42 men; and 10 teachers interviewed, six women and four men) brought gender into the discussion without prompting. Where this happened, the data which emerged seemed particularly valuable, and perhaps more likely to be a true reflection of their feelings on the issue than if they had come in response to a direct question.

Nonetheless, issues of gender, and power doubtless did play their part in the way that the meetings with head teachers were managed – certainly from my own perspective, and probably from that of my subjects as well. I was very much aware when conducting the interviews of the difference in professional status between myself as a middle manager and the head teachers. Processing the experience afterwards, I realized the dimension that our respective genders had probably added. As Mickelson (1994: 139), says:

> ... when feminists engage in research on men ... and those with considerable power, they are likely to demand less from their subjects. It is crucial, however, that feminist researchers persevere and consciously probe.

During the process of transcribing and analyzing the interviews, I recognized that there were, indeed, areas where I had not "probed" as I should have done, and statements that I had left unchallenged. Although some of this may have been unconscious, it was in part at least deliberate – a result of my "gender-neutral" strategy, and my feeling that in avoiding overtly feminist interventions I would encourage my subjects to talk more openly, to be less on their guard. Certainly, without exception, the head teachers I interviewed spoke fluently and without apparent restraint on a range of issues related to recruitment and selection, and equal opportunities. However, this openness could, equally, have been a manifestation of the tendency commented on by Deem (1994: 157), when she described the different reactions shown to female and male researchers during a project involving school governors:

> ... it is ... possible that men revealed more about their views ... to the women in the team ... precisely because the women researchers were regarded as relatively unimportant and therefore entrusted with the kinds of confidences to which men's secretaries and wives may also be made party.

Once the head teacher interviews were complete, and preliminary analysis had taken place, four schools were made the subject of closer examination. A questionnaire and an interview schedule were devised which sought both to look at recruitment and selection from the perspective of mainstream teachers, and to test some of the head teachers' assertions – particularly those concerning equal opportunities issues – against the perceptions of their staff. Eighty four teachers responded to the questionnaire; of these, 10 gave an interview. The data gathered during this phase of the research not only conflicted with some of the assumptions made by the head teachers, but also indicated that there were significant differences in the professional experiences of women and men.

Head teachers and the selection process: autonomy and control

One of the most striking aspects to emerge from the first phase of the research, the interviews with the head teachers, was the nature and extent of their authority within the promotion system. Without exception, the head teachers acknowledged that they both sought and enjoyed substantial autonomy in operating selection in their schools. They all saw it as their role to orchestrate the process, and in so doing, they made a series of decisions which could be seen as crucial: (a) they defined the nature of a post, and decided its position within the school hierarchy; (b) they chose where and in what terms the post should be advertised; (c) they set the time scale for applications; and (d) they devised and wrote the job specification. The accounts that they gave suggested that their role throughout was both dominant and very much "hands on". Governing bodies (or at least, their Staffing Committees), whose task it is, nominally at least, to oversee the procedure, were actively involved by few head teachers in the early stages. As one head teacher said:

> Amongst ourselves, we would decide what sort of a person or role we were looking for . . . Before you took it to governors, because otherwise, if you were not clear in your own mind, you'd get driven.

Although one or two head teachers in the study made it clear that they had striven to involve governors in the selection process thoroughly and from the outset, in most cases governors did little more than "rubber stamp" the decisions presented to them by the head.

At interview, the autonomy of the head appeared to continue. Although it was usually a governor who chaired the selection panel, and might be expected for this reason to have a casting vote, most head teachers were confident that, should there be a difference of opinion over which candidate to appoint, they would carry the day. Articulating his autonomy, one head reflected:

> I've never had a governor overrule me . . . sometimes you've got to fight for it; you've got to argue your case. We've got some strong governors – I'm not saying they're all wishy washy, wimpy governors . . . But they will accept your case.

Those who had, on occasion, bowed to pressure from the rest of the panel to appoint someone who was not their first choice said, without exception, that their intuition had been correct; in each case, the offending appointment had been glaringly unsuccessful.

If governors appeared to pose little threat to the autonomy enjoyed by head teachers with respect to recruitment, neither, it seemed, did the local education authority (LEA). The schools in this sample were, as explained above, mixed with regard to status, but whether a school was grant maintained or LEA-run seemed to most head teachers, in the wake of Local Management of Schools (LMS), to have little bearing on how this aspect of their jobs, at least, was done. Although most schools, irrespective of status, used standard LEA documentation and those with a commitment to the LEA went through the motions of consultation with education officers, this came across as being more of a courtesy than a genuine sharing of the task.

Bradley (1997: 8), analyzing gender and power in the context of employment, points out that:

Despite the increased numerical presence of women in the workplace, men, utilizing their dominance in authority positions, are still primary definers in the world of employment . . . Men continue to set the rules of the workplace, and to define the meanings of such key terms as "worker", "skill", "merit" and "competence" . . . Even in feminized cultures, men remain the scriptwriters.

This was certainly true of the male head teachers in this survey, for they were in a position to orchestrate all aspects of the recruitment and selection procedure, and took substantial responsibility for devising procedural and practical initiatives. They also expressed a commitment to the career development of their staff, and saw it as their role (sometimes delegated to a deputy) to nurture and further this. There was, however, disagreement as to how this should be done. Most head teachers claimed to be both systematic and proactive in their approach, making a point of encouraging staff (female and male) who they felt were ready for a move, to seek and apply for promoted posts, and, where possible, putting appropriate internal responsibilities their way to enable them to gain necessary experience. Others felt that this was too direct and could lead staff into feeling either unwanted or, on the contrary, over-optimistic about their chances of advancement. These head teachers claimed to use more subtle forms of encouragement, usually through the mediation of one of their senior managers. Whatever the means, they all felt that they treated staff equally and monitored their professional development to the best of their ability.

The gender question: head teachers' perspectives

All bar one of the head teachers had positive things to say about the idea of women in management. They stated a commitment to the achievement of gender equality within the selection system, and demonstrated a level of understanding of the issues involved. All the schools in the study had a predominance of males at senior management (and, generally speaking, in middle management, too). All except one of the head teachers showed concern at this and expressed a desire to effect more equal representation for women, although many of them, having inherited a gender imbalance in staffing terms, found this problematic.

There was no admission in any of the interviews that head teachers considered women to be unequal to the task of senior management: on the contrary, many positive things were said about the variety of experience which women could offer, and for the personal qualities it was felt that they might bring to this role. As one head teacher remarked:

> . . . people say . . . that I'm biased towards women – and I am! Women work harder. My prejudice. More committed, more conscientious.

Some head teachers also claimed that they did not view breaks in service or unusual career patterns in any negative way – on the contrary, they said they valued the breadth of experience which women often bring. Such a perspective came from a head teacher comparing male and female applicants for a recent deputy headteachership:

> [The women's] experience tended to be more varied . . . the married ones had moved around with husbands . . . they'd had career breaks, and so they'd tended to have been in more schools, perhaps had more opportunities to do things . . . [which] . . . certainly for deputy head jobs, demonstrated more managerial skills. The guy who's been head of french, when you look into it, what's he doing, he's actually managed about two or three other people – What does it actually say about him?

There was an awareness of the home/work conflict faced by many women, and a number of head teachers described with frustration how they had observed talented female colleagues letting promotion opportunities pass them by. This, of course, is very much grist to the mill of the deficit model, and it would be unreasonable to suggest that the pressures of family and domestic responsibility do not, at times, force women to curtail or re-direct their career prematurely. The head teachers giving these examples appeared to feel somewhat bewildered and powerless to alter a situation in which, for once, their substantial ability to control events had temporarily abandoned them!

What was evident during the interviews was the lack of thought given to alternatives such as job sharing, and similarly flexible working practices which can sometimes present women and men with a way to combine home and career in at least a partially satisfactory way. Only one head teacher in the sample had actively offered a post as a job share, and this was internally, in response to a direct request from some of his female staff. Others had considered the possibility but rejected it, although when questioned they were unable to articulate why.

The head teachers in this survey, then, appeared on the whole to be extremely open to the notion of appointing women. But in how many cases are good intentions matched by the practice? During the interviews, it became clear that head teachers had identified a number of aspects of procedure to which (they felt) women and men tend to react differently. The effect of these, in the estimation of most of the head teachers, is to hinder women from applying. One example discussed was the job specification, which all the head teachers in the survey identified as a crucial tool within the selection process. Most of them expressed the view (not one, incidentally, confirmed by teachers in the second phase of the research) that the format they used, in which the major aspects of qualification, experience and personality required are divided into categories headed "essential" and "desirable", militated against women. Thus women were seen as less likely than men to apply for a post for which they did not hold all the essential requirements. Although they agonized frequently over the content, it apparently did not occur to the heads to deviate from their standard path and to reorganize their job specifications into a format which they felt might encourage more women to apply – or to make representations to their LEA to do this on an authority-wide basis.

Timing was another issue which generated discussion. In the experience of some head teachers, women tend to take longer to put in an application, and the process of interview is more complex for women than it is for men. As one head teacher noted:

> Women take longer. They've got more things to arrange. It's more complicated being a woman . . . Their appearance is so much more tricky to manage, to give the right message.

Altering the timescale for applications should, in most cases, be entirely possible for appointments to senior positions. These are rarely made in haste, and the timing of each stage would certainly fall within the remit of the head teachers interviewed for this survey. However, only one head teacher had attempted this, resulting in him receiving a larger number of female applicants than usual.

Another problematic variable which emerged was the composition of the interview panel. It was felt that, ideally, the panel should include both men and women, and that applicants should know in advance that this would be the case – since otherwise women might feel alienated. It can certainly seem to a woman coming into an interview situation that she is entering a strictly male preserve. For example, I have experienced interviews where the panel is all male, and find that, however non-threatening they set out to be, there is an inevitable feeling of isolation, which adds to the vulnerability felt in this sort of situation. There was little evidence from head teachers, however, of any effort to get a mixed selection panel; participants are usually invited on the basis of their position, and those with sufficient status to merit a place on the selection panel for a senior post are, of course, generally men.

On the whole, though, the head teachers interviewed presented a series of positive messages concerning their feelings about women and management. Most of them professed to want more female managers, and to consider that women have valuable qualities to bring to a management team; some, at least, showed an understanding of, and a respect for, non-traditional career paths. What was less clear is whether, and how, they were attempting to get this message across, both to the women on their staff, and to potential female applicants – establishing this was part of the purpose of the second phase of the research.

Career development and equal opportunities: rhetoric versus reality

The data for the second phase was gathered, as mentioned above, from 84 completed questionnaires and 10 interviews. The staff concerned ranged widely in age, experience and subject background. Many of the themes covered had emerged out of the head teacher interviews and much of what the teacher respondents had to say on these issues directly contradicted the perceptions and assumptions of their head teachers.

Some of the concerns felt by head teachers about the procedural aspects of the selection process appear to have been unfounded. For example, there seems to be no significant difference in the attitude of women and men to the layout of a job

specification – on the whole, men are just as concerned to meet the essential requirements as women. Equally, there was little suggestion that women take longer to
apply for jobs than their male counterparts. However, the positive feelings expressed
by many of the head teachers regarding the competence and desirability of women
managers, and the potential benefits of career breaks and non-traditional career paths,
were not getting across to their staff. A majority of the teachers in the sample felt
that being male was still an advantage within the selection process, and that career
breaks were detrimental to their chances. As one woman said:

> I know, with having had such a patchy and a peculiar sort of career pattern,
> that . . . schools that want someone that's just gone the traditional way up
> the ladder . . . [are] . . . probably unlikely to look at me.

None of the women surveyed seemed to have less confidence in their ability than
their male colleagues; nor did they find the thought of the selection process unduly
daunting. They did, however, appear to feel on balance that they had received
comparatively little help or support with their career development – most identified
themselves as their main source of help, whereas men were more likely to cite a
senior colleague, or their partner. Also, the men surveyed felt that their head teacher
viewed them in a positive light, whereas the women were less certain. As one
woman explained:

> I feel like he doesn't really know what I'm doing. You know, I think some-
> times he's a bit distanced from it . . . There is a lack of communication.
> So like I say, I'm not really sure what, what . . . [he] sees as my job, or that
> he really understands what I'm doing.

Few of the staff surveyed seemed aware of the head teachers' avowed commitment to the career development of their staff. Although they recognized that some
help was available, generally in terms of assistance with applications and interview technique, the vast majority of them tended to feel that this was too *ad hoc*
and unstructured to be of real value. Time, or the lack of it, was recognized as a
major factor that militated against the provision of effective help with career issues.
Appraisal was seen as a potentially helpful device in this regard, but one which
was, at present, not used to maximum benefit.

Crucially, however, it became clear from my interviews with mainstream staff
that there was one major difference in the way in which women and men were
experiencing their professional lives. All of the men interviewed had, at some stage
during their career, been offered the types of internal, whole-school responsibilities
which are generally seen as fundamental to the development of an impressive curriculum vitae, and therefore essential for promotion. Examples given included liaison
roles, timetabling, interviewing experience, and a range of other junior management and administrative experiences. One man claimed to be "on cloud nine" when
I interviewed him, having recently been offered by a deputy (apparently at the
suggestion of the head teacher) what he considered to be a prime opportunity:

He said, "Have you ever done any timetabling?" and I said, "No." He said, "Well, have you got ambitions beyond this role . . . it would be a good one to get under your belt if you have". That was his exact words. Which is very flattering. I've been very fortunate in that there's been somebody like [him] . . . in this case, who's done that to me at every stage of my career.

Another male teacher had already turned down one or two opportunities but, as is recorded below, remained confident that more would come his way:

I was offered a couple of whole school responsibilities, which I turned down, because at the time, I couldn't have taken anything more on; I was a bit under the weather.

I've been offered a . . . there's . . . a middle schools liaison job is coming up again, so I've been told . . . I think I'm going to get that, if it does come up.

A third male teacher related how the head had given him a number of chances to lead curriculum developments, including this one:

I was asked, would I like to introduce the GCSE, as it came in, the GCSE Co-ordinated Science course, along with another person . . . together, we, sort of, had to lead the science team through the changes that were needed to introduce the course.

In contrast, none of the women had been offered such roles, although they recognized their importance. Indeed, one woman teacher indicated that due to restructuring in the school, she was losing opportunities that had previously been available to her:

I think a lot of it is to do with the changes that have happened in the structure . . . I feel because they're taking away some of the whole school stuff, and the management stuff there, that actually I'm being pushed into, into a corner, because you need those skills to then move further. So it's actually, I think, limiting me . . . I mean, I go to the management meetings every week, but I'm not one of the management team there any more . . . I just go anyway. But I never get an agenda, or anything like that.

There are two aspects of particular importance here. First, there is a set of messages related to worth and competence which are implicit in the bestowing of such responsibilities. Secondly, and on a more practical level, there are the opportunities that such responsibilities provide people in acquiring valuable and necessary experience. As has been noted, most teachers, irrespective of gender, are reluctant to apply for posts for which they cannot demonstrate the requisite "track record". What emerged strongly from my data was that men are being offered this experience during the normal course of their professional lives – women are not. Although mine is a relatively small-scale survey, which makes no claims to be replicable, the point is clearly made that if this pattern is the same in other schools and other authorities, it is small wonder that men feel equipped to apply for more posts than women. Certainly, the situation found in these target schools is very similar to that described by Collinson et al. (1990: 117) in their broader industrial survey:

> ... with regard to informal training in the workforce, women were not given the sort, or the variety of tasks that would ensure their promotion. Consequently they gained neither the breadth of organisational experience and technical knowledge, nor the confidence to accept the responsibility for decision-making.

There is no suggestion in my research that there is a deliberate policy by the head teachers of excluding women from senior management positions by limiting their access to developmental experiences – far from it. What seems apparent is a more subconscious process, which is, however, no less potentially damaging to women's career progress. The reasons for it are not immediately obvious. Perhaps, as the woman quoted earlier suggests, head teachers simply notice their female staff less. Or possibly, it is a manifestation of the tendency identified by some of the head teachers surveyed to think in gender terms without always being overtly aware of doing so. As one head teacher admitted:

> ... it's difficult to break the mould that most head teachers are still men ... they like people like themselves; they appoint people with their own qualities, as they see their own qualities.

The compulsion to appoint in one's own image is now well documented. Morgan et al. (1983), noted, in their detailed study of the selection of secondary-school head teachers, that:

> ... a candidate's suitability was judged through the different colour filters of selector perceptions. The only filtering process shared by many lay selections was that derived from recollections of their own experiences of headteachers. The fixed mental impression which many demonstrated appeared to be influenced by their own schooldays, acquaintance with other headteachers or reports from the neighbourhood. ... Additionally, they appear to be influenced by perceptions of the previous head of the appointed school, and the ability of a candidate to fit the local peer group of headteachers. (cited by Delamont 1989: 173)

This tendency has been discussed by other writers. For example, Homans (1987: 104), described discrimination against female scientists employed by the National Health Service thus:

It was not . . . that men were *better* at the tasks which led to promotion, but that they possessed qualities which male managers already in post regarded to be essential to management . . . Moreover, certain managers tended to select candidates with characteristics similar to their own (i.e. some kind of mirror image).

Southworth (1990: 11–12), from a slightly different perspective, has this to say about the selection of primary school staff:

> Having done reasonably well out of the selection process themselves, are heads in danger of putting too much faith in the process, thinking if the present system of selection picked me it must be alright?
> Selection implies approval; having been approved it might seem perverse to question the means by which one is approved. As a result, head (and others) may be more willing to maintain selection as it is than to alter it.

Whether the reasons behind women's exclusion are overt or covert, what does seem clear is that the head teachers' rhetoric with regard both to career development and equal opportunities is not matched by the reality. The glass ceiling remains in place, ready to catch out women who try to reach "too high". It would be unreasonable, of course, to suggest that this is always the case. A proportion of women do climb a substantial way up the promotion ladder; indeed, 16 per cent of them reach the level of secondary-school head teacher. It seems, however, that their progress is still, despite the avowed commitment of head teachers to the contrary, a more complex one than that experienced by men. It is also evident that the obstacles that they face are not just the "self-inflicted" ones of home and family commitments, career breaks, and the like, as so many men managers would have us believe.

The challenges of management

When women do make it "to the top", their problems are, however, far from over. Far from helping the situation, new management cultures in schools appear to have made matters worse. For example, the opportunities for promotion are generally fewer; head teachers are cautious about committing themselves to permanent appointments; those posts which are available demand an accountability, and a range of practical and financial expertise which could easily put off all but the most resolute of applicants. Head teachers recognize these difficulties as clearly as anyone else:

> . . . now, of course, it means you're managing a declining budget every year, and you've got all that kind of stuff, the public issues, and what happens when the school is slammed in an Ofsted and so on. You can understand people picking and choosing . . . looking a bit harder at the challenges of the school.

There was also an increasing awareness amongst many of the teaching staff surveyed (male as well as female) that the glittering prize of a senior management post was becoming slightly tarnished! At all levels in the hierarchy, respondents were suspicious of the demands which the next step up was likely to make on them. As one woman said:

> I have this feeling that schools are more like businesses now, and the more they can squeeze out of you, the better, for less money, so . . . it sounds very crude, and I, I don't like this prospect at all.

And this from a man:

> I applied to a school which looked as if it was super-keen on everything, and its job specification was 6 miles long, and you thought well, yes, if I wore my underpants on the outside of my trousers, I might stand a chance of getting there! You know, Superman could do it, but I couldn't. There's no way I'm going to apply for a job which I feel from what they seem to be demanding that I couldn't do realistically.

For some respondents then – women and men – the future was not at all clear cut. A few of them were considering pursuing a career outside education. Others were weighing up the potential consequences of concentrating on classroom work, and forgetting management:

> Sometimes I think, well, do I, in 10 years' time want to be being told what to do by very young people who will be in senior positions within the school . . . You know, I'll be 47, and somebody might be 32, and a deputy head . . . And I, I passionately believe that the older you are, the wiser you are, and I think older people are wise people, you know. And I don't want some young upstart telling me.

Although both women and men were aware of the difficulties implicit in taking on a management role, it was an issue which seemed to be in sharper focus for women at all levels of the hierarchy. Perhaps this is because, once they have achieved a level of management success, their struggles seem to be far from over. As well as having to cope with the increased – and increasing – demands of their role, some of the women interviewed cited as a major problem relationships with men who were unprepared to accept their authority. One experienced deputy head, who was excellently equipped in terms both of skill and experience to apply for head-teacherships, was wary of taking this step – not because she doubted her ability, but because she did not want to put herself in a position of constantly having to battle to assert herself with male colleagues. She reflected:

> I've had a couple of experiences since I've been here . . . of people who seem to have taken a disliking to me . . . and I've found those situations really, really difficult to deal with. Because I don't know how to handle them.

And they've both been men . . . and they've both used bullying tactics . . . I've never had problems with a woman yet, I mean, difficult situations, but never, never . . . [such] . . . threatening . . . bullying tactics.

Other women emphasized the difficulty of having to deal with "enemies as well as friends" amongst the staff – and this is, clearly, not a phenomenon specific to teaching. Cockburn (1991: 67–69), in her study of equal opportunities initiatives across a variety of organisations, found a very similar situation within the civil service:

Women found some of their male subordinates unwilling to accept their authority. Most . . . were able to call to mind men who had "got a chip on their shoulder", "were awkward", who "created undercurrents".

There was resentment of women's successes . . . When a successful woman fails or has a setback there is "a lot of crowing over the humiliation".

What appears to be happening here is that men are warning off women, warning them not to compete with men for promotion and authority.

Judi Marshall (1995), too, in her recent study of female senior managers who have left employment, came across tales of prejudice and lack of co-operation, as well as a general distaste amongst her respondents for the type of tasks that they were increasingly being called upon to do. Of the eight women she interviewed, only one cited domestic responsibilities as being amongst her reasons for leaving. The rest were leaving their well paid, high-status jobs because they didn't want to compromise any more. The game was no longer worth the candle – they "wanted their lives back".

A personal conclusion

In talking to the women teachers, I found many resonances with my own professional situation. At the outset of the study, I was newly appointed to the post of head of department in a college of further education. With a firm belief in my own ability, I could see nothing to stop me going higher up the ladder – indeed, I planned to do so. Five years on, I find that my experience has been parallel to that of the women in my survey in some respects, although not others. Working in further education and struggling to make sense of the radical changes in practice and in management imposed on that sector, I didn't, for example, have actively to seek additional responsibilities to fill out my curriculum vitae – I had new responsibilities added to my job description with monotonous regularity, and I responded to this (as, it must be said, did my male counterparts) with singular ingratitude! When I felt that the time was right, I began looking for promoted posts, but, although I applied for one or two, in both schools and colleges, my attempts were half-hearted. On the whole, I found both the content, and the sheer volume, of the job descriptions unappealing. I didn't doubt that I could do the job – I doubted that I wanted to. Within my existing role, I grew increasingly impatient both with the greed of the organization and the nature of the tasks that I was expected to perform: selecting colleagues for redundancy; challenging them about sick leave; cutting their budgets; adding to their class contact time. When an opportunity arose, I left to begin my own business as a trainer and education consultant.

Although I had no regrets on a professional level, I did feel a lingering sense that I had, as a woman, in some way let the side down. In some way, too, it seems that education has failed to make the impact, in gender equality terms, that it might have. As Cockburn (1991: 231) says:

> Schools, colleges . . . and universities with their influence on both the content and the social relations of learning are potentially at the heart of social change. Few have emerged as leaders in sex equality, however.

Certainly, my research shows more evidence of missed opportunities than of progress and optimism. Although it is a profession whose numerous female practitioners might be expected to make substantial career gains, the teaching profession remains – at the top, where it counts – dominated by men and, as this chapter indicates, the opportunities and conditions required for advancement are still granted mainly, though covertly, to men. Women – some at least – are losing patience with the struggle and directing their considerable energies and skills elsewhere. If this sorry tale is not to continue then, first, those who manage and govern schools must become aware that they are not, as most of them claim to be, fully "equal opportunities employers" – and, having recognized this, they must make and follow *conscious* strategies to ensure that women are provided with opportunities to develop professionally, opportunities which are, in one form or another, currently given to men.

References

Acker, S. (1994) *Gendered Education: Sociological Reflections on Women, Teaching and Feminism* Buckingham: Open University Press

Bradley, H. (1997) "Re-conceptualizing gendered power at the micro-level: the example of the workplace", paper presented at the British Sociological Association Conference, University of York, 7–10 April 1997

Burgess, R. (1993) "Event analysis and the study of headteachership", in Schratz, M. (ed.) *Qualitative Voices in Educational Research* London: Falmer

Cockburn, C. (1991) *In the Way of Women: Men's Resistance to Sex Equality in Organizations* London: Macmillan

Collinson, D.L., Knights, D. and Collinson, M. (1990) *Managing to Discriminate* London: Routledge

Deem, R. (1994) "Researching the locally powerful", in Walford, G. (ed.) *Researching the Powerful in Education* London: Falmer

Delamont, S. (1989) *Knowledgeable Women* London: Routledge

Evetts, J. (1987) "Becoming career ambitious: the career strategies of women who became primary headteachers in the 1960's and 1970's", *Educational Review*, **39**, 1, pp. 49–62

Fidler, B., Fugl, B. and Esp, D. (eds) (1993) *The Supply and Recruitment of School Teachers* Harlow: Longman

Grant, R. (1989) "Women teachers' career pathways: towards an alternative model of career", in Acker, S. (ed.) *Teachers, Gender and Careers* London: Falmer

Homans, H. (1987) "Man-made myths: the reality of being a woman scientist in the NHS", in Spencer, A. and Podmore, D. (eds) *In a Man's World: Essays on Women in Male Dominated Professions* London: Tavistock

Marshall, J. (1995) *Women Managers Moving On* London: Routledge

Mickelson, R. (1994) "A feminist approach to researching the powerful in education", in Walford, G. (ed.) *Researching the Powerful in Education* London: Falmer

Morgan, C., Hall, V. and Mackay, H. (1983) *The Selection of Secondary School Headteachers* Milton Keynes: Open University Press

National Union of Teachers (1980) *Promotion and the Woman Teacher* London: NUT

National Union of Teachers (1989) *Promotion and the Woman Teacher* London: NUT

Southworth, G. (1990) *Staff Selection in the Primary School* Oxford: Blackwell

Zimmer, L. (1988) "Tokenism and women in the workplace: the limits of gender-neutral theory", *Social Problems,* **53**, 1, pp. 64–77

CHAPTER FIVE

Power and resistance in the academy: the case of women academic managers

Rosemary Deem

Introduction

This chapter examines issues related to power and resistance that arise from a study of feminist women academic managers working in universities or colleges of higher education in the UK. The analysis draws on data collected from 24 women managers working in a cross-section of higher education institutions (HEIs). The women were interviewed during 1996 as part of a research project focusing on the values and work practices of women managers in HEIs and the organizational cultures within which they worked.[1] All of those taking part in the research expressed a strong commitment either to feminisms or to the pursuit of equal opportunities for women. At the time at which they were interviewed, they held a range of temporary or permanent positions as middle or senior managers (for example, as head of department, faculty dean or pro-vice-chancellor). None of them regarded themselves as career adminstrators in the sense that a university personnel manager or finance director might, although one or two in very senior positions saw themselves as having embarked on a managerial career path. All remained active researchers and a number still had significant teaching responsibilities.

The increasing involvement of women with feminist beliefs in the management of public-sector organizations is a phenomenon that has become of increasing interest to feminist researchers in a number of countries (Yeatman 1990, 1995; Eisenstein 1991; Watson 1992; Blackmore 1995; Itzin and Newman 1995). The question of what happens when femocrats (feminists who enter bureaucracies and other complex organizations) are involved in the management of higher education is an important one for those of us concerned with the future shape and direction of higher educational institutions. Can feminists in these positions use their power to help advance feminist causes? Are they able to resist pressures to conform to other kinds of values and to adopt practices and strategies that are inconsistent with their feminisms? One view of femocrats, held by some in Australia, from whence the term emanates, is that they are feminists who have sold out to the organizations in which they work, thus abandoning their values, although others regard femocrats in a more positive light (Eisenstein 1991). Which of these applies to femocrats in the academy? The interview data used here offers only a partial and rather decontextualized view of the organizations and work practices which make up everyday life and routines for women academic managers. In order fully to explore the various organizational cultures which exist even within single institutions (Alvesson 1993), and the role of femocrats in those, it will be necessary to engage in more detailed fieldwork at the institutional level.[2] Nevertheless, the data presented here illustrate how a small number of feminist academic managers view their work practices and experiences.

Although there is now a growing body of feminist research related to women working in higher education (Acker 1994, 1996, 1997; Morley 1994, 1996; Morley and Walsh 1995, 1996; Yeatman 1995; Weiner 1996; Brooks 1997; Walker 1997), it is more usual to examine the role of women academics *qua* academics rather than to focus on those in management roles. This is despite a growing literature on women managers in general (Tanton 1994), on women managers in other sectors of education (Evetts 1990, 1994; Adler et al. 1993; Al Khalifa et al. 1993; Ozga 1993; Hall 1996) and on masculinities and management (Collinson and Hearn 1996).

Perhaps the absence of feminist research and writing on academic management is a reflection of feminist unease with the idea of academic women in management roles, or maybe it is because many feminists who write about academic women are not themselves in management positions. It may also be indicative of the scarcity of good research on academic management and leadership in higher education in general, since this is a field dominated by personal accounts (Bland 1990, Weil 1994, Slowey 1995, Eggins 1997). In so far as there is a more theoretical dimension, the theories are often rather uninspiring, paying little regard to current trends and debates in the social sciences and rarely looking at feminist research and scholarship. Regrettably, these deficiencies do not just apply to studies undertaken by men (Middlehurst 1993, 1997). It is important that existing feminist research on women and management and on gender and organizations, whether inside or outside public-sector organizations, *is* used as a basis for further investigation of women managers and leaders in post-school education (Marshall 1997). There are also welcome signs that an analysis of masculinities in the management of post-compulsory education is beginning to develop (Kerfoot and Whitehead 1996; Prichard 1996a, b; Whitehead 1996, 1997a, b).

Gender, power and resistance

The analysis of how gender relates to power and resistance is a complex one and, although much discussed, is also a highly contested arena of research (Connell 1987, Hearn 1987, Singer 1987, Weedon 1987, Davis et al. 1991, McNay 1992, Duerst-Lahti and Kelly 1995, Pilcher 1995, Cosslett et al. 1996). At the most basic level, gender is seen to be embedded within many different kinds of power relations, although this varies from concern with forms of collective oppression or power over other groups, to a more microlevel focus on power in connection with individual identities and subjectivities. Within the field of organizations, there is an increasing acceptance that some of the more deterministic formulations of power – for example, as a zero-sum concept or as a property of particular positions – are not particularly helpful (Davis et al. 1991, Savage and Witz 1992, Jermier et al. 1994, Duerst-Lahti and Kelly 1995). There has thus been a tendency recently, amongst both feminists and organizational theorists, to adopt various versions of Foucault's ideas about the close connections between power and knowledge as a way of studying power in organizations:

> By refusing to choose between power as either centred in abstract structures
> . . . or as a possession of individual subjects . . . Foucault offers the promise
> of escape from such dichotomies. (Knights and Vurdubakis 1994: 170)

Use of Foucault's concept of power in the analysis of organizations is not quite such a straightforward exercise (Knights and Vurdubakis 1994). However, it is evident from Foucauldian enthusiasts that power is best explored not as an abstract entity but in particular contexts, so that the local conditions can be fully taken into account. Of course, it also depends on what is being studied; while analyses of decision-making may lend themselves to theories that examine different kinds of decision-making processes and the power thus implicated (Komter 1991, Deem et al. 1995), an investigation of the work practices and experiences of particular managers, as in the data presented in the paper, requires a somewhat different stance.

It is also important that managing is seen as part of a labour process, in just the same way as other jobs are; otherwise some of the complexities of what are involved can be lost. It cannot be assumed *a priori* that the role of managers is one in which no resistance is possible, or that resistance by any employee always takes the form of collective strategies (Jermier et al. 1994). This leads on to the question of how resistance is conceptualized. Resistance, just like some theories of power, also has its roots in some rather deterministic theories of power. But just as power can come in many forms, and is neither an institution nor a structure, but rather arises out of social relations, so resistance is closely linked with the formation of individual subjectivities. Thus, it is perfectly consistent with such a view to argue that, in certain contexts, women managers may engage in resistance to some of what occurs in their organizations; for feminist managers, resistance is likely to be an important aspect of their subjectivities. Indeed, it is this ability to both resist and transform which some writers see as an important characteristic of women managers (Yeatman 1995). Hence this chapter both examines how gender power is embedded in the social relations of higher education and also explores the extent to which individual women managers use forms of resistance to bring about change in their organizations. However, despite the focus in the chapter on the relationship of feminisms to management, there is no assumption here either that what feminist managers do is necessarily part of a wider collective social movement. Although the notion of a critical mass of women managers is thought to be important by some researchers (Clark et al. 1997, Kanter 1977), the study reported here is more concerned with the practices and experiences of individual feminist academic managers.

UK higher education: setting the context

The context of our research is one in which massive changes are currently taking place. UK higher education, in common with higher education systems in a number of other highly industrialized societies, is presently undergoing considerable re-structuring. This has had considerable effects on work practices, work relations and working conditions (Cuthbert 1996, Prichard 1996a, Trowler 1996) as well as impacting upon funding, curriculum, pedagogy, research and student experiences. The kinds of restructuring involved include a much greater focus on external forms of accountability in respect of teaching/learning and research, as well as a continued reduction in the amount of public subsidy available to higher education. There is thus both a growing compliance culture and an emphasis on "doing more for less" which, as Trow (1997) notes, has tended to lead to a rather uncritical assumption that different or better management can be substituted for resources. The overall conditions and constraints affect all UK higher education institutions, but there are many local variations in how the changes have been implemented.

The kinds of institutions which make up UK higher education are more diverse than might be imagined. Thus, amongst the universities established by charter prior to 1992, there are considerable differences between "Oxbridge", the so-called "redbrick" universities, those established in the 1960s, and the former colleges of advanced technology. There are also the post-1992 universities, which were once polytechnics run by local education authorities; and colleges of higher education, which were once mostly teacher training colleges, but which now offer a wide range of courses, often accredited by universities. There are also four different funding agencies for UK higher education. Scotland, England and Wales each have their own higher education funding council, and in Northern Ireland higher education is funded directly by the Department of Education (known as DENI). So it would not be surprising if academic management posts in different universities were to exist in very diverse organizational cultures.

However, the overall position seems to be one in which workers in higher education, whatever the positions that they occupy, have less and less autonomy over the way in which the core activities of higher education are conducted, even if some autonomy remains over the content of teaching and research. It is suggested that this decreased room for manoeuvre affects managers as much as those they manage, even though the popular perception is often of managers as a separate category of people from ordinary workers. However, some recent analyses of higher education have started to address this and to analyze the labour processes of higher education as a whole (Cuthbert 1996). In the research considered done by the author, it was found that feminist women academics who were also managers regarded the latter aspect of their work as just one facet of their work subjectivities and identity. Other aspects of their work, such as research, and sometimes teaching, were also vitally important. Indeed, many management posts in post-compulsory education now involve working at the interface between management and teaching, with managers involved in both activities (Prichard et al. 1998).

"Womanagers" in higher education

Existing research on women managers, both inside and outside public-sector organizations, has examined the extent to which women have begun to break through the so-called "glass ceiling" and actually become managers (Hansard Society 1990, Davidson and Cooper 1992, Taylor 1995, Hall 1996, McRae 1996). There has also been an attempt to explore whether there are many differences in the approaches to management that are adopted by women as compared with those favoured by men (Marshall 1984, 1995; Korabik and Ayman 1989; Bell and Nkomo 1992; Frisby 1992; Adler et al. 1993; Ozga 1993; Powell 1993; Tanton 1994).

Despite the existing body of research, there remain unanswered questions and problems. For example, the investigation of possible links between gender and management style does not always say what is meant by gender (A variable? Gender relations? Gender subjectivities?). Furthermore, research on management veers between, at one extreme, seeing gender as relevant to the whole of management and, at the other, not even regarding it as important. Yet, as others have also noted, gender is sometimes very relevant to an understanding of management and organizations, and sometimes not (Alvesson and Due Billing 1997). Research on gender and management often omits mention of sexuality, yet this was raised by a number of our respondents and is clearly an issue for anyone who teaches (Epstein 1994, Morley and Walsh 1996). Existing studies of women managers do not do always do justice to the complexities of understanding how and why managers manage as they do; nor do they take fully into account either the effects of management roles and responsibilities or the organizational and policy climates within which these are located. Furthermore, although analyses of the connections between gender, organizational cultures and management have begun to emerge (Ferguson 1984, Cockburn 1991, Savage and Witz 1992, Itzin and Newman 1995, Gherardi 1996, Alvesson and Due Billing 1997), these analyses have been less apparent in studies of educational organizations than in research on other kinds of public- and private-sector organizations.

We found that the majority of our interviewees thought that gendered subjectivities, gender relations in the workplace and prevalent ideologies about gender roles were all important either in shaping their work as managers or in affecting how others regarded them and behaved towards them. For our interviewees, both the kinds of power relations within which they were positioned and their resistances to managing in particular ways were seen to be strongly influenced by gender. This was not only because the women themselves saw gender as a political issue, but also because it was perceived that others operated on the basis of certain kinds of stereotypes or were defending particular conceptions of masculinities in their behaviour towards women managers (Hollway 1996). There was not, however, a sense amongst our respondents that gender and sexuality were relevant merely, or only, because management styles were principally based on gender characteristics. Rather, the women interviewed were aware of the extent to which their gender and sexuality affected what they believed in and what they wanted out of their management roles. They saw it as affecting both power flows and resistances. For instance, several women said that they were interested in management as a way of shaping higher education in particular directions rather than as a means to increasing personal status and ego boosting:

> [I] lack . . . traditional ambition, which reduces the constraints associated with intimidation from senior management. (assistant dean, college of higher education)

Their gendered subjectivities as women, in a sector of education which is still primarily male-dominated at the policy and managerial level, were central to the way in which they approached management and to the way they were treated by colleagues. This took several forms. Some women were acutely aware that they looked different, as well as feeling different from the majority of their (male) colleagues, but this was in itself sometimes a source of power:

> I terrify lots of people, I'm very big, noisy and bossy, eff and blind a lot and wear outrageous clothes. (dean, old university)

> I'm not a mother and I'm not a heterosexual . . . I'm more visible than men, large with blond hair. (head of research, college of higher education)

Others noted that it was not necessarily their own gender subjectivities which shaped expectations of them, but the kinds of gender subjectivities that others expected them to have:

> . . . women have to fight off different kinds of expectations of them, if you have to make a hard decision you're put in a "bad mother" scenario whereas a man is not. (head of department, old university)

Lest this should create the impression that women manage largely on the basis of reactions to negative ideas and expectations, it is worth emphasizing that, in many cases, feminism itself was seen to contribute positively to their work:

> . . . the experiences of my life as a woman shaped the kind of manager I am. I've learnt a lot through bad experiences (e.g. at the hands of other managers). Engagement with management literature recognizing its limitations in analyzing women's experience, e.g. the notion of "feminine" manager, . . . trying to write about alternatives. (associate dean, new university)

Secondly, it was suggested by many of our respondents that gender relations in general, but particularly other men's and women's experiences of gender relations, both at work and at home, affect how women managers are regarded, the power relations within which they are positioned and how they are expected to operate:

> It's quite hard – staff will come to you with lots of things, load lots of stuff on to you whereas they don't do that to a man. Women have got to be

much sharper and clever about their boundaries in management situations. (research manager, old university)

Cockburn and Gherardi both suggests that a form of unwritten sexual contract exists in organizations whereby men have tacit understandings of how women should behave in the workplace, and may make moves to block women who do not follow these forms of behaviour (Cockburn 1991, Gherardi 1996). Some of our interviewees had encountered such views:

> You've got to be superhuman in some ways to get noticed. The contradiction of trying to manage when you don't agree with the male management introduces enormous stress. Many women in management want to be able to encourage involvement, make the best of everything, but boys want to play their games and don't like it when you draw attention to that. People want to disguise the reality. Male management is very unhappy with criticism or even critique. It gets very defensive and sneery. (associate dean, new university)

> Acceptable ways of being a manager are still very much patriarchially informed . . . men still prefer to work with men . . . you do operate in a different way with men because you have to use strategies to get male colleagues to do things . . . you must be encouraging and open with them. If you use the same ways that male managers do you wouldn't get the response they do. (dean, new university)

> . . . certain behaviour regarded as normal in men is condemned as careerist in women – I'm excluded from their little networks – whenever I do anything I'm thinking of how men will react – it cramps and restricts what you're able to do. (associate dean, old university)

Although not all of our respondents talked about the impact of sexuality on them and on the organizational climates within which they worked, those that did noted issues related both to heterosexuality and lesbianism and pointed out that female sexuality, of whatever kind, is an organizational issue in a way that male heterosexuality seldom is:

> . . . they're aware you're a woman, not just a person – there's some element of sexualization at some level without surfacing fully – it's not specific to managing – it's happening anyway. (director of women's studies, old university)

> Organizations are highly sexualized and a lot of the relationship between management and work force is about their use of power, sexualized interchange. Universities are heterosexual and homophobic organizations. The experiences of lesbians are ignored. (associate dean, new university)

It is important, however, not to overstate the case for gender and sexuality. Some women recognized that a variety of marginalizing experiences, not simply gender, had contributed to their way of operating in higher education:

> ... not only my gender is influential – I come from a very working class family and have done everything part-time and without funds and would hope this affects how I treat people. (Women's Studies coordinator, old university)

Unlike much of the literature on women and educational management, however, we did not gain the impression that the kinds of managerial roles that women took on were necessarily ones that were sharply influenced by their gender; thus we found women dealing with financial issues as easily as they did matters relating to curriculum or student/staff welfare. The question of the validity of women's knowledges arose in a number of interviews, but the following view was not widely held:

> Men find it difficult to give credibility to women, to believe that they know what they're doing, that they know anything. (assistant dean, new university)

There was evidence from our respondents of considerable recognition of engendered organizational cultures in higher education, and of cultures that are not very sympathetic either to women managers or to women in general as organizational actors. These engendered cultures are closely related not only to different values of the actors involved but also to different practices and ideas about appropriate organizational objectives. In turn, these cultures embrace and support social relations in which gender and sexuality are important dimensions of power flows, although those flows do not necessarily connect to positions held. Indeed, as we have seen from some of the quotes, implicit and explicit questioning of the legitimacy of women managers and their power/knowledge by men (whether in managerial posts or not) was a constant thread in our respondents' comments. In this sense, one can see that even resisting these challenges to legitimacy is, in itself, a significant act of resistance for women academic managers.

Engendered organizational cultures and power

To suggest that some or all of the organizational cultures of higher educational institutions may be suffused by gender and sexuality is still regarded as a somewhat controversial statement within the field of research on higher education. This is despite the greater awareness of the importance of gender and sexuality in organizations in general (Burrell 1984, Hearn and Parkin 1987, Ramsay and Parker 1992, Savage and Witz 1992, Adkins 1995) and a growing literature on gender and sexuality as key elements of educational organizations (Blackmore and Kenway 1993; Epstein 1994; Blackmore 1995; Morley and Walsh 1995, 1996).

Newman, in her analysis of cultures found in public-sector organizations, distinguishes between three different forms. First, there is the traditional, with a mix of administrative and professional discourses and elements of bureaucracy and hierarchy. Next is the competitive, where the emphasis is on entrepreneurial activity, market orientation and short-term goals, with the successful rewarded and other employees "downsized". Finally there is the transformative, where there are flatter structures, an emphasis on people and people skills, and a focus on longer-term visions (Newman 1995). Higher education institutions do not correspond closely to any of these, but it is possible to see the elements of collegiality, as in the old universities, as an extension of the traditional model, and signs of market-driven, resource-starved organizations, like some of the former polytechnics, in a liberal interpretation of the competitive model. Few of our respondents felt that they worked in an institution that was anything like Newman's transformative model. Some felt that their institution was close to her description of a competitive organization:

... very macho, very male. (head of department, new university)

An equal number of women thought that their institutions were a mix of collegial and hierarchical structures:

[The] VC likes line management but not all the managers agree ... at faculty level [it is] more collegial and team based. (head of department, old university)

Hybridization of cultural forms is much in evidence in UK higher education: there are pockets of traditionalism, evidence of entrepreneurial activity and aspects of newer, less bureaucratic organizational forms, within the same institution.

Academics, even those not significantly involved in administration and management, are likely to be part of more than one organizational culture – including those based on, for example, their subject or discipline, the organizational unit(s) to which they belong, their teaching, professional organizations and trades unions and their friendship networks. Not all of these will be suffused by gender, but the importance of subject orientation, organizational units and friendship networks were emphasized by a number of our respondents, particularly those who were involved in some way in women's studies. The latter provided a knowledge, power and friendship base from which to operate, no matter how marginal women's studies seemed to higher education institutions as a whole:

... women's studies – we don't belong anywhere. There are no feudal barons who protect our interests ensuring long-term visibility. (women's studies coordinator, old university)

Researchers not sensitized to gender do not see gender as an issue that affects the cultures and social relations of higher education (including definitions of knowledge) in the same way as, for example, they recognize the impact of the external assessment of teaching or research on higher educational organizations and their staff. Although Halsey took account of gender as a variable in his most recent study of British academics, he did not really consider the cultural implications rather than the demographics (Halsey 1992). Kogan and Henkel, in their research on changes to academic life and values, discuss academics and their identity as though academics were all of one gender (Henkel and Kogan 1996). Some of our interviewees were acutely aware that their values differed from those of many of their colleagues and that these differences could have real practical consequences, if only there were greater access to the mechanisms of change:

> ... women academics on the whole identify less with the system and unlike men, feminist academics are less preoccupied with order and power. If we had more space to teach in different ways, we could empower more women to think independently and critically. (director of women's studies, old university)

> I've liked being a feminist manager. It is interesting to get into senior levels, to get a sense of power plays, to see how political it is, how much information senior people have. My feminism allows me to make sense of it, but what worries me is I'm not in a position to help women. (head of department, new university)

The second respondent in particular conveys a sense of a glimpse of how to change things without being able to do anything. Compare this with someone who has reached the level of running an institution:

> There is not an equal opportunities policy which satisfies me and this is being worked on. There is only one clear commitment – to raise the proportion of female professors to 30% by the end of the decade and this is probably achievable but this was the only thing in place . . . On the whole my experience has been quite positive – the fact that there is no stereotype of a woman VC means that I have a lot of freedom to do things the way I want to. In another sense everything I do looks odd because people don't usually see women doing those jobs but most people don't have an image of a female VC. It is different to other male VCs but it is hard to say if it is because I am a woman.

It is clear here that the power to change is both relational and positional, and that resistance is not necessary. Other women interviewed perceived that there were still many cultural barriers to women's advancement, even though these have clearly been breached in other institutions:

> I think there is something to do with the glass ceiling – women can go so far, and no further. Such heavy handed patriarchal authority, using informal wooing (taking me out to dinner) to persuade me to carry on

being responsible for research even when I wasn't shortlisted for a Dean's post in the university. There are some women who are threatening, even sexually threatening to men in power. (head of research, new university)

Finally, much of the research on changes in higher education as a result of greater accountability, a more corporatist culture and drives towards greater "efficiency" has focused on the ways in which collegiate cultures or traditional academic values and concerns have responded to those changes. Although some have recognized that collegial cultures have problematic elements (McNay 1995), only one writer (Bensimon 1995) seems to have understood that collegiality is actually gendered. Some of our respondents agreed, noting the extent to which it can be a convenient cloak for forms of male sociability and patriarchal exclusion:

[If more women were to be part of senior management] we'd have to redefine the culture. It would take an enormous amount of emotional, psychological and structural change to make very senior management comfortable for women – it's such a boys' club. (head of research, college of higher education)

I don't think the culture of higher education has changed much over twenty years. We've still got a vice-chancellor who says we want the best man for the job and means just that. (dean, old university)

Although there was clear commitment amongst our interviewees to trying to achieve more diverse student populations and a more diverse staff at all levels, quite a few wondered if they could actually achieve what they wanted. Obstacles, past and present, were identified:

. . . the previous vice-chancellor wouldn't allow adverts to mention the [equal opportunities] policy. (faculty dean, old university)

(Equal opportunities) policies might not survive a concerted backlash:

. . . all changes have an impact and tend to make the institution revert to the familiar. (associate dean, new university)

Awareness of the nature of power relations amongst our respondents in higher educational institutions was widespread, but their perceptions of it differed widely. Fashionable theories of power talk about its fluidity and positive qualities, and this is reflected in some replies:

. . . power depends in part on position, in part on control of resources and in part on personal qualities. It is therefore quite widely distributed. (pro-vice chancellor, old university)

The formal hierarchy has a lot of power but networking (especially between boys) and the length of time people have been here are relevant – many have been here a long time and are quite senior so the formal reinforces the informal. (director, women's studies, old university)

... the principal and various people choose to use power because of their personalities – I'm aware of different sources of power. In my department people who are disillusioned exert power by exuding an air of depression and refusing to co-operate. (associate dean, old university)

However, there were also some more old-fashioned ideas of power in a number of other responses:

It's a tight knit oligarchy – a few have power if they choose to exert it and others fill the vacuum if they don't – Does power equal the resource base or is it power by default? (head of department, old university)

... general power lies with the VC – he exerts it strongly over a limited set of issues, e.g. fundraising, external links, university image – specific power lies with the management teams over their own areas. (provost, new university)

... it's patriarchal, a classical pyramid, vice chancellor with ultimate power. Rigidly structured, hierarchical layers. Senior managers have this idea that it's a flattened structure. When you're on top of the pile you see it all very differently. (assistant dean, new university)

If some of the plans of our women managers were unlikely to come to fruition because of the social relations, power flows and organizational cultures of the institutions in which they worked, were there alternative ways in which these women managers could respond? One form of resistance to institutional pressures to conform to male norms was to seek subjectivities that were not based just on academic management.

To be or not to be an academic manager?

Unlike the women FE managers whom we also interviewed in 1996, the women academic managers in HE more often had an alternative aspect of their work, research, which sustained their non-managerial identities at work. The desire to remain a researcher is both motivating and a reason for some very long working hours (the average working day of our respondents exceeded 12 hours). The data that we have suggest that research is also a form of resistance in at least two ways: to being a full-time manager and to being the kind of manager that male colleagues expect. Finally, it provides a mechanism by which feminist women managers try to stay closer to the colleagues whom they are intended to "womanage":

I'm very clear about what I want to achieve . . . most people are expected to choose between management and research – I want to do both. (head of research, college of higher education)

My own teaching and research are still very important to me and provide an alternative focus to the management tasks. (assistant dean, new university)

Thus, in many ways, these women academic managers, except at the most senior levels, still regard themselves as workers involved in the core activities of higher education, as well as being part of management. Although this is an apparently freely chosen route, and one which is almost certainly not exclusive to women managers, it also has other consequences. Those choosing it are thus subject both to the pressures of working in higher education and are also expected to "manage" those pressures and the difficulties that they give rise to, as they impact on other staff working within their institutions. Where such academic managers are also women, there may be additional pressures on them, in the form of expectations based on prejudice or gender stereotyping, which make the tasks involved in managing even more demanding than usual. Many of the women whom we interviewed were aware of the costs of the route that they had chosen, but wanted to retain the dimension of "otherness":

. . . the harder jump to make is that it's possible to be senior, to be feminist, but it's no good pretending you're marginal any more. You have to take responsibility – I worry about forgetting and being incorporated, so beleaguered I can't get a political purchase on it. (head of section, old university)

The women whom we interviewed derived their subjectivities from very complex sources. Their gender, sexuality, social class origins and academic interests were all important. For those who were mothers, this provided a further dimension (Leonard and Malina 1994, David et al. 1996). Despite the growing literature on masculinity (Brittan 1989, Hearn and Morgan 1990, Seidler 1994, Connell 1995), there has been little attempt to explore male academic life from this perspective except where managers are concerned (Prichard 1996a, b), the reverse of the situation on research about academic women.

In the former polytechnics, academic management tends to be viewed as a permanent specialism attached to a specific job, although this does not necessarily preclude the individuals concerned from engaging in research in the very limited time that they have left. Nor does it prevent them from applying for posts in which they can revert to a more academic role; two of our interviewees from new universities have done this since we interviewed them. In the "old" university sector, all except the most senior posts tend to be allocated on a temporary basis, sometimes for as little as two years. Thus subjectivities and time spans spent as managers may themselves only be transitory. The absence of a permanent identity as an academic manager does, however, mean that the institution and its failings can be viewed from a more detached perspective. Some of the managers whom we interviewed were very critical of their institutions. One said, of industrial relations in her university:

[It's] pretty awful really . . . the trades unions have little participation and are not consulted much . . . instead there's an unofficial newsletter . . . and people meeting in the corridor. (department head)

Others were scathing about their institutions' approach to external change:

. . . it's a jittery institution . . . geographically isolated, a bit claustrophobic, wants to retain its status . . . but with falling numbers. (assistant dean, old university)

The ability to voice such criticisms may itself be a form of resistance, as it distances those making the criticisms from those who toe a party line outside the institution. It also indicates the extent to which some women academic managers, despite their responsibilities and job titles, still feel marginal and somewhat resistant to the enterprise of managing higher education.

Conclusion: womanagers – coping good citizens or resisting, positive and powerful?

Are the various resistances and power plays of feminist academic managers no more than a token gesture, or do they provide a basis for an alternative approach to management? Acker's research on female Canadian teacher educators notes the emphasis often given to caring in describing feminized occupations such as nursing. The women academics whom she interviewed also saw themselves as occupying a caring role (Acker 1996), although this may be as much a product of the expectations of those who interact with women academics as the views of those academics themselves (Skeggs 1995). Acker found women teacher educators working long hours, taking responsibility for others and acting as good citizens in their departments. To a considerable extent, the women whom we interviewed also displayed such characteristics, although in our research they were doing so voluntarily, rather than reluctantly as in Acker's research. But these qualities and practices do not mean that women academic managers are passive or lacking in initiative. Such assumptions have sometimes been made about women in other professions who take on management roles. Acker and Yeatman wonder whether, if more women enter academic life, administration and management will come to be regarded as inferior to other activities in higher education (Yeatman 1995, Acker 1997). In fact, our respondents implicitly recognized this, in their desire to retain their research even when becoming managers. But it did not make them passive in the face of the many obstacles that they had to overcome – indeed, those very difficulties seemed merely to produce a stronger desire to succeed.

The research reported here was partly concerned with asking whether femocrats entering academic management were selling out their values and political commitment or extending them to new arenas. There is certainly no evidence that the feminist managers interviewed in the research reported here had given up or compromised their values on becoming managers. Although the data only partially support Yeatman's contention that femocrats' position as outsiders enables them to move more quickly in changing the culture and practices of educational organizations (Yeatman 1995), nevertheless there are some grounds for optimism. All of the women whom we interviewed were still committed to changing their institutions in feminist ways, and some were managing to achieve this. Despite the cultural hurdles that feminist academic managers are likely to encounter, particularly as a consequence of their distance from patriarchal organizational cultures, at the same time they may prove, even in spite of themselves, to be more powerful change agents than most of their male counterparts. Furthermore, it is apparent that resistance is as an important dimension of the possibilities of change as power itself.

Acknowledgements

I thank Jocey Quinn for her work on the telephone interviews, and our respondents for sharing their experiences of academic management with us. An earlier version of this paper was presented at the British Sociological Association Conference on "Power/Resistance", held at the University of York on 7–10 April 1997 and thanks are also due to the participants in the discussion that took place on that occasion.

Notes

1. The research was conducted by the author together with Jenny Ozga (University of Keele); Jocey Quinn (Lancaster University) was research assistant on the project.
2. The author, together with Oliver Fulton, Mike Reed and Stephen Watson (all of Lancaster University), began an Economic and Social Research Council funded research project on new managerialism in UK higher education in 1998; this research includes a strong gender element.

References

Acker, S. (1994) *Gendered Education* Buckingham: Open University Press

Acker, S. (1996) "Doing good and feeling bad: the work of women university teachers", *Cambridge Journal of Education*, **26**, 3, pp. 401–22

Acker, S. (1997) "Becoming a teacher educator: voices of women academics in Canadian faculties of education", *Teaching and Teacher Education*, **13**, 1

Adkins, L. (1995) *Gendered Work: Sexuality, Family and the Labour Market* Buckingham: Open University Press

Adler, S., Laney, J. and Packer, M. (1993) *Managing Women: Feminism and Power in Educational Management* Buckingham: Open University Press

Al Khalifa, E. et al. (1993) *Equal Opportunities in School Management* National Development Centre for Educational Management, Bristol University

Alvesson, M. (1993) *Cultural Perspectives on Organizations* Cambridge: Cambridge University Press

Alvesson, M. and Due Billing, Y. (1997) *Understanding Gender and Organizations* London: Sage

Bell, E.L. and Nkomo, S.M. (1992) "Re-visioning women managers' lives". See Mills and Tancred (1992)

Bensimon, E.M. (1995) "Total quality management in the academy: a rebellious reading", *Harvard Educational Review*, **4** (winter), pp. 593–611

Blackmore, J. (1995) "Policy as dialogue: feminist administrators working for educational change", *Gender and Education*, **7**, 3, pp. 293–313

Blackmore, J. and Kenway, J. (eds) (1993) *Gender Matters in Educational Administration and Policy* London: Falmer

Bland, D. (1990) *Managing Higher Education* London: Cassell

Brittan, A. (1989) *Masculinity and Power* Oxford: Blackwell

Brooks, A. (1997) *Academic Women* Buckingham: Open University Press

Burrell, G. (1984) "Sex and organizational analysis", *Organizational Studies*, **5**, 2, pp. 97–118

Clark, H., Chandler, J. and Barry, J. (1997) "Movement and organization: a study of gender in two universities", paper presented at the British Sociological Association Annual Conference, 7–10 April, University of York

Cockburn, C. (1991) *In the Way of Women: Men's Resistance to Sex Equality in Organisations* Basingstoke: Macmillan

Collinson, D.L. and Hearn, J. (eds) (1996) *Men as Managers, Managers as Men: Critical Perspectives on Men, Masculinities and Managements* London: Sage

Connell, R.W. (1987) *Gender and Power* Cambridge: Polity Press

Connell, R.W. (1995) *Masculinities* Cambridge: Polity Press

Cosslett, T., Easton, A. and Summerfield, P. (eds) (1996) *Women, Power and Resistance: an Introduction to Women's Studies* Buckingham: Open University Press

Cuthbert, R. (ed.) (1996) *Working in Higher Education* Buckingham: Open University Press

David, M. et al. (1996) "Mothering and education: reflexivity and feminist methodology", in Morley, L. and Walsh, V. (eds) *Breaking Boundaries: Women in Higher Education* London: Taylor & Francis

Davidson, M.J. and Cooper, G. (1992) *Shattering the Glass Ceiling* London: Paul Chapman

Davis, K., Leijenaar, M. and Oldersma, J. (eds) (1991) *The Gender of Power* London: Sage

Deem, R., Brehony, K.J. and Heath, S. (1995) *Active Citizenship and the Governing of Schools* Buckingham: Open University Press

Duerst-Lahti, G. and Kelly, R.M. (1995) *Gender Power, Leadership and Governance* Michigan: University of Michigan

Eggins, H. (ed.) (1997) *Women as Leaders and Managers in Higher Education* Buckingham: Society for Research into Higher Education/Open University Press

Eisenstein, H. (1991) *Gender Shock: Practising Feminism on Two Continents* Sydney: Allen & Unwin

Epstein, D. (ed.) (1994) *Challenging Lesbian and Gay Inequalities in Education* Buckingham: Open University Press

Evetts, J. (1990) *Women in Primary Teaching* London: Unwin Hyman

Evetts, J. (1994) *Becoming a Secondary Headteacher* London: Cassell

Ferguson, K. (1984) *The Feminist Case Against Bureaucracy* Philadelphia: Temple University Press

Frisby, W. (1992) "Women in leisure services management: alternative definitions of career success", *Loisir et Société*, **15**, 1, pp. 155–74

Gherardi, S. (1996) "Gendered organizational cultures: narratives of women travellers in a male world", *Journal of Gender, Work and Organization*, **3**, 4, pp. 187–201

Hall, V. (1996) *Dancing on the Ceiling: a Study of Women Managers in Education* London: Paul Chapman

Halsey, A.H. (1992) *Decline of Donnish Dominion: the British Academic Professions in the Twentieth Century* Oxford: Clarendon Press

Hansard Society (1990) *The Report of the Hansard Society Commission on Women at the Top* London: Hansard Society

Hearn, J. (1987) *The Gender of Oppression: Masculinity and the Critique of Marxism* Brighton: Wheatsheaf

Hearn, J. and Morgan, D. (eds) (1990) *Men, Masculinities and Social Theory* London: Unwin Hyman

Hearn, J. and Parkin, W. (1987) *"Sex" at "Work": the Power and Paradox of Organization Sexuality* London: Wheatsheaf

Henkel, M. and Kogan, M. (1996) *The Impact of Policy Changes on the Academic Profession* paper presented to the Society for Research in Higher Education, University of Wales Institute, Cardiff

Hollway, W. (1996) "Masters and men in the transition from factory hands to sentimental workers", in Collinson, D.L. and Hearn, J. (eds) *Men as Managers, Managers as Men: Critical Perspectives on Men, Masculinities and Managements* London: Sage

Itzin, C. and Newman, J. (eds) (1995) *Gender, Culture and Organizational Change* London: Routledge

Jermier, J.M., Knights, D. and Nord, W. (eds) (1994) *Resistance and Power in Organizations* London: Routledge

Kanter, R.M. (1977) *Men and Women of the Corporation* New York: Basic Books

Kerfoot, D. and Whitehead, S. (1996) *And so Say All of Us? The Problematics of Masculinities and Managerial Work* Occasional Papers in Organizational Analysis, **5**, (special issue), Department of Business and Management, University of Portsmouth

Knights, D. and Vurdubakis, T. (1994) "Foucault, power, resistance and all that". See Jermier et al. (1994), pp. 167–98

Komter, A. (1991) "Gender, power and feminist theory", in Davis, K., Leijenaar, M. and Oldersma, J. (eds) *The Gender of Power* London: Sage

Korabik, K. and Ayman, R. (1989) "Should women managers have to act like men?", *Journal of Management Development*, **8**, 6, pp. 23–32

Leonard, P. and Malina, D. (1994) "Caught between two worlds – mothers as academics", in Davies, S., Lubelska, C. and Quinn, J. (eds) *Changing the Subject: Women in Higher Education* London: Taylor & Francis

McNay, I. (1995) "From the collegial academy to corporate enterprise: the changing cultures of universities", in Schuller, T. (ed.) *The Changing University* Buckingham: Open University Press, pp. 105–15

McNay, L. (1992) *Foucault and Feminism* Cambridge: Polity Press

McRae, S. (1996) *Women on Top: Progress over Five Years: a Follow-up Report to the Hansard Society Commission on Women at the Top* London: Hansard Society

Marshall, C. (ed.) (1997) *Feminist Critical Policy Analysis: a Perspective from Post Secondary Education* London: Falmer

Marshall, J. (1984) *Women Managers* Chichester: John Wiley

Marshall, J. (1995) *Women Managers Moving On* London: Routledge

Middlehurst, R. (1993) *Leading Academics* Buckingham: Open University Press

Middlehurst, R. (1997) "Leadership, women and higher education", in Eggins, H. (ed.) *Women as Leaders and Managers in Higher Education* Buckingham: Open University Press

Mills, A.J. and Tancred, P. (eds) (1992) *Gendering Organizational Analysis* London: Sage

Morley, L. (1994) "Glass ceiling or iron cage: women in UK academe", *Journal of Gender, Work and Organization*, **1**, 4, pp. 194–204

Morley, L. (1996) "Interrogating patriarchy: the challenges of feminist research". See Morley and Walsh (1996), pp. 128–48

Morley, L. and Walsh, V. (eds) (1995) *Feminist Academics: Creative Agents for Change* London: Taylor & Francis

Morley, L. and Walsh, V. (eds) (1996) *Breaking Boundaries: Women in Higher Education* London: Taylor & Francis

Newman, J. (1995) "Gender, and cultural change". See Itzin and Newman (1995), pp. 11–29

Ozga, J. (1993) *Women in Educational Management* Milton Keynes: Open University Press

Pilcher, J. (1995) "The gender significance of women in power", *The European Journal of Women's Studies*, **2**, pp. 493–508

Powell, G. (1993) *Women and Men in Management* London: Sage

Prichard, C. (1996a) "University management: is it men's work?" See Collinson and Hearn (1996), pp. 227–38

Prichard, C. (1996b) "With my body I thee work: the changing embodiment of managerial work in a reconstructing UK higher education", paper presented at the Society for Research in Higher Education Conference, December, University of Wales Institute, Cardiff

Prichard, C., Deem, R. and Ozga, J. (1998) "Managing further education – is it still men's work too?", paper presented at Gender, Work and Organization Conference, UMIST, Manchester

Ramsay, K. and Parker, M. (1992) "Gender, bureaucracy and organisational culture", in Savage, M. and Witz, A. (ed.) *Gender and Bureaucracy* Oxford: Blackwell

Savage, M. and Witz, A. (ed.) (1992) *Gender and Bureaucracy* Oxford: Blackwell

Seidler, V. (1994) *Unreasonable Men: Masculinity and Social Theory* London: Routledge

Singer, L. (1987) "Value, power and gender: do we need a different voice?", in Genova, J. (ed.) *Power, Gender and Values* Edmonton, Canada: Academic Press

Slowey, M. (ed.) (1995) *Implementing Change from within Universities and Colleges* London: Kogan Page

Tanton, M. (ed.) (1994) *Women in Management: a Developing Presence* London: Routledge

Taylor, A. (1995) "Glass ceilings and stone walls: employment equity for women in Ontario school boards", *Gender and Education*, **7**, 2, pp. 123–42

Trow, M. (1997) "More trouble than it's worth", *The Times Higher Education Supplement*, 24 October 1997, p. 26

Trowler, P. (1996) Academic responses to policy change in a single institution: a case study of attitudes and behaviour related to the implementation of curriculum policy in an expanded Higher Education context during a period of resource constraint, unpublished PhD thesis, Lancaster University

Walker, M. (1997) "Women in the academy; ambiguity and complexity in a South African university", *Gender and Education*, **9**, 3, pp. 365–81

Watson, S. (1992) "Femocratic feminisms", in Savage, M. and Witz, A. (ed.) *Gender and Bureaucracy* Oxford: Blackwell

Weedon, C. (1987) *Feminist Practice and Post-structuralist Theory* Oxford: Blackwell

Weil, S. (ed.) (1994) *Introducing Change from the Top in Universities and Colleges* London: Kogan Page

Weiner, G. (1996) "Which of us has a brilliant career? Notes from a higher education survivor", in Cuthbert, R. (ed.) *Working in Higher Education* Buckingham: Open University Press

Whitehead, S. (1996) "Men/managers and the shifting discourses of post-compulsory education", *Research in Post Compulsory Education*, **1**, 2, pp. 151–68

Whitehead, S. (1997a) "The gendered transition of education management", paper presented at the Gender and Education International Conference, 16–18 April, University of Warwick

Whitehead, S. (1997b) "Identifying the subject at work: arenas of power/resistance in education management", paper presented at the British Sociological Association Annual Conference "Power/Resistance', 7–10 April, University of York

Yeatman, A. (1990) *Bureaucrats, Technocrats, Femocrats* Sydney: Allen & Unwin

Yeatman, A. (1995) "The gendered management of equity-oriented change in higher education", in Smyth, J. (ed.) *Academic Work* Buckingham: Open University Press, pp. 194–205

CHAPTER SIX

How does it feel? Women managers, embodiment and changing public-sector cultures

Joanna Brewis

This chapter examines the extent to which women managers in the UK public sector experience their work as embodied subjects: how influential do they see their bodies to be in terms of their working lives? Moreover, do they believe that their bodies represent obstacles or useful resources to them at work? The question of how it feels to be a female manager in what might be seen to be a more efficiency-oriented and managerialist public sector is central to the analysis. The chapter draws on qualitative research conducted in higher education, the social services, local government, the NHS and the Probation Service.

The body, women and work

Clegg (1990) suggests that the discursive basis of the modern Western organization, which elsewhere has been labelled "scientific modernism",[1] represents an early appropriation of Enlightenment thought by thinkers such as Saint-Simon and Comte. Its premise is that humans cannot make adequate decisions about how their world should be managed if they do not *subdue* their "lower order" functions, and by so doing develop their capacity for reason; thus humans must become less "bodily" and more intellectually oriented. Scientific modernism therefore places, claims Clegg, particular importance on the need for human beings to be able to: ". . . respond to a changing environment and to manage complex systems" (Clegg 1990: 28). Its emphasis on the need to repress our physicality/biology makes the human condition a battle against the "threat" of our bodies, deemed to be the carrier of dangerously animalistic instincts (Watts 1975: 168; Bauman 1983: 36).

The onset of the division between public and private spheres during the eighteenth century can be seen to bear testimony to the powerful effects of scientific modernism (Foucault 1980). Martin describes the public sphere as a site:

... where "culture" ... is produced, where money is made, work is done, and where one's efficiency at producing goods or services takes precedence over one's feelings about fellow workers. (Martin 1989: 16)

The private sphere, on the other hand, became the arena:

... where "natural" functions like sex and the bodily functions related to procreation take place, where the affective content of relationships is primary.... (ibid.)

Weber (1964, 1968, 1970) famously identifies the organizations established in the public sphere during this period as bureaucratic, suggesting in fact that the purest form of bureaucracy is to be found in the "modern European states" (Weber 1970: 204). This bureaucratization of the public sphere was apparently intended to ensure that processes of production, education, health provision and so on were at all times governed by reasoned thinking, buttressed against the more "unpredictable" components of the human condition. This theme – that the design of the modern organization is such that there is an attempted foreclosure of the possibility that our bodily "drives" might "impinge" on the "cool rationality" (McDowell and Court 1994: 729) demanded in the public sphere – is a common one in organizational studies. Marcuse (1969: 200–1) argues that modernity, and the onset of capitalism in particular, has brought about the desexualization of the public body; he attributes this to the objective of controlling the body and rendering its labour power useful (see also Gramsci 1971: 297; Burrell 1984, 1992). Importantly, this "quelling" of the body in the modern workplace has been identified by (pro)feminist organizational theorists as problematic for women, given that they have historically been considered to be more closely connected with their bodies, because of their role in carrying and giving birth to children (see, for example, Martin 1989). It has been suggested, therefore, that what is being "refused admission" to modern organizations are the supposedly "feminine" elements of the human condition. Thus scientific modernism, and the type of organizations that have been established as a result of its powerful effects, are identified as masculinist; the scientific modernist degradation of the body is used to explain, at least in part, why the modern workplace is a "man's world" (Martin 1989, Mills and Tancred 1992, Hearn 1993, Parkin 1993). Consequently, scientific modernism can be seen to constitute, in a Foucauldian sense, organizational subjects who relate to themselves and to others in ways which consolidate the myth that women are less capable of reason than men, and thus less suited for organizational life. A prominent example is sexual harassment, often conceptualized as a technique used by men to reinforce the construction of women as bodily much more than they are rational (Schneider 1982; Konrad and Gutek 1986; Collinson and Collinson 1989: 99–103, 107–9).

The body itself is also a contentious issue for feminism; for example, the controversy within radical feminism as to whether female biology is oppressive (Firestone 1971, Brownmiller 1975) or life-enhancing (Daly 1984). However, there are well established difficulties with arguing that physiological differences represent the basis of "femininity" and "masculinity", as radical feminists seek to do (Jaggar 1983, Eisenstein 1984, Hutcheon 1988, Moore 1988, Tong 1989). At what is conceivably the other end of the theoretical spectrum, Foucauldian analysis suggests that there is nothing stable enough in the human condition to permit generalizations based on some kind of gendered essence; rather, that gender differences are constituted by the powerful operations of discourse such that we come to think of ourselves, and to interact with others, in ways which reflect dominant understandings of what it means to be female/male (Foucault 1980; Butler 1987, 1990, 1993; Bordo 1990, 1993; McNay 1992; Grosz 1994). Given this continuum of feminist theorizing about the female body, particular attention will be paid later in this chapter to the implications for the female respondents of their sense of the origins of their embodiment.

This chapter now moves to analyze the ways in which public-sector women managers experience their bodies at work. The 12 women respondents (for whom pseudonyms are used throughout) whose accounts are discussed here participated in a series of in-depth qualitative interviews during the summer of 1997. Appendix 1 offers brief biographical details for each respondent. Given the use of convenience sampling to select respondents, the size of the respondent group and the nature of the interviews, no attempt is made to generalize from the experiences of these respondents to the experiences of women managers in the wider public sector. Rather, the aim is to provide insight into *these* women's experiences of managing in the public sector and what *their* experience of embodiment seems to mean in their working lives.

Listening to women managers: public-sector management and the gendered body

The public sector post-1979

The respondents pointed to several key dimensions of recent public-sector change, which are echoed in the relevant literature. The remit of this chapter does not permit extended discussion of these issues, but a brief summary is required to set what follows in context. The three main themes raised by the women were that:

- The public sector has become much more like the private sector (see Pollitt 1993: 44; Farnham and Horton 1996d: 15–17).
- There is a new emphasis on the use of resources in terms of efficiency, effectiveness and economy, a decline in the unit of resource itself and emerging demands for accountability and performance monitoring (see Flynn 1993; Pollitt 1993: 44; Farnham and Horton 1996d: 15–17).
- The market has become a major preoccupation (see Farnham and Horton 1996a) and there is a burgeoning consumerism amongst service users in housing and higher education (see Pollitt 1993: 44; Farnham and Horton 1996d: 15–17).

Implications for the role of the public-sector manager were, consequently, seen to be:

- Growing demands for resource consciousness, and for the achievement of precise outcomes (see Flynn 1993; Keeling, cited in Farnham and Horton 1996a: 36).
- A requirement to be much more consumer/market-oriented (see Aucoin, cited in Pollitt 1993: 49; Flynn 1993; Keeling, cited in Farnham and Horton 1996a: 36).
- A need to develop more generalist, or professional, managerial skills, as opposed to relying on clinical, social work or educational expertise. Pollitt attributes this to the Conservative belief in the "ideology" of managerialism:

> Managerialism is a set of beliefs and practices, at the core of which burns the seldom-tested assumption that better management will prove an effective solvent for a wide range of economic and social ills. (Pollitt 1993: 1)

The overriding feeling amongst the respondents, moreover, was that the changes had simply gone too far; that they had negatively impacted on both service to the public (seen to be the "bottom line" of the public sector) and on the quality of working life for staff in the sector. The respondents implied, therefore, that the emphasis within the public sector is now on formal rationality at the expense of substantive rationality (Merton 1957: 202–3; Weber 1968, 1994: 230; Willmott 1993: 532; Watson 1995: 79). The women here were also, in the main, less than optimistic that Labour will introduce any positive changes to the public sector, in the near future at least (see Farnham and Horton 1996c: 259, 1996d: 23). However, they did welcome the growth in openness, accountability and resource consciousness, and the decline in wastage; no one suggested that a return to the 1970s public-sector model was appropriate.

Having established the general direction which the female respondents see the public sector – and managers within it – taking, the discussion now turns to their experiences of having a female body in management within changing public-sector cultures.

Management, masculinity and femininity

The managerialism which now prevails in the public sector arguably demands skills which men have traditionally been seen to possess, due to their particular physiological configuration. These are rationality, objectivity, efficiency, precision, measurement, discipline, competitiveness, assertion and so on, as indicated in the respondents' own accounts, and summarized by Brenda:

> . . . [Management is], you know, making decisions, having control of other people, um, those sorts of things you tend to equate more with males than females.

Kerfoot and Knights (1996: 7–8) agree that managerial prerogative in modern organizations is premised on an ability to control, quantify, examine and grade – that is, on masculine forms of behaviour (see also Pollitt 1993: 8–9). This masculinity renders the environment, others and the self objects for the individual to control, as is also evident in what commentators on gender difference identify as powerful definitions of masculinity:

> Traditional masculinity focuses on dominance and independence, an orientation to the world which is active and assertive, which valorises competitiveness and turns its face from intimacy, achieving esteem in the glorification of force. (Glaser and Frosh 1988: 24)

Femininity, on the other hand, is seen to consist of:

> . . . the values of caring and sharing; the prioritizing of feelings; the reality and value of the non-marketable and non-material; the importance of the imaginative and creative; a vision of the wholeness and interdependence of the world, and a knowledge of and faith in the creative potential of stillness, rest and silence. (Hines 1992: 314)

According to these definitions, the masculine is premised on closing events and processes down, the feminine on opening them up (see also Ragland-Sullivan 1991: 75–6; Brewis et al. 1997). One might conclude, then, that the women respondents are operating in a difficult environment – one that requires skills which they are, by and large, seen not to hold. However, a more detailed analysis of the data regarding their experiences of managing, and their bodies in relation to this process, suggests that their situation is actually more complex.

Kerfoot and Knights (1995) argue that those who identify predominantly with the feminine (who, by virtue of the power of gender discourse(s), are female in the main) have tended to disengage from work, and management in particular, because prevailing organizational values are so alien to them:

> By contrast with men dominated by competitive masculinity, many women resist the bureaucratic displacement of intimacy and refuse to allow organizational goals and career aspirations to dominate their lives. (Kerfoot and Knights 1995: 19)

However, these women respondents did not perceive, by and large, that they personally have any difficulty in being more "masculine". Holly argued that:

> . . . the manager's role, it's about "can you be tough with these people if you have to?" And I think I can equally do that as any male can. . . .

Belinda, while suggesting that, for her, "masculinity" is very much a performance, still emphasized that she has little difficulty with appearing to be masculine in environments where it is demanded:

> . . . the classic for me is that inside I can be dying a million deaths and on, on the outside I can be very cool, very professional, very matter-of-fact.

Some respondents implied that femininity for them is perhaps easier because they are biologically female (Brenda suggests that she tends to be more lenient towards her students than her husband might be), and others that their socialization has made them more people-oriented. Nonetheless, their stance on the origins of masculinity and femininity suggests an equally strong sense that these bundles of characteristics are not necessarily locked into biology in any significant way.

Moreover, there was a strong sense on the part of many of the respondents that, despite the growing prevalence of a more masculine model of management in the 1990s public sector, traditionally feminine skills and attributes were a central component of their managerial work. What emerged here was a suggestion that effective public-sector management should now follow an ideal type HRM model, with the necessary combination being one of "hard" strategic skills and "soft" people skills (Guest 1989; Storey 1989, 1992, 1995; Legge 1995) – Marie, in fact, making this exact point.

Helen said that:

> You also actually are very reliant and dependent upon the skills of other people around you, close to you . . . I'm very dependent upon both Sandra and Molly [secretarial staff] . . . who will, will do the sort of tidying up and reminding and the checking up and remember [what] you've got to do. . . .

Helen also implied that she does not see her environment as something to be controlled in her present role:

> Um, I think you also probably need to have the ability to be able to juggle lots of different balls in the air and *not worry actually too much if you don't catch all of them at any one time* and you just have to let . . . some go. (emphasis added)[2]

The references here to depending on others and to the need for flexibility seem to be at odds with the definition of successful modern management as reliant on controlling others and environments. Moreover, Hines's "vision of the wholeness and interdependence of the world" is a key dimension of *femininity*.

Furthermore, Brenda said that her role required:

> . . . the ability to communicate, interpersonal skills of all kinds, writing skills, um, presentation skills, um, meeting skills, groupwork skills. . . .[3]

She also said that an important part of her role on the master's course is what she describes as "handholding" or "mothering" the students when they have problems. Interestingly, Alimo-Metcalfe (1995: 6) suggests that women managers tend to see an effective manager as being sensitive to the effect that their behaviour has on others. Furthermore, this reflects Hines's (1992: 314) reference to "caring and sharing; [and] the prioritizing of feelings" in femininity.

In a similar vein, Tracey suggested that public-sector managers need to empower their staff (as opposed to "dumping on" them) in order to achieve their objectives – since it is now, in a resource-constrained environment, much more difficult to motivate simply by using money. Meg also emphasized her preference for an enabling and empowering style of management. Rosener (1990) identifies an emphasis on staff participation in decision-making as part of her "transformational leadership" model, which she associates more with women than with men (see also Eagly and Johnson 1990; Alimo-Metcalfe 1995: 6; Brown, cited in Gherardi 1995: 90).

Given these claims that effective public-sector management is feminine perhaps as much as it is masculine, and the respondents' position on biology and gender, they seem overall to echo Epstein's argument that:

> . . . women ought to be in management because they are intelligent, adaptable, practical, and efficient – *and* because they are capable of compassion, as are other human beings. . . . (Epstein 1991: 151, emphasis added)

These women suggested that the management that they are required to perform is multifaceted – requiring a mix of masculine and feminine skills (cf. Rosener 1990; Siegel 1991: 154; Rosenbach and Taylor, cited in Alimo-Metcalfe 1995: 8). They also argued that they have no real difficulty with adopting a more masculine approach as and when it is required. Indeed, the respondents here seemed to imply that the experience of management might be instrumental in producing, reproducing and sustaining forms of gender identity which are relatively non-sex specific (see also Cohen 1991: 158; Epstein 1991: 151; Brewis and Linstead 1999).

Back to the body: others' perceptions at work

The above notwithstanding, Helen remarked that gender is undoubtedly a powerful organizing principle in terms of the way that we relate to each other:

> . . . you see someone and actually you're not certain whether they're male or female and you sort of look at them and it almost requires me, it's the sort of, *it's such a first thing* in the way in which you perceive people . . . it's an unconscious aspect I think about classifying people that, when you can't classify it, it sort of really diverts and focuses, well, certainly my attention. (emphasis added)

While the women respondents share a sense that their gender identities (and therefore their behaviour, thoughts and feelings) are not biologically prescribed in their entirety, they also acknowledge that powerful discourses around managing the new public sector, and around gender itself, constitute subjects who expect managers to be men, in the most essentialist sense of the word. Thus they may have to work to draw attention away from their female bodies and towards their managerial capabilities.

Brenda described her efforts to "blend in" in her previous management position:

> I felt more comfortable if I dressed in a similar way to the men. If I actually wore a jacket at a meeting with other men, um, I felt, err, that they might

have perhaps more respect for me . . . it gave me increased confidence in that environment, that I was perhaps on more equal terms with them.

Brenda's "power dressing" seems to represent an attempt to downplay the gender-signifying effects of her body (see also Lurie 1992: ix–xi; McDowell and Court 1994: 745; Brewis et al. 1997). The woman who power dresses appears more masculine; her curves hidden under the lines of a tailored suit, her shoulders emphasized by padding (Williamson 1980). Thus her body shape is transformed to signify a masculine orientation to working life – rational, objective, efficient and so on.

Holly commented that she also dresses for work to downplay her female body, in particular as a signifier of her sexuality:

I'd never go into work in a short skirt or anything like that just because I work in a very male-dominated environment, with clients as well . . . it's alright in the office, we work in a sort of like quite a sanitized, equal opps . . . environment, but you could go out working at the weekend and even supervisors, supervising the people on community service, make comments and I think I've always sort of shied away from that. . . .

She also commented that her male colleagues' and clients' perceptions of her attractiveness frequently make her angry:

You can be more acceptable if you're ni[ce], if they think you're nice looking and at the same time they can dismiss it a bit more, do you know what I mean? It's because you can't really understand . . . [you're] a bit of a girly and you're only a young thing [laughs] . . . sometimes it can just rile you up and you think "complete tosser" don't you? You know, and you just want to sit and give them your CV, don't you? [laughs].

Melissa suggested that the association of management, masculinity and the male body is a potential source of humour for her; that when a senior job had become vacant at work, she was joking with a woman colleague that they couldn't apply for it:

. . . 'cause we haven't got a todger. Um, you know, . . . it was a technical, plant maintenance job, you know, very much todger orientated. So we wrote "todger" on the advert, you see: "todger required". . . .

However, she acknowledged that having a female body can put her at a disadvantage in her managerial role; that clients very often refuse to believe she is a manager at all. Similarly, many of the women managers interviewed by Sheppard (1989: 146) suggested that the prevailing perception on the part of their male peers or clients was that of a dualism between "feminine" and "businesslike" (i.e. masculine). Thus they laboured to present themselves so as to imply that they were capable of behaving in a more businesslike manner than their bodies may have suggested. Here bodily appearance and demeanour is moulded to send out certain signals about capabilities; for women managers, this project is intended to undermine the meaning-laden properties of their biologically sexed bodies. This undertaking of a more masculine identity project can be seen to render the individual a "successful" organizational subject, someone who is "fit" to join the ranks of management; there is pressure to appear outwardly masculine in one's working life, even if one is biologically female.

In a related set of comments, Rachel, like Brenda, Holly and Melissa, argued that her body is potentially problematic with regard to her managerial role, given the demands that she perceives are placed on her in the changing environment of social services. Talking of her weight in particular (Rachel perceives herself to be overweight), she commented that:

> ...I think there are instances where people kind of equate body size with being a slob...How can you control circumstances if you can't control your body?

To be perceived as lacking control, a key dimension of the managerialist discourse which is so powerful in the contemporary public sector, clearly has ramifications for Rachel. Importantly, she suggests that men are better able to be larger and not be punished for it at work. Rachel also suggested that women's perceived attractiveness, which she sees as partially dependent on their size, is a major determinant in them finding and keeping employment. Olivia made a similar point:

> ...the downside of that [her size] is *higher* management I would say possibly think I'm as laxadaisical [*sic*] about my job as I am about my size...that I've let myself go to seed or whatever they are saying. (emphasis Olivia's own)

Olivia suggests here that her size perhaps signifies to her managers that she is unable to control her body shape and therefore raises questions about her work performance *per se*. Olivia agrees with Rachel that the same would not be true of a man who was overweight.

Respondents also commented that the size of the female body presents another set of difficulties in the working environment. Belinda said that her height sometimes works against her, because she frequently has to look up at people who may be junior to her in the organization. Rachel agreed with Belinda's analysis of her petite "femaleness" having a "minus side", because she says she is hardly in a physical position to confront violent clients successfully.

By way of contrast to the above, Meg seemed to suffer, not from being defined as physically female, but from being classified as "one of the boys". She is often put in an awkward position by her male colleagues' tendency to classify other women as sex objects; they frequently make sexist innuendos in her presence. However, Meg does not challenge these men because:

. . . it would be "Oh, blooming, you know, social worker, ex-social work",
you know, sort of "lefty" or I dunno, you know, "feminist" or something . . .
I know if I was very what they would perceive as radical then I wouldn't
get anywhere, probably.

This situation is clearly a dilemma for her. Holly, in a related comment, suggested
that:

. . . if you act in the same way as a man you're tougher or it's unfeminine
. . . or that you're hard faced or something like that, whereas a bloke that's
just some sort of natural authority that people assume it's OK to have. . . .

Meg's account of being complicit with sexist innuendo hints at the rigours of a
"blending in" strategy, as do Holly's remarks. Similarly, Sheppard (1989: 146, 148)
suggests that many of her female respondents had to work to appear feminine *at the
same time* as appearing to be businesslike. Otherwise they were punished for being
too masculine, for stepping too far out of their ascribed gender role, such as being
labelled a "lesbian" or a "castrating bitch" (see also Bartky, cited in Martin 1989: 21;
Yount 1991; Gherardi 1995: 135; Brewis 1998). For Tracey, however, being perceived
as more masculine or, as she puts it, "neuter" (because of her less than traditionally
feminine demeanour and body shape), works in her favour. She suggests that her
more misogynist male colleagues accept her, although they have problems with
other women.[4]

On the other hand, the female body was also seen to represent a potentially useful
organizational resource – not least in its attractiveness to men. Marie, for example,
made the point that:

. . . I think it helps me to look presentable and reasonably attractive to
industry . . . I just think being a *female* in a male's world can't be a bad
thing. (emphasis Marie's own)

She talked of a male colleague who says:

"If you're a male out there, you spend most of your day . . . meeting and
talking to other boring middle aged males" . . . "So how would you react
if you get a, you know, a female coming in of whatever age really?"

It is significant that Marie feels this way because it suggests that, for her, her
female body is somewhat "double-edged" at work. She suggests that she, like many
of the other respondents, has "suffered" from preconceptions about women and work;
thus her body can precede and define her, but it can also prove useful in terms of
marking her out as different and interesting in the work environment. Similarly, Hilary
talked of flirting with male colleagues to get her own way at work – "fluttering" her
eyelashes, for example. She says that this helps with the daily running of the hospital,
as well as keeping "stress levels down".

It is interesting to note, with the above in mind, claims in the organizational literature that women are caught in a sexist economic trap such that their only means of survival in employment is to offer themselves as sexual commodities. This strategy supposedly has the effect of reinforcing prevailing definitions of women as less rational and more bodily than men – and results in outcomes such as sexual harassment (Renick 1980: 660; see also Grauerholz 1989, Martin 1989, Bremer et al. 1991, Yount 1991).

However, this somewhat deluded offering of sexual self is not what these respondents are talking about. Marie suggested that:

> . . . it's not been unhelpful to, to, um, hopefully look reasonably, you know, appealing but I, I wouldn't say there's an allurement element to that. I don't think I've ever kind of gone in to *allure* anybody or . . . use it, um, overtly. (emphasis Marie's own)

Hilary says that she knows when to flirt and when not to, as did Melissa, who mentioned that part of her repertoire of persuasion at work is to be "a little bit girly", putting her head on one side and adopting a wheedling tone. However, she also stated that she only does this with her team, whom she knows well and is close to. Melissa also spoke disapprovingly of a colleague of hers who used her body as a "control, um, type mechanism", leaning over desks wearing low cut tops. Appearing *overly* sexy, then, is unwise, according to these respondents. Their feminine attractiveness is a resource that must be carefully managed, not exploited – otherwise they risk censure apart from, it is implied, a loss of belief in their own abilities.

Melissa, Belinda and Rachel also all made comments about women's bodies being less threatening and therefore useful for defusing tension in the working environment. Melissa commented that, in her organization, it is usually women who are sent to deal with violent clients: ". . . because . . . historically it's been quite a calming influence, you know, and, and, people actually start to talk to a woman rather than talk to a guy . . .".

Belinda recalled an incident dating back to her work as a psychiatric nurse. A male patient who was over six foot tall had spent the day trying to escape from the ward. He ran off again when Belinda's night shift took over, and she told of how she had chased after him, with no one else accompanying her:

> We got to the end of this corridor and he stopped and looked down at me and I looked at him and I said, I said "Please come back". I said "There's nothing I can do". I mean men had been jumping on him all day, you know, to try and restrain him . . . and he looked at me, and he was mad as houses he was, he looked at me, he said "Alright then" and we walked back, we just linked arms and we walked back to the ward. . . .

Belinda is, as she pointed out, only five foot one. She suggested that sending a "big burly man" into this kind of situation often "makes people frightened". This relates to Lamplugh's (1996: 67) research, in particular her suggestion that women

94

are less likely to be the target of violence from the public both in and out of work because they are good at either avoiding or defusing aggression, whereas men tend to "meet aggression with aggression" and so spark confrontation. Moreover, here it seems that Belinda's tactics of persuasion *combined with* her small stature worked better than the more physicalized techniques employed by her male colleagues. In a comment which might be seen to be related to these issues, Hilary identified a strong perceptual association between the female body and looking after and caring for someone – therefore claiming that patients adapt more easily to female nurses.

Another issue initially raised in the comments about problems caused by perceptions of the female body at work was pregnancy. Brenda, however, offered another take on this. She talked of how her body had become "public property" during her pregnancy; colleagues feeling able to comment on her body shape and to touch her stomach. In addition to comments about how this was occasionally wearing, she also said:

> . . . it's nice in a way because we all like attention and it's nice to get that attention . . . most of the time it's quite nice 'cause it means, you know, that people are actually concerned and are excited for you and wanting to talk about it and that's basically what they're saying, isn't it?

Brenda's changing body shape during her pregnancy seems to some extent to have allowed her to sense her colleagues' feelings about her – they had been able to express their concern and affection for her, and this had been a largely positive experience. Marie, in the same environment, made a similar point about feeling:

> . . . just probably more warmth or concern . . . [I] just generally felt very, very kind of supported really.

while she was pregnant. Olivia also commented that many of her colleagues enjoyed following the progress of her pregnancy and that.

> . . . my *top* boss was actually pregnant when she came to work in the department, when she first moved, and it acted, acted as a real ice-breaker, because people were asking her about that, whereas probably normally people wouldn't speak to . . . a new boss. . . . (emphasis Olivia's own)

In sum, then, it seems as if the body as biologically gendered and, more specifically, feminine, plays a complex role in the working environment in terms of others' perceptions. It acts, however inaccurately, as a signifier to others of (the lack of) certain attributes, but can also, sometimes simultaneously, prove beneficial. It is also true that these women, while preferring in the main to suggest that biology/physiology has little to do with one's ability to be rational, logical or objective – or caring, sensitive and a good communicator at work – did suggest that certain biological functions presented obstacles for them at work.

95

Female biology and work

Several respondents talked about the potential difficulties caused by menstruation at work. Helen, for example, said that:

> ... if you've got a heavy period and you have to be, you have to be careful about how long you're going to spend in any one particular place at one particular time, then you sort of have to excuse yourself from a meeting and I think that's a pain. ...

Helen's comments reflect Martin's (1989: 94) argument that women trying to conceal their menstrual cycle from colleagues are "being asked to do the impossible"; to hide the fact of their periods in an environment where the organization of time and space pays little attention to such bodily events.

Rachel told an anecdote resulting from the juxtaposition of her biological cycle and the demands of her working life. She had been away on a training day at a remote location, and her period had started "with a flood". She was wearing a white skirt and, because the weather was warm, did not realize she had begun to menstruate until someone told her. As Rachel says, by this time her skirt was "covered with blood" and she could not obtain tampons:

> ... that was just *dreadful*. I went home [i.e. left early] ... I felt dreadful. I felt dirty, stupid, unclean, the, the whole thing really ... and angry, angry that my body had got in the way, yeah. (emphasis Rachel's own)

Rachel's account in particular bears testimony to the embarrassment that menstruation can cause for women at work, and reflects Martin's (1989: 93) conclusion about her respondents' accounts of menstruation in this environment – that women feel it is imperative never to be seen dealing with the "mechanics" of menstruation and, above all, never to allow menstrual blood to be seen on clothes, furniture and so on. The notion of menstrual blood having to be hidden from others stems, suggests Martin (1989: 92), from the powerful medical definition of periods as "failed [re]production" and therefore as unacceptable and dirty.

Hilary, in a different vein, talked of how painful and heavy her periods have been in the past, and that they frequently forced her to leave work early or to take time off, and Belinda mentioned another "classic" problem connected to women's biology, suggesting that pre-menstrual symptoms can affect work performance. She says that her symptoms include feeling neurotic, paranoid and "hating everybody". This connects to Martin's (1989: 121–2), point that pre-menstrual symptoms are very often perceived as a temporary loss of discipline – so prized in the modern workplace, amongst managers especially. Belinda also notes that, while living in a nursing home in close proximity to other women, their periods synchronized. She wondered whether this group's pre-menstrual symptoms had also synchronized and whether this had affected their collective decision-making and their coping strategies at work during these times. Meg said that her pre-menstrual symptoms had worsened as she has become older; that she is now "not coping as well with, with the stress" prior to her period.

Harriet also referred to the issue of PMT impacting on work performance:

> ... I mean I do think this whole biological cycle thing *is* different. I mean that I'm just not conscious that, that men *swing* in, in quite the same way [as women] ... that's clearly got to have implications for work ... [for] performance, and it's not at all clear that institutions in any sense are equipped to pick up on this, that they can use you when you are creative and leave you alone when you're not. (emphasis Harriet's own)

Harriet is explicit here that organizations are, as in the instance of menstruation and the use of time and space at work, not structured to easily encompass the "swings" that she associates with the pre-menstrual period. Belinda also made this point, as did Rachel, who, like Meg, suggested that her pre-menstrual symptoms have worsened as she gets older:

> ... certainly for *me* I have dreadful period pains and, um, alongside that more recently I'm getting migraines as well. Not necessarily the headaches but flashing lights, um, which just make life very difficult on those days. (emphasis Rachel's own)

Again, Rachel says that her working life means that she cannot organize her day to suit her physical condition; that if she has a migraine she is unable to cancel a meeting, for example, although she will be much less effective because she has difficulty concentrating. On the issue of the inflexibility of organizations in these circumstances, Martin comments:

> Women are perceived as malfunctioning and their hormones out of balance rather than the organization of society and work perceived as in need of a transformation to demand less constant discipline and productivity. (Martin 1989: 123)

Another respondent who has suffered from serious pre-menstrual symptoms is Hilary. She, like Rachel, gave an evocative account of how difficult this was for her:

> ... I'm usually OK now, um, but, yes, a few years ago I did get very snappy ... women who have never suffered PMT don't understand it. They're very lucky if they haven't and they are very lucky if they never suffered from dysmenorrhea, painful periods ... those are two I think of the worst things that God could ever give you, they are miserable and ... you just lose control completely.

Her symptoms included "severe" food cravings; weight gain; sore breasts; spots; and feeling tearful and paranoid. The pre-menstrual symptoms described by the respondents are all recognized as dimensions of "pre-menstrual syndrome", as Lever and Brush (cited in Martin 1989: 114) point out. Lever also suggests that 75 per cent of women suffer from some form of pre-menstrual symptomatology.

Clearly, then, there are issues around the female biological cycle and work which many of the women have faced and continue to face. Nonetheless, it is interesting to note that they all feel that some measure of control can be achieved over these circumstances. For instance, the respondents tend to agree that one should not, as Marie puts it, "give in" to the physical symptoms associated with menstruation in the working environment:

> . . . I don't like that word ["gives in"] because sometimes you don't have a choice, but it's how a woman *copes* and how much she's prepared to absorb some of these problems and still do her job professionally. . . . (emphasis Marie's own)

Hilary, for example, has worked hard to minimize her menstrual symptoms; in the first instance taking strong painkillers, later trying diarrhetics and the pill, and subsequently having acupuncture and taking primrose oil. Because the latter two treatments, while helpful, eventually proved expensive, Hilary now relies on:

> . . . mind over matter . . . [saying] "Look, this is real, but it's not real" . . . you know what the cause is, you just have to put a brave face on . . . I've learnt to take a lot of deep breaths.

Melissa talked of a colleague who has been prone to complain of her period pains and who, because she was pregnant at the time of the interviews, constantly drew attention to her bodily state at work by stroking her "lump". While Melissa was not directly critical of this woman, she referred to other female colleagues who:

> . . . use their body as a[n] um, "Oh, protect me" type thing . . . the poor me syndrome . . . to get people to feel sorry for them, um get attention. . . .

There is arguably something of this in her comments about her pregnant colleague – that this woman exploits her menstrual symptoms and her pregnancy to gain sympathy, and that Melissa does not approve of this strategy.

Rachel, although acknowledging that she has difficulty at work with her pre-menstrual migraines, talked of "living on pills" to minimize period pain, and says that she passes off her pre-menstrual awkwardness as "a clumsy day". Like Marie, she is not sure that "people notice it particularly . . . I just feel, just a bit silly". Unlike Rachel, however, Marie preferred to be more "upfront" about her menstrual cycle; suggesting that women perhaps need to be more open about their periods in the working environment. She says she always asks her colleagues to excuse her for her pre-menstrual aggressiveness. Belinda commented that men are now less "cynical" about menstrual symptoms and, therefore, that it is easier for women to be honest about their experiences.

As well as women themselves coping with the effects of their menstrual cycle at work, Belinda talked of trying to manage her team in a way which minimizes the problems caused by menstruation. Here she is talking about a former colleague's pre-menstrual symptoms:

> . . . she couldn't, err, get her words out right and she couldn't write properly. Yeah, it used to really knock her sideways. So you see as her boss, as her manager, we just used to work round that, um, so, you know, she wasn't writing reports two or three days before her period.

Many of the respondents also implied that menstruation is not necessarily the most significant biological problem that presents itself at work. Helen, for instance, said that people who have weak bladders would experience the same kind of difficulty in lengthy meetings as do women who are menstruating. Hilary talked at length about a recurrent back injury which she said left her with "absolutely no quality of life" and had necessitated frequent absences from work. Others acknowledged that men may suffer from their bodies as well. Meg said that:

> . . . I mean I have some, um . . . empathy with the, you know, supposed sort of male menopause.

And Belinda referred to:

> . . . how their [men's] moods are quite cyclical too and how insecure they can be and how emotional they can become. . . .

Belinda also pointed out that her management strategy of allowing for individual differences extends to men as well; for example, to a colleague who has childcare responsibilities.

The mothers, likewise, were reluctant to overplay the difficulties that pregnancy had caused them at work. Belinda, for example, offered the following comment about her nausea:

> . . . the very important point here, um, [was that] I felt that I had to keep going, you know, 'cause I had the mentality "If you're pregnant, you're not ill". I was sort of a bit intol[erant], intolerant of women who sort of played the sick role when pregnant. . . .

It was only when the symptoms became too difficult to cope with that Belinda consulted her doctor and he ordered her to take sick leave.

One could speculate that these women are being stoical about the difficulties that their biology causes in an effort not to underplay the contribution that they feel women can make at work. However, if this is the rationale behind their accounts of their bodily processes in the work context, it is possibly justified. In the nineteenth century, menstruation was seen as pathological and thus properly disbarring women from productive activity during their periods; a similar argument relating to PMT emerged in the early years of the Depression (Martin 1989). What seems more significant, though, is that these respondents agree that female biology can affect performance at work, but that organizations are often not structured in ways that take account of this. Moreover, they emphasize that individual women can act to minimize their own symptoms and control them, as well as accommodating others who are suffering. While this does not necessarily have an impact on the wider organizational frameworks that they work within, it seems to have beneficial effects for the individuals who experience the symptoms that they identify – such as Belinda's ex-colleague not being hampered by requests for reports at times when she felt physically unable to write them. Given this understanding of organizational processes, it is pertinent to return to Foucault, who argues that addressing oneself to the specific nuances of power as experienced in one's own particular situation (such as an individual woman striving to conceal her menstruation from colleagues because of wider discourse constituting the process as aberrant and disgusting) is crucial so as to resist what we perceive to be unacceptable effects of power at the "... most basic levels ..." (Foucault 1980: 99; see also Foucault 1979: 157). The micro-level of experience is where, for Foucault, the effects of power are felt – thus it makes the most sense to resist power at this level. The women here, then, constituted in particular ways as bearers of certain biological processes, *resist* these definitions to some extent by being:

- open about these processes to colleagues (Marie asking her colleagues to excuse her PMT, for example)
- challenging the dominant definitions of the processes (Belinda's refusal to define pregnancy as an illness, for instance)
- making efforts to manage the processes as they happen (such as Hilary's "mind over matter") and
- enabling other women to do the same (for example, Belinda's account of accommodating problems caused by menstruation)

Moreover, there is a strong theme in Foucault's work that the body can be closed off/opened up/re-fashioned in certain ways by different discursive regimes and, consequently, varying understandings of the body (see also Baudrillard 1993: 105; Brown, cited in Miller 1993: 275). Foucault (cited in Miller 1993: 277) declares that the power effects of discourse have resulted in us underestimating the plastic potential of our bodies, in the sense that we are constituted to place artificial boundaries around what our bodies are and can do. This is relevant here in terms of understanding the ways in which several of the women respondents seem to refuse to understand themselves as somehow tied into an oppressive and rigid biology. Their understandings of their biologies can be seen to interact with the physiology of menstruation, pregnancy and menopause to produce the lived experience of these phenomena (Lewantin et al., cited in Martin 1989: 12). Consequently, a woman who understands her biological processes as being something separate to her, as something entirely involuntary and outside of her control, will, we can suggest, experience these phenomena differently compared to a woman such as Marie or Hilary, who understands these processes as something that can be redefined, consciously managed or accommodated.

However, it is also true that there is something of what Martin (1989: 77–9) refers to as separation of body and self in the respondents' accounts of their biologies, which she also located in her own data – themes such as "Your body is something your self has to adjust to or cope with . . . Your body needs to be controlled by your self . . . Your body sends you signals." This indicates, on the one hand, less of a sense that menstruation, pregnancy and the menopause are things that women actually do, and more that they are events which they have to manage. Nonetheless, these women's sense of being able to redefine, direct and accommodate these processes, as opposed to simply tolerating them, does indicate some understanding of a more active role in these bodily events, as suggested above (Martin 1989: 86). Furthermore, unlike Martin's respondents, these women often suggested that organizations *should or can* be run in such a way as to legitimate these bodily processes. This implied reappropriation/redefinition of women's biology is something that Martin (1989: 130–5) emphasizes as potentially liberating for women. The respondents were also, on the whole, eloquent on what Martin (1989: 110) refers to as the "phenomenology" of these processes; often describing in vivid detail how it feels to menstruate, or to be pregnant. This led to a positive evaluation of pregnancy in particular, with descriptions such as "exciting", "extraordinary", "a miracle", feeling "privileged" or in "awe" being common to the mothers' accounts.

Conclusion

We have seen that, for these women, their bodies play a complex role in the working environment. While they differed as to how embodied they felt during the working day, many suggesting that this often varies depending on mood in any case, several important themes emerge from their accounts of "how it feels" to have a feminine body in the contemporary public sector:

- These women acknowledge that the changing world of public-sector management requires skills and attributes which are usually considered to be masculine.
- However, they have little truck with the notion that their biological sex makes them any less fit for managing, also suggesting that a significant part of their managing draws on more conventionally feminine attributes. They espouse a relatively fluid model of gender identity which acknowledges that women can strive to be masculine much as men can to be feminine.
- The women do, nonetheless, accept that their bodies act as signifiers in terms of their gender and that this has both benefits and drawbacks in the working environment.
- In terms of biology in its basest sense, they also acknowledge that their female bodily processes do occasionally cause problems for them at work, but they feel on the whole that these are manageable and, moreover, that organizations can and should make space for such processes.

It is therefore useful to ask the two-part question that Martin poses regarding women, their bodies and work:

> ... are women, as in the terms of our cultural ideology, relegated by the functions of their bodies to home and family, except when, as second best, they struggle into wartime vacancies? Or are they, drawing on the different concepts of time and human capacities they experience, not only able to function in the world of work but able to mount a challenge that will transform it? (Martin 1989: 137–8)

On the basis of the data reviewed here, the answers would appear to be a definite negative, followed by a qualified affirmative. The women here seem to be living out Gherardi's (1995: 94–5) "dual presence", her alternative to an "either/or" model of gender identity, which consists of the notion that women's identities may be "cross-wise" – subverting but not abandoning conventional feminine role models by operating in many arenas across the social. The respondents are aware of themselves as women and may enjoy the various bodily experiences that their biological sex affords them, as well as their socially constituted identities as feminine – but, at the same time, they do not acknowledge that these feminine bodies and identities are so rigid as to disbar them from full participation in the organization, a world which in any case they, through their evidently active participation, subtly reconstitute away from an otherwise predominantly masculine/masculinist mode.

Appendix 1: Respondents' details

National Health Service

Hilary is a staff nurse in an intensive care unit. **Meg** is a service manager within an NHS Trust. **Belinda** manages a substance misuse team within an NHS Trust.

Local government

Tracey is responsible for communications strategy and policy, and manages a communications team, in a local authority. **Olivia** manages a team whose main remit is housing benefit in a local authority. **Melissa** manages a team whose main remit is overseeing council housing in a local authority.

Higher education

Brenda is responsible for the first year of a Master's programme within a university management school. **Marie** manages a division of the profit-making arm of a university, her main remit being to generate income from non-governmental sources. **Helen** has overall responsibility for a group of degree and diploma programmes within a university management school. **Harriet** is involved in different levels of course management in a university management school.

Social services

Rachel is responsible for the childcare division within a geographical region of the social services, overseeing two teams of social workers.

Probation Service

Holly supervises a team of personnel who are responsible for arranging and overseeing community service.

Notes

1. Brewis (1996); following Geuss (cited in Reed 1985: 80–1).
2. Belinda actually suggested that this ability to manage several different tasks at once is a female skill.
3. Many of the respondents suggested that their bodies play a crucial role in communication at work – that body language (stance, gesture, tone of voice, even touching others) is a vital part of their communications "toolkit". Olivia, for example, stated that: ". . . probably if I was seeing a *landlord* and I wanted them to be aware that I was acting on government legislation, non-negotiable, then I've noticed myself that my whole stance, . . . the whole way I sort of hold myself . . . [is] quite different." (emphasis Olivia's own)
4. Rachel also argued that her body has advantages in her managerial role; when she is larger, she is seen as almost "genderless", whereas when slimmer she experiences sexual harassment from both colleagues and clients. However, as we have seen, she also feels that her size signifies to others that she lacks self-control.

References

Alimo-Metcalfe, B. (1995) "An investigation of female and male constructs of leadership and empowerment", *Women in Management Review*, **10**, 2, pp. 3–8

Baudrillard, J. (1993) *Symbolic Exchange and Death* London: Sage

Bauman, Z. (1983) "Industrialism, consumerism and power", *Theory, Culture and Society*, **1**, 3, pp. 32–43

Bordo, S. (1990) "Feminism, postmodernism and gender-scepticism", in Nicholson, L.J. (ed.) *Feminism/Postmodernism* New York: Routledge, pp. 134–53

Bordo, S. (1993) "Feminism, Foucault and the politics of the body", in Ramazanoglu, C. (ed.) *Up Against Foucault: Explorations of Some Tensions Between Foucault and Feminism* London: Routledge, pp. 179–202

Bremer, B.A., Moore, C.T. and Bildersee, E.F. (1991) "Do you have to call it 'sexual harassment' to feel harassed?", *College Student Journal*, **25**, 3, pp. 258–68.

Brewis, J. (1996) *Sex, Work and Sex at Work: a Foucauldian Analysis* PhD thesis, UMIST, UK

Brewis, J. (1998) "What is wrong with this picture? Sex and gender relations in *Disclosure*", in Hassard, J. and Holliday, R. (eds) *Organization/Representation: Work and Organizations in Popular Culture* London: Sage

Brewis, J. and Linstead, S. (1999) "Gender and management", in Fulop, L. and Linstead, S. (eds) *Management: a Critical Text* Melbourne: Macmillan

Brewis, J., Hampton, M.P. and Linstead, S. (1997) "Unpacking Priscilla: subjectivity and identity in the organization of gendered appearance", *Human Relations*, **50**, 10, pp. 1275–304

Brownmiller, S. (1975) *Against Our Will: Men, Women and Rape* London: Secker & Warburg

Burrell, G. (1984) "Sex and organizational analysis", *Organization Studies*, **5**, 2, pp. 97–118

Burrell, G. (1992) "The organization of pleasure", in Alvesson, M. and Willmott, H. (eds) *Critical Management Studies* London: Sage, pp. 67–88

Butler, J. (1987) "Variations on sex and gender: Beauvoir, Wittig and Foucault", in Benhabib, S. and Cornell, D. (eds) *Feminism as Critique: Essays on the Politics of Gender in Late Capitalist Societies* Cambridge: Polity Press, pp. 128–42

Butler, J. (1990) *Gender Trouble: Feminism and the Subversion of Identity* New York: Routledge

Butler, J. (1993) *Bodies That Matter: on the Discursive Limits of "Sex"* New York: Routledge

Clegg, S. (1990) *Modern Organizations: Organization Studies in the Postmodern World* London: Sage

Cohen, A.R. (1991) "Debate: ways men and women lead", *Harvard Business Review*, January/February, p. 158

Collinson, D.L. and Collinson, M. (1989) "Sexuality in the workplace: the domination of men's sexuality". See Hearn et al. (1989), pp. 91–109

Daly, M. (1984) *Gyn/Ecology: the Metaethics of Radical Feminism* London: The Women's Press

Eagly, A.H. and Johnson, B.T. (1990) "Gender and leadership style: a meta-analysis", *Psychological Bulletin*, **108**, 2, pp. 233–56

Eisenstein, H. (1984) *Contemporary Feminist Thought* London: Allen & Unwin

Epstein, C.F. (1991) "Debate: ways men and women lead", *Harvard Business Review*, January/February, pp. 150–51

Farnham, D. and Horton, S. (1996a) "Managing public and private organizations". See Farnham and Horton (1996b), pp. 25–46

Farnham, D. and Horton, S. (eds) (1996b) *Managing the New Public Services* Basingstoke: Macmillan

Farnham, D. and Horton, S. (1996c) "Public service managerialism: a review and evaluation". See Farnham and Horton (1996b), pp. 259–76

Farnham, D. and Horton, S. (1996d) "The political economy of public sector change". See Farnham and Horton (1996b), pp. 3–24

Fineman, S. (ed.) (1993) *Emotion in Organizations* London: Sage

Firestone, S. (1971) *The Dialectic of Sex: the Case for Feminist Revolution* London. Cape

Flynn, N. (1993) *Public Sector Management* New York: Harvester–Wheatsheaf

Foucault, M. (1979) *The History of Sexuality, Volume One: Introduction* London: Allen Lane

Foucault, M. (1980) *Power/Knowledge: Selected Interviews and Other Writings 1972–1977*, Gordon, C. (ed.). Brighton: Harvester

Gherardi, S. (1995) *Gender, Symbolism and Organizational Cultures* London: Sage

Glaser, D. and Frosh, S. (1988) *Child Sexual Abuse* London: Macmillan

Gramsci, A. (1971) *Selections from the Prison Notebooks* London: Lawrence & Wishart

Grauerholz, E. (1989) "Sexual harassment of women professors by their students: exploring the dynamics of power, authority and gender in a university setting", *Sex Roles*, **21**, 11–12, pp. 789–801

Grosz, E. (1994) *Volatile Bodies: Towards a Corporeal Feminism* St Leonards: Allen & Unwin

Guest, D. (1989) "Personnel and HRM: can you tell the difference?", *Personnel Management*, January, pp. 48–51

Hearn, J., Sheppard, D.L., Tancred-Sheriff, P. and Burrell, G. (eds) (1989) *Sexuality of Organization* London: Sage

Hearn, J. (1993) "Emotive subjects: organizational men, organizational masculinities and the (de)construction of emotions". See Fineman (1993)

Hines, R. (1992) "Accounting: filling the negative space", *Accounting, Organizations and Society,* **17**, 3, pp. 314–41

Hutcheon, L. (1988) *A Poetics of Postmodernism: History, Theory, Fiction* London: Routledge

Jaggar, A. (1983) *Feminist Politics and Human Nature* Brighton: Harvester

Kerfoot, D. and Knights, D. (1995) "The organization(s) of social division: constructing identities in managerial work", paper presented to the European Group on Organization Studies Colloquium, University of Bosphorus, Istanbul, Turkey, 6–8 July

Kerfoot, D. and Knights, D. (1996) "The best is yet to come: searching for embodiment in managerial work", in Collinson, D.L. and Hearn, J. (eds) *Men as Managers, Managers as Men: Critical Perspectives on Men, Masculinities and Management* London: Sage

Konrad, A.M. and Gutek, B.A. (1986) "Impact of work experiences on attitudes towards sexual harassment", *Administrative Science Quarterly,* **31**, 3, pp. 422–38

Lamplugh, D. (1996) *Gender and Personal Safety at Work* Occasional Papers in Organizational Analysis, **5**, (special issue), pp. 64–79, Department of Business and Management, University of Portsmouth Business School

Legge, K. (1995) *Human Resource Management: Rhetorics and Realities* Basingstoke: Macmillan

Lurie, A. (1992) *The Language of Clothes* London: Bloomsbury

McDowell, L. and Court, G. (1994) "Performing work: bodily representations in merchant banks", *Environment and Planning D: Society and Space,* **12**, 727–50

McNay, L. (1992) *Foucault and Feminism: Power, Gender and the Self* Cambridge: Polity Press

Marcuse, H. (1969) *Eros and Civilization: A Philosophical Inquiry into Freud* London: Allen Lane

Martin, E. (1989) *The Woman in the Body: A Cultural Analysis of Reproduction* Milton Keynes: Open University Press

Merton, R.K. (1957) *Social Theory and Social Structure* New York: The Free Press

Miller, J. (1993) *The Passion of Michel Foucault* New York: Simon & Schuster

Mills, A.J. and Tancred, P. (1992) "Introduction", in Mills, A.J. and Tancred, P. (eds) *Gendering Organizational Analysis* London: Sage

Moore, S. (1988) "Getting a bit of the other: the pimps of postmodernism", in Chapman, R. and Rutherford, J. (eds) *Male Order: Unwrapping Masculinity* London: Lawrence & Wishart

Parkin, W. (1993) "The public and the private: gender, sexuality and emotion". See Fineman (1993), pp. 167–89

Pollitt, C. (1993) *Managerialism and the Public Services: Cuts or Cultural Change in the 1990s?* Oxford: Blackwell

Ragland-Sullivan, E. (1991) "The sexual masquerade: a Lacanian theory of sexual difference", in Ragland-Sullivan, E. and Bracher, M. (eds) *Lacan and the Subject of Language* New York: Routledge

Reed, M. (1985) *Redirections in Organizational Analysis* London: Tavistock

Renick, J.C. (1980) "Sexual harassment at work: why it happens and what to do about it", *Personnel Journal,* **59**, 8, pp. 658–62

Rosener, J. (1990) "Ways women lead", *Harvard Business Review,* November/December, pp. 119–25

Schneider, B.E. (1982) "Consciousness about sexual harassment among heterosexual and lesbian women workers", *Journal of Social Issues,* **38**, 4, pp. 75–98

Sheppard, D.L. (1989) "Organizations, power and sexuality: the image and self-image of women managers". See Hearn et al. (1989), pp. 139–57

Siegel, M.R. (1991) "Debate: ways men and women lead", in *Harvard Business Review,* January/February, p. 152

Storey, J. (ed.) (1989) *New Perspectives on Human Resource Management* London: Routledge

Storey, J. (1992) *Developments in the Management of Human Resources: an Analytical Review* Oxford: Blackwell

Storey, J. (ed.) (1995) *Human Resource Management: a Critical Text* London: Routledge

Tong, R. (1989) *Feminist Thought: A Comprehensive Introduction* London: Unwin Hyman

Watson, T. (1995) *Sociology, Work and Industry* London: Routledge

Watts, A. (1975) *Psychotherapy East and West* New York: Vintage

Weber, M. (1964) *The Theory of Social and Economic Organization* New York: Free Press

Weber, M. (1968) *Economy and Society: an Outline of Interpretive Sociology* New York: Bedminster Press

Weber, M. (1970) "Bureaucracy", in Gerth, H.H. and Wright-Mills, C. (eds) *From Max Weber* London: Routledge & Kegan Paul

Weber, M. (1994) "Bureaucracy", in Clark, H., Chandler, J. and Barry, J. (eds) *Organization and Identities: Text and Readings in Organizational Behaviour* London: Chapman & Hall

Williamson, J. (1980) *Consuming Passions: the Dynamics of Popular Culture* London: Marion Boyars

Willmott, H. (1993) "Strength is ignorance, slavery is freedom: managing culture in modern organizations", *Journal of Management Studies*, **30**, 2, pp. 515–52

Yount, K. (1991) "Ladies, flirts and tomboys: strategies for managing sexual harassment in an underground coal mine", *Journal of Contemporary Ethnography*, **19**, 4, pp. 396–422

CHAPTER SEVEN

In the company of men

Jenny Ozga & Lynne Walker

Introduction

In this chapter, we discuss the connections between the growth of managerialism in the public sector and the characteristics of heterosexual masculinity, suggesting that managerialism reflects a particular formation of masculinity that is competitive, ritualistic, unreflexive and false. Furthermore, we suggest that both "first-" and "second-" wave public-sector managerialism are gendered in ways that work against women. By this, we mean that both the thrusting, competitive, cost-cutting entrepreneurialism of the early 1990s and the team-building, empowering and envisioning of the late 1990s are interdependent and represent two "performances" of the same managerialist text. The insecurity created by the first wave created the necessary conditions for the contrived collegiality of the second.

Of course, we recognize that in naming "men" as the "problem", we are simplifying complex social relations and formations. It is more accurate to say that we are concerned here with the "problem" of hegemonic masculinity; that is, with conventionally constituted, heterosexual and heterosexist masculinity, and the opportunities for its enactment that are presented by the new formations of work. We also acknowledge the suppression of masculinities and the oppression of men by these constructions and performances of masculinity. But our focus here is on their consequences for women, particularly for women managers, although we hope that some of what we say has relevance to organizational life in general.

We have chosen to focus on hegemonic masculinity and its impact on women because, despite the encouraging growth of explorations of masculinities in the social sciences, and the parallel growth of studies of organizational life as gendered and sexualized, there is little sign of serious challenge to masculine hegemony in public-sector organizations in general, and in educational organizations in particular. It is also noteworthy that women remain the majority of the education workforce, while the majority of its managers, particularly at very senior levels above "middle" management, are men. Indeed, it is possible to argue that the new managerialism as it is played out in public-sector management may be understood as a "recuperative project of patriarchal power globally" (Mahony 1997: 100), as men use its enabling/disabling discourses to push back gender equity policies. We attempt to illustrate this argument through examples of women managers' recent experience in education. Before doing this, however, we need to set out briefly the central place that the education sector occupies as a site both for the production of differentiated neo-Fordist workers and for the performance of managerialism.

The economizing of education

Education is at the centre of the dominant economically driven policy discourse. The economic function of education systems is prioritized now as never before. For New Labour, the effective service of the economy is the main function of education. This is seen to be necessary because of the transformation of capitalism, following crisis in the 1970s, into flexible, post-Fordist regimes. That transformation led to new demands on education systems. It was assumed that the low competitiveness of the UK economy was directly related to unreformed processes and, in particular, to the old-fashioned and self-interested beliefs of public-sector workers who privileged process over output.

There are three key policy areas designed to ensure the successful harnessing of educational organizations to the post-Fordist economizing project; the first involves the clear articulation of educational outcomes to national economic priorities, the second requires the redefinition of professionalism in the education workforce, and the third concerns organizational restructuring modelled on a corporate managerial approach (Soucek 1994). All three areas have been pursued actively in all education sectors in recent years. For the purposes of this chapter, we shall be concerned with corporate managerialism, but there is very strong evidence of considerable policy activity since the 1980s in the other two areas.

Management becomes managerialism

> Government's hope must be that the implantation of the systems and ethos of management will take root sufficiently to legitimise new mechanisms and routines and to make them appear to be self-imposed, or collaboratively adopted, from top to toe. . . . (Raab 1991: 16)

Managers are the carriers of the transformative process required by the economizing of education. Their roles and responsibilities are much enhanced, despite the apparent democratization of educational bureaucracies that accompanies the flattening of hierarchies, and the delayering, downsizing and mainstreaming of the new managerialism. It is impossible to review in this chapter all of the policy developments that have contributed to this cultural shift in education, and to the accompanying increase in managerialism. Instability is a component, of course, and provides effective leverage in a context of increased public accountability, increased productivity, decreased public funding, and demands for efficiency and effectiveness. Devolution, as a component of the process of transformation, adds to instability by removing central planning and overt state management from the sector, so that inter institutional competition is enhanced, and internal institutional relations are problematized. As Peter Watkins puts it, "the crisis is faxed down the line" (Watkins 1994).

The new managerialist system is steered through a combination of legislative controls and internal, institutional mechanisms, notably performance indicators and inspections, which ostensibly provide consumers with a basis for selection but, more importantly, provide powerful managerial imperatives. Devolution and deregulation greatly enhance the significance of management, because it is now at the level of the institution (rather than, for example, the local education authority) that the forms and processes of control and surveillance of the workforce are installed. These are not simply formal mechanisms, such as inspection, assessment and appraisal, but embrace a whole repertoire of assumptions and relationships that change the nature of educational work. These new processes and structures mirror economic change, and echo changes already made, in the 1980s, in business and industry. The manufacturing of consent is a key intention: for example, human resource management uses it in attempting to manipulate professional cultures to serve managerial purposes. Mutuality is aimed at ensuring compliance and this produces economic efficiency. Tensions between individualistic professional work and teamwork are resolved by a strong corporate culture in pursuit of its mission, creating a cohesive workforce, but avoiding solidarity. Management is all-pervasive, culture and cohesion are achieved through managerially sanctioned values, activity is integrated and coordinated, and commitment is ensured by an "enabling" or "empowering" management. These intentions are not always realized, of course, particularly where they are confronted by strong professional cultures. Resistance and subversion are always possible, though difficult within the totalizing corporate culture of the new managerialism.

We want to emphasize the point that the changes outlined above, although common throughout the public sector, are experienced acutely in education. There, the drive against professionalism has been particularly strong, and traditional work practices have been stigmatized as producer-dominated, lacking accountability, and unresponsive to consumer needs because of the need to eliminate professional orientations to educational work if the economizing of education is to be achieved successfully.

New gender regimes: silencing equalities

The stripping out of the old public-service cultures of education has gender-specific consequences because, first, those cultures included the use of formal procedures and processes to support gender equality in education and, secondly, those cultures also encompassed values other than the rational and selfish calculation of benefit. Put differently (by policy-makers), these cultures are mired in a normative context that creates unrealistic expectations (Pusey 1991) and endless demands for resource.

In education, these norms have included entitlement, universality and equality of opportunity. Equality of opportunity in relation to gender has been a motivating factor for many women managers in education, and some recognition of the principle had been won in the UK context (Farish et al. 1995), even if there were gaps in practice. However, new managerialist discourses are intolerant of appeals to social justice and equality of opportunity. It is not simply that marketization and new funding regimes make equal opportunities policies more difficult to sustain; there is also a sense in which the economizing of education excludes these issues as legitimate concerns of educational organizations and their managers (Blackmore 1997, Eyre and Roman 1997). This is readily illustrated by the closure of Equal Opportunities Units in LEAs, of the Education Unit at the Equal Opportunities Commission, and by the loss of designated staff in schools and colleges. The process may also take the more subtle form of co-option through corporate managerialism, as Yeatman indicates:

> Equal opportunity in this context comes to be reframed in terms of what it can do for management improvement, not in terms of what it can do to develop the conditions of social justice and democratic citizenship. (Yeatman 1990: 341)

The co-option or silencing of voices speaking for gender equality is also evidenced in the "international epidemic of equality for boys" (Mahony 1996), and the accompanying proliferation of common-sense assumptions about female success in achieving credentials and employment. All of these factors undermine the position of feminists in education, and make the work of feminist managers in education particularly conflicted (Blackmore 1996, Acker and Feuerverger 1997, Deem and Ozga 1997).

Hegemonic masculinity and the crisis of patriarchy

In arguing that managerialism in education is gendered, and may be understood as a reassertion of patriarchy, we are drawing on Gramscian analysis which stresses the dynamic process through which groups claim and sustain power. In Connell's terms:

> ... hegemonic masculinity can be defined as the configuration of gender practice which embodies the currently accepted answer to the problem of the legitimacy of patriarchy, which guarantees (or is taken to guarantee) the dominant position of men and the subordination of women. (Connell 1995: 77)

The important ideas here concern the need to legitimate patriarchy, which, in turn, produces constant pressure to find the right "answer" to the problem of legitimacy, the instability of hegemony, and the need to use and maintain power relations that sustain it. Thus we may understand the relatively recent growth of representation of women in some sectors of education management (Deem and Ozga 1996, Prichard et al. 1998) as presenting a problem, the answer to which is managerialism, as currently enacted. This is because managerialism disallows gender equality and the pursuit of social justice as aims for education managers, and because it co-opts women managers into using their "people and process" skills in improving economy and efficiency. In doing these things, it allows men to colonize the language of people and process-oriented management, and empty it of meaning. It also enables the group-based performance of the new social relations of work to be dominated by men who use various strategies, including sexuality, to retrieve and reinforce their power.

In the next section, we attempt an assessment of the current state of play of hegemonic and counter-hegemonic forces in education management, looking at the experiences of women managers at the meeting point of those tensions; that is, in areas where women have achieved greater representation.

Caught in the middle

It is interesting that numbers of women have increased in the "buffer zone" of middle management. Data are extremely hard to collect, because of the reconfiguration of management structures, but there is some evidence of feminization of this zone of management in primary schools (where women are co-opted on to emergent senior management teams), and in further education (FE) and higher education (HE). The extent of the impact of managerialism on the FE sector cannot be overestimated. Since incorporation in 1993, FE colleges have been overseen by the Further Education Funding Council (FEFC), with local control in the hands of the board of governors and chief executive. There have been changes in funding that increase input, output and throughput (to use the language of the Funding Council) in the context of severe underfunding. Downsizing and increased flexibility, particularly through the use of part-time, contract staff, have been a major feature of the sector. All of this has been accompanied by restructuring of management that has replaced heads of department with team leaders, project heads and coordinators. It is in these positions that we see more women being appointed (FEDA 1997), and it is they who are directly responsible for increasing the level of educational activity while resources to support it are reduced. The comments below, that come from interviews with feminist women managers in FE/HE,[1] illustrate their difficulties:

> [The management system] is intensely hierarchical but is currently embarking on management development in total quality management. This is an utter contradiction and absolute nonsense in the way we have been "told" to do it . . . [Employer/employee relations] are absolute hell, there have been two or three strikes, NATFHE have done a survey on stress with horrific results, they intend to present it to the Principalship but it will have no effect whatsoever . . . it's no longer about students, it's just bureaucracies driving absolutely everything. (centre director, FE)

... at some point my principles and integrity will be stretched too far. Once you enter anything you feel competitive within it – but I wouldn't want to be a Principal for very long. At the moment it's one of the most destructive posts you could take, implementing untenable policies on people already stretched too far. (centre director, FE)

It's not exactly the favourite job in my life. Were I not fifty I would change career. Women are being used in this climate as managers in FE, that is something I would like to say. Quite a few women senior managers are being used to bulldoze the terrible changes because they're desperate to get on and they've never been offered promotion before, and because you don't recognise a poisoned chalice when it's offered to you. (programme manager, FE)

Similar evidence can be found from research in the primary-school sector, where women have been incorporated into emergent senior management teams and find themselves coping with greatly increased responsibility (particularly in relation to Ofsted inspections and reporting procedures for statutory pupil assessment) but without increased reward. Indeed, their morale and job satisfaction may be considerably diminished, because their new responsibilities get in the way of teaching (Menter et al. 1997).

In HE, Pat Mahony's discussion of the gendered nature of new public management (Mahony 1997) raises strong concerns about the impact of managerialism on feminist work in teacher education. That sector of provision has a history of engagement with the pursuit of social justice as part of the formation of critical, reflexive professionals. For that very reason, it has been the focus of over fifteen years of reforming policy that has produced enormous intensification of work, along with very considerable insecurity, and very real penalties for continued engagement with social issues, or indeed with anything that falls outside the narrow confines of teacher preparation and development as defined by the Teacher Training Agency. As one of the HoDs in her study comments:

... when you're worn to a frazzle with all the battles, you're meant to develop the faculty mission statement, empower staff and develop flat structures. (Mahony 1997: 95)

Mahony also documents the difficulties for these women managers of coping with an extremely hostile context, both within and beyond their institutions. This could include an unfavourable Inspection Report or a sudden withdrawal of funding for a specific set of activities – for example, professional development – followed by budget deficit, and the management of staff redundancies. These commonplaces of management in teacher education throw into high relief the gap between the rhetoric of managerialism and the reality. That gap is nicely illustrated in the following quotations from the Mahony study. The first is about empowerment:

One head complained bitterly that the person (a man well-versed in management theory) who shouted loudest about non-hierarchical ways of managing and who raised most questions about empowering staff was also the least inclined to do any of the extra work this entailed and the most demanding of her time. She felt that he used the rhetoric of the trans-formational culture to enhance his own position, and his insistence that as a "transformational leader" there were things she "had to do" left her "unusually speechless with fury". (Mahony 1997: 96)

The second quotation relates to management training, and we have included it because it brings to life the gendered nature of team-building and the ways in which these exercises "simulate relatedness" (Casey 1995), and highlight financial economy as the primary concern of management (although they usually cost a great deal). The last phrase also raises many questions about what is permissible in these debates, and how the attempted revival of equal opportunities and social justice issues is dismissed as physically (and sexually?) threatening:

My management training consisted of a week in the country with thirty other heads of department. It was useless. All I really remember was searching for some radioactive brick with some bloke as our leader. In the debriefing we discovered he hadn't listened to anyone . . . Well I didn't need to get soaked to learn that. A lot of the week was spent learning about financial management and I remember feeling quite angry at the way the whole thing seemed to reduce to this. When I suggested that there might be other things at stake in higher education the lecturer asked "like what?" I said "values" and the others laughed and said my comment was below the belt. (Mahony 1997: 96)

These findings illustrate a powerful dynamic against women managers, either through opposition or through co-option into masculine modes and practices. This supports Whitehead's argument that management is being "remasculinized" (White-head 1999), and extends it beyond the FE sector. We want to continue our account of managerial pressures on women to abandon the "people and process" orientation to management (Yeatman 1990), or to collude in using it to serve managerial ends. We do this in the next section through an exploration of the connections between sexuality and managerialism.

Sexuality and its uses

Sexuality . . . is not . . . a stubborn drive but an especially dense transfer point for relations of power: between men and women, young people and old people, parents and offspring, teachers and students, priests and laity, an administration and a population. (Foucault 1978: 103)

113

Sexuality is a neglected aspect of organizational life, yet it is present as a constant undercurrent, part of the social processes that are linked to and underpin management – workforce relations. Heterosexual masculinity produces particular forms of sexuality that dominate workplace relations and reinforce male power and claims to authority and status (Collinson and Hearn 1994). Heterosexual masculinity creates solidarity in workplace relations in a particular form (Acker 1992).

Sexuality was officially "ruled out" in bureaucratic organizations, as it was understood to be a disruptive force that challenged hierarchy and procedures based on abstracted rationality. However, the new social relations of work are based on proximity rather than distance, on engagement rather than detachment, on interdependence rather than isolated expertise. New work formations recognize emotion and demand considerable emotional labour; however, they also require the exploitation of feelings (of loyalty or guilt, for example) in the service of effectiveness. Catherine Casey has documented the effects of these apparently benign and inclusive structures and processes on workers in a large American corporation (Casey 1995). She points to the artificial "sociality" of teamwork, which is supposed to be empowering but which feels false and competitive, and identifies the fostering of some emotions but the denial of others; for example, nurturance and patience. In this climate, we suggest that sexuality is available to men as a resource for exploitation in their reassertion of patriarchal relations in the workplace. In developing this argument, we are drawing on Cockburn's idea of the unwritten sexual contract in work and the home, representing:

> ... the understanding that men have historically entered into concerning women ... [there are] two clauses in this contract. The "domestic clause" ... is an understanding that in ideal circumstances each man may have authority over the person and labour of a wife as housekeeper, child-rearer and sexual partner in the home. There is also a "workplace clause" ... Men guarantee each other rights over women in paid employment and in the organisations in which they work. (Cockburn 1991: 62)

Evidence of the incorporation of heterosexual male sexuality into workplace relations is particularly striking where women are not occupying traditional, "feminized" work roles. In such a situation (for example, where women are managers) the sexual aspects of women are seen by men as their primary characteristic (Gutek 1983). Women prefer to "leave sexuality out of the workplace" (Gutek 1985), but this is particularly difficult when they occupy non-traditional roles.

From these ideas, and from informal, shared experience among women managers in education, we argue that the interaction of power and sexuality produces a dynamic from which these consequences follow:

- women are recognized only in subservient mode
- powerful, authoritative women create confusion
- powerful, authoritative women are "caught" by the sexualized exchange
- women who stand outside the heterosexual power exchange are labelled as "problems"

Although the discussion that follows elaborates these points, we are unable to draw on formal research, as work on sexuality in education is uncommon, and is also hedged about with difficulty that is "the stuff of which scandal can be made" (Epstein and Johnson 1998). There is a growing body of work on sexuality and schooling (Harris 1990, Epstein 1994, Mac an Ghaill 1994, Epstein and Johnson 1998), but little on sexuality and the management of educational organizations. So we are drawing here on conversations with women managers in education, and on our own experience of a range of educational organizations, in order to try to illustrate some of the day-to-day difficulties of managing within the new social relations of work.

Women are recognized only in subservient mode

Here we want to conjure up the element of display in asserting hegemonic masculinity. Formal and informal meetings become arenas for the enactment and approval of assertive masculinity; they are the performance of power, with its particular, arcane language, its sporting metaphors, public "private" jokes and physical and intrusive dominance of space. Performance demands an audience, and women's engagement in these rituals is mediated through their enactment of exaggerated, and sexualized, subservience, requiring the physical display of acknowledgement of the wisdom and prowess of the holders of power.

Subservience is even called forth from apparently powerful women, who evidently feel that they have transgressed if they engage in masculine performance; for example, the female professor cited by Kaplan (1993), who moves from the magisterial style of a public lecture to "a flirtatious girl, a silly chatterbox, a pure and simple coquette" before the older male professor whom she has sought out at the end of her public performance (Kaplan, in Holloway and Jefferson 1996). Variations on this scenario may be observed at academic conferences across the globe, where male "organizers" engage in assertive display of exaggerated "academic" characteristics, while thanking women for their competence in menial tasks. The women then smile, and enact further rituals of subservient femininity that confirm the performance of these gendered scripts.

Women who fail to enact subservience appropriately are invisible and inaudible. For example, on one occasion both of the authors were present at a meeting of all senior managers in the institution in which we then worked. There were approximately forty people expected, of whom six were women. We were early, and pouring tea for ourselves when a male colleague entered the room. We looked up, as from the doorway he surveyed the room and announced: "I see no one is here yet." He then left. Some minutes later he re-entered the room at the same time as another male colleague arrived, and said to him, "I'm glad you're here. Now I have someone to talk to."

Powerful, authoritative women create confusion

In the new workplace relations, female authority is highly problematic. Authority is unwelcome, as it derives from expert knowledge and is value-driven. Underneath the veneer, the new workplace relations are all about power, not authority. The author-itative woman is a source of puzzlement and fear to men. For example: "How are things in general now that there is a close-knit team of politically motivated women in charge?" was a question once asked by a very senior manager after the office move of one member of an all-woman executive management team closer to the other two members. He asked the question in all seriousness; it was not a joke. A group of senior women working together is evidently threatening, and is assumed to be "politically motivated". One way of dealing with the fear is for men to characterize the woman as "difficult". Various strategies are employed to undermine her in the group context. Her speech patterns are mocked – "She speaks in paragraphs" – and she is constantly interrupted; even when silent there is reference to her through in-appropriate, personal questions – "Why are you smiling?"; "Are you bored?" – that reveal the acute tension and discomfort experienced by the male who is not receiv-ing appropriate messages of compliance. Comments designed to undercut authority and reveal the woman behind it are attempts to restore that relationship: "I know I shouldn't say this but I like your hair/ring/dress etc." Strenuous efforts are made to persuade her to enact the rituals of subservience described above; for example, through pressure to engage in administrative housework such as note-taking, message transmission or coffee-making. At the same time, the tension generated by female authority seems to exacerbate ritualistic masculine behaviour, so that exaggerated masculine bonding rituals – joke-telling, physicality and noisy assertiveness – are all displayed. The authoritative woman is thus isolated within the group to the extent that other group members, including women, find it difficult to show solidarity with her. That the confusion created by authoritative women is often "resolved" by men through labelling of the woman as lesbian reflects the importance of the dimension of sexuality in these artificially close relationships, and also suggests that heterosexuality generally works in this context as a transfer point of relations of power that advantages men.

Powerful, authoritative women are "caught" by the sexualized exchange

Here we are referring to the serious difficulties encountered by women managers who attempt to leave sexuality out of the workplace. Once again, we would point to the contrived sociality and false intimacy of new work relations, in which defence of privacy is difficult, and women managers are offered details of private and personal issues by men as a way of calling forth the nurturance and attention that they expect from women. The artificial sociality of the team erodes private space, and the loss of hierarchy reduces the distance between the manager and the managed. Women who welcome this apparently open and democratic style of working are seen by men as offering the possibility of intimacy, understood by them as eroticized. Thus women become "caught" by an exchange in which the currency is not shared, and find themselves understood by men as colluding in sexualized exchange through small gestures of recognition (eye contact, touch) that they may offer to the men (and women) whom they manage.

Women who stand outside the heterosexual power exchange are labelled as "problems"

Women are obliged to collude with the performance of heterosexual masculinity to varying degrees. Their refusal to do so creates difficulty, as indicated above. Lesbians are unable to collude because hegemonically constructed femininity is a performance that is not available to them; nor can they fake it successfully (Jeffreys 1994). There exists a heteropatriarchal eroticism that focuses upon difference, the other, the exotic, the alluring, and that seeks completeness by a desire for union with that "other" (Hall 1989). Not only do lesbians not provide for men that view of the "other", but they are seen by men as de-sexualized, not-women. Yet at the same time they are subjected to an unavoidable and unending eroticism (Hall 1989), that describes and defines lesbians exclusively by reference to sexual activity. When the "other" is not available, then, it may be that sexism and homophobia interact synergistically. Gay men and lesbians at work generally connect to other gay and lesbian workers with whom openness and honesty are possible, but for lesbians in management this is extremely difficult. Isolation is inevitable, even for those who are open about their sexuality. In the various message systems through which sexuality acts as a "transfer point", they are not receiving or transmitting in appropriate and accepted ways. They often, therefore, come to be perceived as "problematic" and "difficult" because male managers and male workers cannot imagine a performance of work relations that is not (hetero)sexualized. We have observed that aggressively heterosexual men may also deny the very existence of the lesbian manager, and maintain this fiction throughout team meetings, where all exchange is avoided, and no contribution made by her is responded to – sometimes even in the face of a direct question.

Conclusion

In this chapter, we have focused on sexuality as a way in which patriarchy is being reasserted in the workplace, within the new social relations of work. We have done this because we think that sexuality is neglected in studies of educational organizations. We also wanted to produce a sharply critical picture of managerialism, one that points up the exploitative and penetrative potential of the new forms of work relations, and that raises questions about the (limited) feminization of management roles within them. Because we have been concerned to sound a warning note about the gendering of managerialism, there is little comfort in this treatment for feminist managers. This is a bleak picture, but we would defend it on the basis that it foregrounds the project of patriarchal restoration, which can then be opposed and subverted. Those counter-hegemonic capacities continue to exist, and are clearer when the agenda of managerialism is stripped of its empowering rhetoric.

Feminist managers in education live within powerful constraints, but seek to use their status and influence to achieve particular ends that challenge masculine hegemony. They also seek to achieve those ends through particular processes, processes that challenge conventional power relationships. The overarching framework is one that seeks to transform organizational priorities towards the pursuit of justice, equality and emancipation. In particular, it is necessary to restate the emancipatory potential of feminism, even in these difficult times.

As Cocks argues:

> If history does not turn out to be a matter of an inevitable or even a possible progression from domination to freedom, it does seem to move in a jolting way between ordinary and abnormal times ... isn't it possible to say that history fluctuates between periods when things continue on, at least on the surface, very much as they had been before, according to the same rules, engagements and constraints, and moments when, for a variety of possible reasons order becomes disorder, and entirely new desires, ideas and actions become explicitly possible and quite conceivably actual? Might it not be such abnormal times that we can still hope and work for inside a mode of life that is oppressive in the way that the atmosphere in a room can be both ugly and close? (Cocks 1989: 221)

Note

1. This research has been carried out with Professor Rosemary Deem, Lancaster University, and involves interviews with feminist managers in further and higher education.

References

Acker, J. (1992) "Gendering organization theory", in Mills, A. and Tancred, P. (eds) *Gendering Organizational Analysis* London: Sage

Acker, S. and Feuerverger, G. (1997) "Enough is never enough: women's work in academe", in Marshall, C. (ed.) *Feminist Critical Policy Analysis: a Perspective from Post-secondary Education,* London: Falmer

Blackmore, J. (1996) "Doing emotional labour in the education marketplace", *Discourse: Studies in Cultural Politics of Education,* **17**, 3

Blackmore, J. (1997) "Disciplining feminism? Australian perspectives on feminism and the backlash in tertiary education", in Eyre, L. and Roman, L. (eds) *Dangerous Territories: Struggles for Equality and Difference* New York: Routledge

Casey, C. (1995) *Work, Self and Society: After Industrialism* London: Routledge

Cockburn, C. (1991) *In the Way of Women* London: Macmillan

Collinson, D. and Hearn, J. (1994) "Naming men as men: implications for work, organization and management", *Journal of Gender, Work and Organization,* **1**, 1, pp. 2–22

Connell, R.W. (1987) *Gender and Power* Cambridge: Polity Press

Connell, R.W. (1995) *Masculinities* Cambridge: Polity Press

Cocks, J. (1989) *The Oppositional Imagination* London: Routledge

Deem, R. and Ozga, J. (1996) "Carrying the burden of transformation: the experiences of women managers in UK further and higher education", European Conference of Educational Research, Seville, September

Deem, R. and Ozga, J. (1997) "Women managing for diversity in a post-modern world", in Marshall, C. (ed.) *Feminist Critical Policy Analysis: a Perspective from Post-secondary Education* London: Falmer

Epstein, D. (1994) *Challenging Lesbian and Gay Inequalities in Education* Buckingham: Open University Press

Epstein, D. and Johnson, R. (1998) *Schooling Sexualities* Buckingham: Open University Press

Eyre, L. and Roman, L. (eds) (1997) *Dangerous Territories: Struggles for Equality and Difference* New York: Routledge

Farish, M., McPake, M., Powney, M. and Weiner, G. (1995) *Equal Opportunities in Colleges and Universities: Towards Better Practice* Buckingham: Society for Research into Higher Education/ Open University Press

Further Education Development Agency (FEDA) (1997) *Women at the Top in Further Education* Coventry: FEDA

Foucault, M. (1978) *The History of Sexuality* (vol. 1) Harmondsworth: Penguin

Gutek, B.A. (1983) "Interpreting social–sexual behaviour in a work setting", *Journal of Vocational Behaviour*, **22**

Gutek, B.A. (1985) *Sex and the Workplace: the Impact of Sexual Behavior and Harassment on Women, Men and Organisations* San Francisco: Jossey-Bass

Hall, M. (1989) "Private experiences in the public domain: lesbians in organisations", in Hearn, J., Sheppard, D., Tancred-Sheriff, P. and Burrell, G. (eds) *The Sexuality of Organisations* London: Sage

Harris, S. (1990) *Lesbian and Gay Issues in the English Classroom* Oxford: Oxford University Press

Holloway, W. and Jefferson, T. (1996) "PC or not PC?: sexual harassment and the question of ambivalence", *Human Relations*, **49**, 3, pp. 373–93

Jeffreys, S. (1994) *The Lesbian Heresy* London: The Women's Press

Kaplan (1993) "Hierarchies, sexuality and social control", *Human Organisation*, **44**, 1, pp. 83–8

Mac an Ghaill, M. (1994) *The Making of Men: Masculinities, Sexualities and Schooling* Buckingham: Open University Press

Mahony, P. (ed.) (1996) Changing schools: some international feminist perspectives on teaching girls and boys, *WSIF*, **19**, 4 (special issue)

Mahony, P. (1997) "Talking heads: a feminist perspective on public sector reform in teacher education", *Discourse: Studies in the Cultural Politics of Education*, **18**, 1, pp. 87–102

Menter, I., Muschamp, Y., Nicholls, P., Ozga, J. and Pollard, A. (1997) *Work and Identity in the Primary School; a Post-Fordist Analysis* Buckingham: Open University Press

Prichard, C., Deem, R. and Ozga, J. (1998) "Managing further education – is it men's work too?", paper presented at Gender, Work and Organization Conference, 9–10 January, UMIST, Manchester

Pusey, M. (1991) *Economic Rationalism in Canberra: a Nation-building State Changes its Mind* Cambridge: Cambridge University Press

Raab, C. (1991) "Education policy and management: contemporary changes in Britain", paper to International Institute of Administrative Sciences, Copenhagen, July

Soucek, V. (1994) "Flexible education and new standards of communicative competence", in Kenway, J. (ed.) *Economising Education: the Post-Fordist Directions* Deakin: Deakin University Press.

Watkins, P. (1994) "The Fordist/Post-Fordist debate: the educational implications", in Kenway, J. (ed.) *Economising Education: The Post-Fordist Directions* Deakin: Deakin University Press

Whitehead, S. (1999) "From paternalism to entrepreneurialism: the experience of men managers in UK postcompulsory education", *Discourse: Studies in the Cultural Politics of Education*, **20**, 1

Yeatman, A. (1990) *Bureaucrats, Technocrats, Femocrats: Essays on the Contemporary Australian State* Sydney: Allen & Unwin

PART II

Unmasking men and management

CHAPTER EIGHT

Men, managers and management: the case of higher education

Jeff Hearn

Historical connections

The connections between men and management are numerous and intense. The historical development of management, and especially management as an identifiable professional group, cannot be understood without naming most managers as men. Indeed, in the early years of the modernization of management, the late nineteenth and early twentieth centuries, management was an almost exclusively male social category.

The growth of the size and complexity of capitalist organizations in the nineteenth century was accompanied by the separation of ownership and control of enterprise (Nichols 1970, Clegg and Dunkerley 1980). This process involved and indeed was (in a sense, reflexively) managed by the newly created occupational group of man agers. Managers were clearly linked to, but distinct from, owners, and were also distinguished from workers and other waged employees. This new group of modern managers were an intermediate class (Wright 1985). They may have their own inter ests of ownership in the form of shares, corporate possession or other privileges, and yet they may also be salaried rather than rewarded by time worked or by piecework. Thus throughout their modern development, managers and management have been both structure and process. Managers have been the product of the separation of ownership and control, and have had the responsibility of managing and mediating across that boundary (Giddens 1981). Not surprisingly, this has led to an extensive debate on the extent to which managers and management can be said to serve the interests of capital and capitalist classes. Debate as to what extent men managers serve the interests of men is less developed and is itself seen as a relatively marginal issue (if it is noticed at all) in malestream analysis. Perhaps most important of all, managers (that is, men managers) began to be not just the champions of their own corporations, but became linked together with others similar to themselves; became available for working in different industrial and other sectors; and developed their own specialisms and internal division of labour. These changes accelerated in the

1910s, with the formation of the national associations of Sales Managers, Office Managers and Industrial Administrators (Child 1969). In 1919, specialist management education was begun in Manchester, Oxford and Cambridge. Modern management was well and truly under way.

A somewhat similar process is observable in the state and state re-formation in the late nineteenth and early twentieth centuries. Not only was the state taking on new and expanding functions – for example, in public health, the military, policing and post office communications – but it was also being structured and organized through larger and more complex administrative units. "The State" (so beloved of functionalist analysis) was in fact a series of mini-states and multi-organizations – an organizational trend that has proceeded with some intensity since (Rose 1987), and threatens to become paradigmatic of late modernity (Rose 1993).

Complementing these late nineteenth century state expansions were the beginnings of the modernization of the civil service, and particularly civil service management. The basis of the modern civil service was set out in the Trevelyan–Northcote Report of 1854, in which proposals were made to replace the then-existing system of patronage with a system based on merit. Some limited reforms of this kind were made in the 1850s and 1860s; however, it was not until 1870 that recruitment to the civil service was moved to the so-called "open [for men] competitive examinations" in some departments at least – even then, all vacancies in the Foreign Office and the Home Office were filled by patronage. The open system – that is, open to men system – was more or less in operation by 1890. Meanwhile, the Marriage Bar had been introduced for all women, except for subpostmistresses, "charwomen" and women factory employees, in 1876. The MacDonnell Commissioners, reporting in 1912–13, still considered that women should not be eligible for "open competition" in the civil service, and that the Marriage Bar should be retained so that women were requested to resign on marriage (Cohen 1965: 65). The First World War and the Sex Disqualification (Removal) Act of 1919 changed this to an extent (Walby 1986: 157), although the Marriage Bar itself was not completely removed until 1946 (Hearn 1992: 153–60).

These reforms were further paralleled in the modernization of the military, with the introduction of mass recruitment of the young adult "citizen" in the Boer and First World Wars, the creation of the General Staff concept and the tentative introduction of management methods and more complex military strategy. Of special importance was the increasing awareness of the interconnections of military, commercial and domestic organization in the preparations for and implementation of war. Concerns for the health (or lack of health) of men for fighting ("manpower") and the commercial flow of chemical and other strategic commodities brought the beginnings of a closer relationship between capitalist planning, state national planning and male management.

It was in this historical context of societal transformation just after the turn of the century that also the universities' dependence on public funding was established, with the setting up of the University Grants Committee in 1911 (de Groot 1997). All of these developments point to the complex interlinks between social changes in capital, state, the profession of modern management and men's domination of the various public realms (Hearn 1992), in particular (management) education.

The place, and especially the interests, of managers in the state is of course open to many different interpretations. Some of these derive from well established disputes on the relation of state and capital (see, for example, Gough 1983). Major driving forces in these debates have been the tensions between Marxist and non-Marxist approaches, and between functionalist and political approaches. Clegg and Dunkerley (1980) conclude that there is likely to be a close affinity between capital, capitalist managers and state managers, who still have to work within budgetary restraints controlled by capital. Again, the relevance of gender, male domination and the interests of men is characteristically absent from such analyses.

Managers and men managers do not just organize the organizational, technical and personnel matters in their charge; significantly, they set and create the ideological scene, although of course not without resistance. In effect, this involves the creation of knowledges, both in the local sense of organizational and managerial knowledge, and in the broader, more pervasive sense of knowledge in and of society – indeed, of what counts as knowledge. This latter activity is especially important in the management of universities, as one set of key institutions contributing to (gendered) production and reproduction of (gendered) knowledge in society.

Gendering management

Changes in capitalist, civil service and military organization and management involve structures and processes, practices and ideologies, managements and managerialisms. But, importantly, they reflect and entail a historic male domination, and often monopoly, of management, and particularly top management. The historical legacy of this male "modernization" of management remains in the methods and systems of management, in language and imagery around management, and in dominant understandings of what management is. So, as I will proceed to elaborate, when talking of the "modernization" of management, "modern management" and its future direction in respect of higher education, what is being referred to is the male modernization of male management, and not to some more universal neutral social process.

To be more precise, the dominant and diverse genderings of management have now been the subjects of extensive research and analysis. Feminist and other critical feminist-influenced studies have spelt out the explicit and implicit genderings of organizations and management (for example, Hearn and Parkin 1983, 1995; Ferguson 1984; Powell 1988; Acker 1990; Mills and Tancred 1992). These sociological analyses have been accompanied by social psychological studies of men and women managers, their characteristics and experiences; and by more interventionist prescriptions for what women managers should do – the so-called "women in management" literature. This latter genre has itself been subject to some qualified critique from feminist commentaries on organizations and management (see, for example, Adler and Izraeli 1988, Calás and Smircich 1993).

The overwhelming finding is that men continue to dominate management, and especially top management. Men comprise about 95 per cent of senior management in the UK and the US. In some countries, the figure is even higher (Sinclair 1995). The domination of men is even more pronounced at the level of boards of directors, and especially for large public companies. By 1990 (Hansard Society 1990), of 100 top Confederation of British Industry (CBI) companies, only 3 per cent had women on their boards at all. Furthermore, there is some evidence that the number of men may be increasing even further at the highest levels of management (Calás and Smircich 1993, Institute of Management 1995).

Men managers are more likely than women managers to be better paid, to be in secure employment, to be on higher grades, to be less stressed, and to have not experienced prejudice and sexual discrimination (Davidson and Cooper 1984, Davidson 1989, Young and Spencer 1990, Institute of Management 1995). In the UK as learnt, men managers are more likely than women managers to be married, to be younger, to have children and to go on to have more children, and not to be separated or divorced (Alban Metcalfe 1984, Davidson and Cooper 1984).[1]

For all of these and other reasons, management and effective management have often been assumed to be consistent with characteristics traditionally valued in men. This has occurred in both organizational and managerial practice, and in research on management (see Schein 1973, Alimo-Metcalfe 1993, Hearn 1994). While some studies have in fact found few differences between women and men managers (for example, Boulgarides 1984), others have found men to be less participative in their management style (for example, Jago and Vroom 1982). Rosener's (1990) work has been especially important in contrasting men's greater tendency to adopt "transactional" styles of leadership (in which rewards and punishments are exchanged for performance) and women's greater tendency to adopt transformational leadership (facilitating participation, sharing power and information, and encouraging self-worth). Accordingly, in this and other studies, men are more likely to use power from organizational position and formal authority (see also Vinnicombe 1987). These contrasts should not be interpreted too simply. A number of authors (for example, Donnell and Hall 1980, Powell 1988) have noted how women managers can often be more achievement-motivated than men managers, perhaps in order to survive and progress in a relatively hostile organizational climate. And a study by Ferrario (1990) found women managers to score higher than men on *both* people orientation and task orientation in terms of structure initiation. Women managers' propensity for a team management style (Ferrario 1990) is to be understood alongside other research findings on men's domination of groups, especially where men are numerically dominant (Alimo-Metcalfe 1993). Men's ability to fail to hear women's comments in groups, or their tendency to attribute them to men participants, can be understood as one part of broader processes of harassment (Hearn and Parkin 1995), abuse (Itzin 1995) and silencing (Harlow et al. 1995).

These gendered studies have led to more focused analyses of men managers. Relevant studies have examined men's cultures in organizations (Parkin and Maddock 1995); discourses and practices of masculinity in management (Collinson and Hearn 1994); men's individualism and homosociality in management (Roper 1993); and men's methods for blocking equal opportunities policies (Cockburn 1990, 1991). The study of "men as managers, managers as men" is now established (Collinson and

Hearn 1996). These understandings of "men in management" and men/managers should not, however, be read in a one-dimensional way. Men/managers may generally convey power and yet can also carry ambivalence, express reluctance (Scase and Goffee 1989), perform long working hours, and retain a concern for more "balanced lives" (New Ways to Work 1995).

Gendered higher education

Universities have grown as organizations and institutions characterized by definite hierarchical patterns, themselves defined by and reproducing other social divisions and social relations of age, class, disability, ethnicity, gender and sexuality. Similarly, management in higher education is not immune from all of the historical and cultural constructions of management that have been more generally outlined already. Above all, higher education management is severely and chronically gendered. The historical homogeneity (or homosociality) of management previously described was also to be found in the university sector, as well as in the capitalist civil service and military sectors. The universities – institutions which were supposed to be founded on the production of knowledge – did not have the "self-knowledge" to include over half the population – women – within their knowledge base. Women were "admitted" on a limited basis as students at the universities of Cambridge, London and Oxford in the 1860s and 1870s, sometimes initially in separate classes and examinations for women (Vicinus 1985: Ch. 4).[2] Women were first appointed as a university lecturer and professor in 1893 and 1894 respectively (Rendel 1980: 143, cited in Brooks 1997: 11); and the first woman vice-chancellor (in what have now become known as the "old universities") was installed in 1995.[3]

Many of the various forms of gendering of organizations and management have also been catalogued within universities and academia more generally. For example, universities have been analyzed as sites of sexual discrimination (see, for example, Aisenberg and Harrington 1988), sexual harassment (for example, Dziech and Weiner 1984, Paludi and Barickman 1991), feminist responses to male domination (for example, Morley and Walsh 1995), and indeed anti-feminism (see, for example, Clark et al. 1996). Similar processes apply not only within the universities but also more broadly in publishing and journal production, even with the considerable growth of "feminist", "women's studies" and "gender studies" publishers' lists (Ginsberg and Lennox 1996). Most recently, the interconnections between men's power and managerial power have also been analyzed in university settings (Davies and Holloway 1995, Martin 1996, Prichard 1996, Roper 1996).

Of both special and general interest is the place of universities in the production and reproduction of dominant ideologies in society, including the very process of knowledge formation, and that is undoubtedly gendered knowledge formation (see, for example, Rose 1994, Keller and Longino 1996). The ideological climate and contribution of universities is severely complicated by *tensions* between three main forms: moral/political ideologies, economic/financial ideologies and knowledge ideologies. These ideologies may respectively emphasize:

- the interest of providing education to a broad range of students, often as part of the liberal democratic project
- the interest of delivering education and other "outcomes", such as research, within a given resource base or by expanding that resource base, say, by increased private-sector "income", and
- the interest of creating (what might be potentially emancipatory) knowledge

Whereas the first two ideologies are broadly demand- and supply-led respectively, the knowledge interest for greater (potentially emancipatory) knowledge operates in a more complex relation to these conditions. While knowledge is certainly socially produced and is in many ways the product of social relations, it may also carry the possible interest of changing those conditions, and leading to somewhere that is not known. However, for the most part universities do not produce neutral, less still emancipatory, knowledge; much of their effort has quite explicitly been devoted to the furtherance of various forms of "technological politics" (Fay 1975) and "scientific knowledge" framed by the discourse of "performativity" (Lyotard 1984, Whitehead 1998). It is not difficult to discern a more explicit shift in these directions with the increasingly applied, technological, vocational and utilitarian character of the "mission" of higher education in the UK, becoming apparent in the 1970s and accelerating in the 1980s and 1990s.

These general patterns are now examined in more detail through a critical life-history approach (Jackson 1990), in which I attempt to consider historical changes in higher education management through my own mediated experience of them.

Tradition, modernization and change: varieties of collegial fraternity in the 1960s and 1970s

The 1960s were a crucial decade of transition for higher education in the UK. The sector was modernized, or rather the foundations of that modernization were laid. This particular "modernization" was of a different kind to that of management in the late nineteenth and early twentieth centuries. Whereas in First Wave modernization (First Wave Feminism), management was being introduced as a specific identifiable activity, in the Second Wave modernization of the 1960s and the 1970s (Second Wave Feminism) management itself was subject to modernization. At the national and international level these changes can be related to both technological advances and sociopolitical transformations; in the case of the university sector the Second Wave modernization involved a greater consideration of national higher education planning, a redefinition of the interests and "missions" of individual universities within that context, an overall expansion of student and staff numbers, and a great emphasis on the promotion of technology, education and research. The universities were being shifted, often somewhat reluctantly, from being state-funded autonomous institutions to state-funded semi-autonomous members of a national university system. The main vehicle of this change was the Robbins Committee Report of 1963 and the subsequent reforms (see Robbins 1963). These made the case for wider access to higher education in keeping with policies and practices of academic competitors in Europe, North America, Asia and Australia. Both working-class men and women across classes could be expected to benefit, in line with thinking on comprehensive schooling in the secondary education system.

Having said that, this was only a modified challenge to the "gentlemanly" ways of managing universities that went back to the nineteenth century and earlier. When I went to university in 1965, some of my contemporaries were among the early entrants to what were then called the "new universities",[4] founded on their out-of-town campuses in Sussex, Staffordshire and elsewhere. These were insistently modern, and supposedly more "integrated" in gender relations. Their foundation fitted well within the postwar "green field" planning of new towns, holiday camps, out-of-town shopping centres and, later, hypermarkets. Social exigencies were to be resolved through spatial segregations.

Meanwhile, my own experience was of leaving a single-sex grammar school and becoming a student at an Oxford college that was traditionally men only, as were almost all of the colleges at the time. All of college "dons" were of course men; High Table was male. The liberality of my particular college was demonstrated by its admission of one woman postgraduate theology student (accepted because the Congregational Church, unusually at that time, included women ministers), and by the wife of one of the "dons" giving some tuition and playing the chapel organ. In the photograph of the First Year cohort for my subject, geography, there were 12 women and 54 men, one of whom was black. In this setting, contact between staff and students was assumed to be male and relatively formal. Rather unusually, my first tutor (from outside the college) was a woman who was married to one of the senior dons in another college. And yet this was soon to be the time of "student revolution". Some graduate colleges, and a newly founded college, did admit women, and several colleges were beginning to "integrate".

Politics, especially international politics, was important to some students. JACARI (Joint Action Committee Against Racial Intolerance) had lively lunchtime meetings that I found very inspiring. My study of "The Geography of Southern Africa" and "The Social and Political Geography of the Former Commonwealth Territories" confirmed my Marxism. In May 1968 I sat my finals. Management was at that time very distant and, in the Oxford case at least, generally a male matter. Apart from the women's colleges (five at the time), the "exceptional women" in the mainstream/malestream university structures, and indirectly in various family niches, principally as wives, the university management was by men.

My own next move was a short one geographically but a long one socially. I turned down the possibility of doing research at "Oxford" and instead went "up the hill" to the Polytechnic (now Oxford Brookes University) to study urban planning and sociology. This was a very different world, and one much more in keeping with the Robbins era. There was more concern for the students, easier staff–student relations, and more open-mindedness on educational methods. But there were still not many women staff. One of the best lecturers was a woman, who in due course left her lecturer husband for one of the students on my course. But the key decision-makers seemed to be men, men, men still, and at least one of the senior staff seemed pleased to be able to demonstrate his aggressive masculinity in a way that might have been considered "ungentlemanly" "down the hill" in the university. I later heard that he went on to become a vice-chancellor.

I found a rather similar situation when I returned to university, this time in Leeds, in 1973. Men were definitely in charge, and for most of the time a fairly liberal regime appeared to reign. As far as could be seen, staff managed to have a high degree of autonomy over what they did and how they did it. In the "old universities", managerial control, largely by men, and largely of men, seemed to be a form of loose fraternalism. The past autonomies of the universities were reproduced within the university mainly by and for men staff. "The university" effectively operated through a series of relatively autonomous departments.

The picture that I found when I joined Bradford University, as a member of staff in 1974, broadly followed the same pattern. The university had upgraded from a College of Advanced Technology (CAT) in 1966. It also had a distinctly technological emphasis, and a rather unusual Charter that spoke of the need to apply knowledge to social problems. Looking back from the 1990s, academic life in the 1970s was indeed much easier. Staff–student ratios were less than half the present levels. There was a lot of individual tuition with students. And the participatory ideologies of the 1960s were to an extent being worked out in practice on the academic "shopfloor". Territorial autonomy ("academic freedom") was a value around which many (male) staff could agree and coalesce. Thus different departments in different universities within a given subject area could have quite different theoretical perspectives, and a similar mixed pattern was able to develop between subjects within the same institution. This was generally a form of male liberal pluralism. Managerial practice tolerated the fact that a minority of staff, usually men, did not research or publish very much or at all (Davies and Holloway 1995: 9). It all ran a bit like a relatively enlightened men's club, which also happened to have a few women members. The organizational base of this club was generally the department, sometimes confusingly called "the school". Departments or "schools" were also the bases for degrees and other courses; in those pre-modular days students were organized in years or cohorts, and staff similarly viewed their teaching responsibilities in this way. In marked contrast to my initial experience at Oxford University, the school/department was the organizing unit of the university, and management, in its rather restrained form, was channelled through what were called in Bradford "Named Persons", who owned staffing resources and were the university personified. Top management beyond that was remote for students and most staff alike. One reason why women were excluded from management was simply that there were not many women there in the first place.

One powerful way of understanding this kind of organization and managerial structure and climate in the universities is in terms of "collegiality" or, more accurately, white middle-class male collegiality. Carpenter (1995), writing in the Australian context, has recently analyzed the "collegiality" of universities within the framework of patriarchy. She argues, drawing on Waters (1993), that universities can be understood as collegial, polycratic institutions, with authority exercised through expertise, peer equality and consensus decision-making, all operating through white middle-class male academics. She suggests that "collegiality creates a unique culture akin to a fraternity" (Epstein 1970, Lorber 1989) "which mirrors patriarchal relations in the wider society" (Pateman 1988: 3–4, see also Carpenter 1995: 62). Such an analysis seems to fit closely the state of UK academia of the 1960s and 1970s. On the other hand, it could be argued that laterally defined relations between men are more typical of fratriarchy than patriarchy. Either way, both fratriarchy and patriarchy may themselves be considered as subsets of androcracy (Remy 1990) or viriarchy (Waters 1989) As such, universities had considerable autonomy, simultaneously as mini-fratriarchies and mini-patriarchies. These relative autonomies were, however, soon to be disrupted with the growth of a new set of patriarchal relations.

The intensification of male management: towards technocratic patriarchies in the 1980s

The modernizations of the 1960s and 1970s were followed by a number of pro-nounced and more centrally directed shifts in the early 1980s. The election of the Conservative government in 1979, economic uncertainties, and the subsequent re-structuring of the state and the welfare state led to a phase of financial, educational and disciplinary cuts in the early 1980s. From January 1980, the University Grants Committee met with the senior staff of universities to discuss their financing, and in particular the possible shift from level funding. In December 1980 the policy of level funding was abandoned, with the announcement of reductions in funds for home students, and this was exacerbated in March 1981 by additional cuts of 8.5 per cent, along with cuts in overseas students, making a total cut of about 13 per cent. The famous 1 July circular letter from the University Grants Committee to (old) univer-sity vice-chancellors began:

> As you may be aware from my letters of 30th December 1980 and 15th May 1981, the Committee has been grappling for some months with the problems of how the present university system might be reshaped within the financial constraints determined by Government for the period up to 1983/84 ... The aim of a revised system should be to offer good educational opportunities to students of all ages who may enter it, as well as career prospects and research opportunities for its staff. (Parkes 1981: 1)

This "opportunities" (equal or otherwise) rhetoric in fact meant an overall reduc-tion in planned student numbers (from 260 970 home and EC full-time students in 1979–80 to 248 720 in 1983–84 in Great Britain), and an overall cut in recurrent grant (from £128.69 million in 1981/2 to £119.85 million in 1983/4). These umbrella figures, however, included considerable variation in the percentage cut across the universities. Bradford, where I then worked, had a planned cut from £11.91 million in 1981/2 to £9.64 million in 1983/4. While Bradford had a 19 per cent cut, Salford fared worst with a 27.5 per cent cut.

The way in which these targets were achieved was through the national centralized control of both student numbers and financial expenditure – a method that has since become part of normal university life. The immediate message was delivered by the UGC through the giving of "advice" to the universities. In the Bradford case, the "advice" on "arts" (including the social sciences), reads as follows:

> The Committee suggests that the University should concentrate on Languages and on maintaining European Studies and Interdisciplinary Human Studies. It recommends a small increase in undergraduate numbers in Business and Management Studies and invites the University to consider discontinuing courses in Education. The Committee recommends a substantial overall reduction in student numbers in other subjects and invites the University to explore with the University of Leeds the possibility of increased collaboration in Social Studies. (Parkes 1981: Appendix)

In effect, this was central control, not just of total student numbers for a given university but by coded "advice" for each university for the management, occasional expansion, reduction and occasional abolition of subjects, departments and knowledges. The individual university could find the same overall savings from elsewhere, but the central calculation had been done on the basis that they would follow the UGC "advice". In Bradford's case, a number of degree programmes were closed and the Postgraduate School of Research in Education was abolished. The biggest cuts in the social sciences just happened to be in those subjects where there were women professors. In the manner of a self-fulfilling prophecy, these subject areas happened to be defined by men as suitable for reduction. By their association with women, the academic assessment of these subjects was defined by management men as "vulnerable", although no evidence for this was given or offered. Nationally, 250 courses were lost in the "old universities". The earlier autonomy and discretion of the universities as to how to organize and manage themselves had declined and perhaps gone.

More interestingly still, national planning of universities was eventually reproduced *within* the universities themselves, with newly important "planning units", "resource methodologies" and "financial systems". Rather similarly, there was increasing central government attention to the specific funding of research (Davies and Holloway 1995: 9), and to the evaluation of research performance.[5] Decision-making became more centralized in many universities with "top management teams" and "strategic review bodies" planning future retrenchments, with faculties and boards of studies playing a less influential role than previously.

Ironically, this was at the very time at which attempts were being made to make decision-making in faculties and boards of studies more politically informed and more responsive to equal opportunities. Indeed, the central government attack on higher education brought a surprisingly concerted response from the members of the Association of University Teachers and the other campus unions, including a memorable mass lobby of parliament in London. One possible consequence of this was that the male collegiality was to an extent broken, with different staff identifying separately as managers, workers, academics, teachers, researchers or professionals.

Staff also became segregated in other ways. Rather like the modules that they were soon to teach within modularization structures, some were defined as suitable for early retirement and voluntary severance; a few entered as "new blood"; and numbers of short-term, temporary and part-time staff increased. A number of important consequences flowed from the events of the 1980s, although they are not altogether consistent in their effects. First, academic accountancy (although not necessarily in a professional sense) became as important as academic quality. Secondly, the information upon which decision-making was made, or was said to be made, became more transparent. At least there were now figures to argue about, whereas before there had been very little at all by which to explain or rationalize decisions. Thirdly, the initial cuts in student numbers of the 1980s led on throughout the 1980s and early 1990s to student expansion at a lower unit cost, and especially in the polytechnics, soon to become the "new universities", following the 1992 Further and Higher Education Act. Fourthly, and perhaps most importantly, the 1981 and subsequent cuts in fact ushered in the era of intensification of university work, particularly in teaching but also soon too in demands for increased research and publication output. In 1994, the AUT reported a 64 per cent increase in student numbers, and an 11 per cent increase in staff over ten years (see AUT 1994). This intensification of the academic and "non-academic" (for example, secretarial and administrative workers) labour process happened to coincide with the loss of "academic tenure" enshrined in the 1988 Education Reform Act and, interestingly, the establishment of university equal opportunities and sexual harassment policies. Finally, it almost goes without saying that the influence of students in university politics and decision-making declined greatly during this period, other than in appearances, for example, the ubiquitous "student feedback form".

The overall organizational and managerial structure that was created in the late 1980s and the early 1990s is summed up in the dreaded word "modularization". Academic teaching was redefined as "fitting into" predefined "flexible" modular structures, with the consequence that staff now no longer know who the students are. Whereas in the 1970s differences developed between different departments, with different ideological or disciplinary emphases – for example, "Marxist", "ego psychology" and so on – in the late 1980s and the 1990s difference was incorporated within broader managed structures. Thus "Feminism" is now a module, like everything else.

Meanwhile, women were becoming more visible in the universities, not least by the academic development of women's studies, but also through the commitment of more women staff to considerable time and effort within university decision-making and trade union structures. Usually this involvement extended to membership of faculty boards of studies, although rarely beyond that to deanships, pro-vice-chancellorships, or vice-chancellorships. Equal opportunities might be introduced in policies, but the general climate was no longer collegial (Duke 1997) – a technocratic patriarchal form was becoming more common, displacing the gentlemanly fraternities of earlier years. Indeed, one other effect of this intensification of male management in the universities was the reduced tolerance in management for those staff, men and women, who were (assumed to be) less productive in research or less effective in other ways. This criterion of research productivity was not of course always applied by those, usually male, managers to themselves.

This extended surveillance in turn interacted with the spread of staff appraisal systems in the universities. While these could be used to further careers and wider interests of individual staff and groups of staff, particularly where the appraiser was benevolent, their introduction at a time of increasing insecurity meant that they could be used directly or indirectly to punish or even force out staff (Thomas 1996). Equally interesting is the intersection of these dynamics of managerialism and appraisal with the loss of male fratriarchal collegiality. To put this slightly differently, managerial control of staff, usually male managerial control, was developing at the time of increasing challenge and confidence from women staff; thus patriarchal managerialism was introduced for both women and men staff in a way that was unthinkable in the earlier fraternal or fratriarchal days of male collegiality.

In many ways, the university reforms of the 1980s can be understood as part of the processes of structural change in the relation of the state, the professions and the market (Flynn 1990, Pollitt 1990) – changes that were gendered, and have led to new gender regimes and organizational cultures in universities (Davies and Holloway 1995). On the one hand, this could be said to involve a shift from the state to the market, or to internal markets within and around the state (Prichard and Willmott 1997). On the other hand, the universities themselves have become more closely surveilled, more bureaucratic, more centralized, and more precisely defined and codified. They remain mini-patriarchies, but in a different way; they are less collegial, less fratriarchal and less fraternal. Women's voices are heard more; women are less easy to ignore. Indeed, in a paradoxical way, some of the new managerial practices of the universities in the late 1980s and 1990s have led to a re-examination of old taken-for-granted "truths", more accountability, more emphasis on the distribution of labour, and even now, more collective ways of working, organizing and managing. Some of these have created the spaces for women to do more management and to do management in different ways (Davies and Holloway 1995, Prichard 1996) – but generally without fundamentally challenging the masculinist culture long established in these institutions.

My management

From 1989, my own relationship to this technocratic intensification started to change. I had by that time been at Bradford for 15 years and was one of the longest-serving staff in my department. It was then that I agreed, with some ambivalence, to take on the strange job of Workloads Co-ordinator in the department. This involved gathering information on who does what work, especially what teaching and administrative work. It was also coupled with various other tasks, assisting the head of department, such as planning the agenda of meetings, dealing with part-time staff and drafting notes on her behalf – a kind of political secretary. In 1993, the then head of department left for another university, and I was chosen by the staff to be head of department. I did this for two years, and it proved to be an exceptionally demanding and interesting period.

For a start, the intensification of university labour was proceeding more definitely than ever – modularization and semesterization were in operation. There was considerable pressure from the top university management to accept an imposed reorganization on the department – this was resisted by the staff of the department, and I spoke on their behalf on a number of occasions. In many ways, I was in the classic boundary role position – between the top management and the departmental staff. This involved moving in and between two quite different gendered cultures – a process that was at times difficult, confusing and sometimes even amusing.

The management of the university was, with the exception of one of the most senior managers, exclusively male. All of the heads of the academic departments were men; in addition to the one senior woman manager, a woman dean was also appointed in another faculty during those two years, so making two women out of more than twenty at the head of department level or above. On the other hand, the department's staff was largely women, and indeed over the two-year period a number of men left and were replaced by women. What this meant was that whereas the department's full-time academic staff had for a long time been about half women and half men, this now shifted to very largely women. During the second year there was in my department only one other man on the full-time academic staff apart from myself. While the management of the university was dominated by fairly unreconstructed men, even with the presence of one, and then two, senior women managers, the department was characterized by a variety of feminist positions.

My own position in this was as a man, a manager, and a profeminist. I tried to implement or at least facilitate a form of equality in my relations towards staff, this was in the sense that I was responsible for all staff, about fifty in all, and the well-being of, say, the part-time secretary had to be taken as seriously as that of, say, the full-time senior lecturer. When they were speaking to me, particulary one to one, what might appear a small matter in the context of the whole department's activities might be a very large matter to the individual concerned.

I also tried to be open, as open as I could in collective discussions – one problem here was often that there was confidential information about individual staff that I and perhaps one or two others knew, but that could not be shared with everyone.

This two-year period proved to be one of major change in the department. There was a reorganization of administration and offices; new degrees were planned and introduced; other degrees were reformed; there were significant staff changes; and at last new technology was introduced for almost all staff – all in the context of a considerable squeeze on resources.

The shift to management was a considerable challenge to me: how to be fair and efficient as a manager; how to be a man and a manager and not be oppressive; how to be profeminist within the context of what could reasonably be described as a feminist department and a male-dominated university; and how to be facilitative towards staff at a time of increasing managerial control and managerialism, both in the university and nationally. It also involved working very closely with not only academic but also secretarial, administrative, personnel, financial and management staff.

I experienced the shift to management not so much in terms of adopting different or separate positions – politically or discursively – as living with more accentuated challenges. My identity was certainly challenged, sometimes profoundly so, but somewhat to my surprise, it was not completely disrupted. Perhaps one reason was that I saw this new position (in both the organizational and discursive senses) as strictly temporary. In the first instance, I took on the headship of the department for one year only, and then only agreed to do the second year on gaining certain undertakings on the future staffing of the department from the top management of the university. As a result, I was fairly easily able to know that I was not an "academic manager" for life. This helped, and stands in contrast with the tendency towards longer-term, and even permanent, appointments of managers in higher education.

On the other hand, I did experience what at times seemed like a puzzling mixture of harmony and conflict throughout the two years. At its best, there was a very real sense of collective feminist-inspired effort; but this was coupled with my fair share (sometimes it felt like more than my fair share) of difficult and conflictual situations. Some of these were situations that I inherited; some arose (in my terms) from trying to be even-handed regardless of status; some came from taking and sticking to difficult principled decisions; some came from staff who I had previously known well as colleagues, who were now feeling let down because I did not behave the same with them as before; and some came from differences of opinion.

There was also a cost; that is, a personal cost. To do the job thoroughly and conscientiously, to do all the things that were being asked, and especially so at a time of very tight resources and so-called (not really) devolved budgets, was in some profound ways not possible; there was always more to do than could be done. For example, the financial push to employ more part-time staff coupled with a solid commitment to good equal opportunities practice meant that there was a major increase in the management, administration and support for such staff. Whereas in the past, part-time staff had been recruited by "word of mouth", with all the discrimination that can involve, there was now a consistent attempt to recruit for what was an increasing array of part-time work as fairly as possible.

One particular memory stays in my mind of that period: of returning home from an especially arduous day and meeting some visiting friends whom I had not seen for some while, and of one of them commenting – in fact, emphasizing – how I seemed so much less relaxed and so much more stressed than usual. What stays in my mind is that it was becoming clear that I had remember to change my life from this impossible job.

Personal/political profeminism is certainly in tension with masculinist managerialism; and there were many times when I felt it was difficult, if not impossible, to be all things to all people. However, it would be a mistake to assume that profeminism is necessarily incompatible with management, or that it is impossible to do profeminist management. Perhaps it is more accurate to recognize the specific and variable contingencies – gendered, organizational, hierarchical and so on – that affect the attempt to be both profeminist and a manager. Accordingly, the experience of being, or trying to be, a profeminist manager is likely to be rather different in such different organizational cultures.

In trying to understand the gendered nature of universities and higher education, the autobiographical has its uses in locating one's own story and experiences, but it also has its limitations. In particular, it can divert attention from some of the general features of the whole system, and it is to these that I now turn in this concluding discussion. Crucially, what is clear is that although there has been change, the broad structural pattern is still alarmingly resilient to gender transformation. Thus I will conclude by reviewing the overall gendered state of UK higher education at the end of the 1990s.

Changing university managements?

Changes in management of universities, in their gendered structures and processes, and in the place of men in management are difficult to summarize. The movement could be seen as a shift from a non-bureaucratic male-dominated "feudal" system to a bureaucratic male-dominated "feudal" system, or from collegial fraternity (or fratriarchy) to technocratic patriarchy (Burris 1996). The system is now certainly more fully documented and in that sense at least more open, more accountable, yet still also open to abuse.[6] On the other hand, there are profound contradictions – it could be said to be both more centralized and more devolved.

Universities are in some ways unusual kinds of organizations, and thus managements. They combine together a number of gendered features, that do not always work together in an easy harmony. They also operate within the broader societal context of patriarchal and fratriarchal social relations. While my emphasis has been on gendered relations, universities are simultaneously structured by age, class, disability, ethnicity, racialization, sexuality and other social relations. Indeed, these gendered social relations are also simultaneously racialized, sexualized and so on. So, to conclude, let us consider what some of these major and persistent features of universities look like.

First, universities are *still* incredibly hierarchical institutions, and these hierarchies are gendered, as well as constructed through other social relations. This applies both *between* universities and *within* universities. For example, the higher the status of the university the more men are likely to work there as academics – while Cambridge and Oxford have 3.5 and 3 times, respectively, as many men as women academics, the comparable figures for Manchester University, Bradford University, Central Lancashire University and Chester College are 2.5, 2.3, 2.1 and 2.

Similarly, the internal hierarchies of universities are intense, and indeed, as already noted, in recent years, despite a (somewhat) "more democratic ethos", the gradations of these hierarchies have certainly become more finely drawn and more complex. There are now whole drafts of staff in short-time temporary, part-time, lowly paid, module-paid, tutor, teaching associate/assistant, contract, research-related and other statuses. Between 1983–4 and 1993–4 there was a 71 per cent increase in the number of academic staff on part-time pro rata contracts (de Groot 1997: 136). Often, though of course not always, these more marginal academic statuses are relatively more populated by women, compared with the situation in the primary full-time academic labour market. In a 1995 AUT survey, 16.2 per cent of men respondents were found to be on fixed contracts, as opposed to 31 per cent of women respondents (de Groot 1997: 136). There is, in effect, a new labour market for these floating staffs, who often teach (and sometimes research) in two, three or four different institutions. However, the primary labour market remains amongst the "full-time" academic staff, and this is also profoundly gendered. The current gender composition, depending on precise definitions used, is as follows:

Grade	Women (per cent)	Men (per cent)
Professors	7–8	92–93
Senior lecturers	15–16	84–85
Lecturers	28–30	70–72
Contract researchers	45	55
Postgraduates	48	52

National information collected by the Higher Education Statistics Agency (HESA) (1996) across 38 academic areas, covering 92 700 staff in 1994–5.

Secondly, these general hierarchical distributions still obscure some incredible horizontal segregations and variations in the gendering of different parts and disciplines of the universities.

What is remarkable is the way in which not just a few but many academic areas remain almost exclusively male at the high, and particularly the professorial, levels. For example, in four areas – general science (534 staff), civil engineering (1716), mineralogy, metallurgy and materials engineering (1153) and administration and central services (255) – all of the 256 professors are men. In a further eight academic areas – clinical dentistry (689), pharmacy (642), chemistry (3298), agriculture and forestry (1378), chemical engineering (782), electrical, electronic and computer engineering (3523), other technologies (870) and academic services (1079) – all but one in each area (i.e. eight) of the 850 professors are men. And in five additional academic areas – veterinary science (1422), pharmacology (510), general engineering (1966), mechanical, aero and production engineering (3474) and communication and media studies (435) – all but two in each area (i.e. ten) of the 437 professors are men. What this means is that in these 17 academic areas, almost half of all the 38 areas, there are 18 women professors and 1543 men professors out of the total of 23 726 staff. Male domination remains profound, and especially so in certain identifiable sectors.

Within these different disciplinary and academic areas, and thus different university departments, there may be rather different gender climates and cultures – in terms of their history, traditions, social organization, curricula, relations between staff, between staff and students and between students, and awareness of gender. The greater the domination of men, the more the academic area, discipline or department is likely to be presented to those within it as gender-neutral; the more homosocial, the more it may appear to those who work and study there as a gender-neutral environment.

Thirdly, the *academic* hierarchies, both across universities and within particular disciplinary and other sectors, overlap in complex ways with management. Traditionally, management in the supposedly "collegial" model was very largely in the hands of male professors and other senior staff. To be a professor did not guarantee being a manager by any means, but most of the managers were in effect professors. The movement to the more technocratic model has meant a limited separation of the professoriat and management in some institutions – and especially in the "new universities". However, the intermingling of management and the professoriat remains intense, and is one of the special features of universities as gendered organizations. There are certainly cases of staff being made professors on the basis of their managerial or administrative activity, rather than on their academic achievements.

In some universities there has been a pronounced move towards heads of departments and even deans not being a professor. The power relations here are complex. On the one hand, professors are often happy to avoid the formal and time-consuming administrative commitments of the headship of department, especially when they can always have their say through Senate, professorial meetings, direct lines to the top management of the university, or informal influences. This is especially since the functions of the head of department have become increasingly constrained by the control of the centralized planning from the national to the individual university levels. Thus heads of departments, while carrying some power and authority, may also carry major responsibilities to deliver services (such as degrees) and other outcomes (such as research "outputs" for the Research Assessment Exercise), with insufficient and diminishing resources, while being obliged to operate with centralized planning and financial constraints. It is no wonder that some professors are not that keen to do the job, compared to the old days when it was "naturally" assumed that this was a job for professors – to exert some "leadership" and power.

Despite what I have just said, there remains, especially in the "old universities", the tradition of management positions being made on a temporary basis and thus changing, often every three years. This usually applies to heads of department, deans and pro-vice-chancellors (PVCs). In some cases, individuals will serve two terms and occasionally more. Indeed, there is sometimes a process of finding such management types new management posts when their period as dean or pro-vice-chancellor is nearing its end. One interesting case involved a former dean being made a professor so that he could then become a PVC, as all PVCs had to be professors. There is, meanwhile, in the "new universities", a strong tradition of "permanent" managerial appointments, an approach which is being promoted in a few "old universities". Similarly, heads of department, deans and PVCs formerly appointed in the "old universities" for three years are now in some cases appointed for five years. Additionally, specific *external appointments* to management are now sometimes made on a time-limited basis, sometimes with performance targets, a model extended from that which is well developed in further education (Whitehead 1999).

Fourthly, it is important to address the current ideological climate of universities. In the late 1990s, it can at best be described as contradictory. Even with some limited optimism associated with "New Labour" in government, this remains severely complicated by *tensions* between moral/political ideologies, economic/financial ideologies and knowledge ideologies. In some ways it could be argued that the gendered nature of academia is being undermined as never before (de Groot 1997: 141): For example, there is now a very extensive set of official commitments to equal opportunities policies in universities (see, for example, CUCO 1997, DFEE 1997, Powney et al. 1997, see also Farish et al. 1995), with 96 per cent of universities claiming to have such policies in place (CUCO 1997). In this respect, the "new universities" have often demonstrated a clearer commitment to EOP than the "old universities". However, at the same time there is a need for great caution concening the extent to which EOP can deliver rapid results (Cockburn 1991), and especially so in an institutional system with such a built-in long time lag. Then there is the sheer persistence of male hierarchical domination, particularly in the subject areas outlined above. And in addition there is the continued reconstruction of gendered domination within universities through gendered inequalities amongst academics, gendered employment insecurities, and gendered undermining of identification and collegiality (de Groot 1997: 137, 141).

Finally, there is the question of gendered knowledge formation. Whereas economic/ financial and moral/political ideologies emphasize relatively short-term or long-term conditions respectively, the ideological interest for greater knowledge with the potential for gender emancipation questions these very conditions. In that sense, knowledge production (or more precisely *some* knowledge production) may have its own interests. While universities are characteristically dominated by men, and knowledge produced there is also characteristically dominated by men, I still see the possibility of knowledge being produced that is different, that is not simply reproducing these dominant relations, that provides a counter-gendered view of reality, and that is contributing to gender change – and, in those senses, is more accurate and less pre-scientific than dominant knowledge. But then, being a man, an ex-manager and a member of the universities with their own interests, it is perhaps not so surprising that I would think that.

Acknowledgements

I am very grateful to the editors for their detailed comments on earlier drafts of this chapter, and to David Collinson, Elizabeth Harlow, Liisa Husu and Wendy Parkin for discussions on these and related issues. An early version of these ideas was presented as "Changing men and changing management: personal, political and research agendas" at the Men in Management: Changing Cultures within Education Conference, Thomas Danby College, Leeds, May 1995. A further presentation, "Men and management in the universities: two more challenges for equal opportunities", at the Finnish Universities Equal Opportunities Committees Annual Conference, University of Tampere, September 1996, placed the UK situation in a broader perspective.

Notes

1. This and the following paragraph draw extensively on Alimo-Metcalfe's (1993) excellent article on organizational socialization and assessment practices that prevent career advancement for women in management.

2. The history of women's initial entry in university higher education is a complicated and uneven story, stretching at least from the 1840s to the 1890s. For further details in what is a thorough and lively account, see Vicinus's (1985) *Independent Women*, especially Chapter 4.
3. There are previously women Heads of Institution in the various colleges of higher education and polytechnics that have become known as the "new universities".
4. The term "new universities" refers to those universities newly created in the 1960s, and is not to be confused with those instituted in the 1990s. See note 3.
5. An invaluable record of major national changes in the governance of higher education from 1980 to 1994, along with an expert commentary on gender regimes in this period, is provided by Davies and Holloway (1995).
6. The Nolan Committee into Standards in Public Life was set up by the Conservative government in 1993. Now termed the Neil Committee, in 1997 its remit was extended to include the investigation of fraud, misconduct and unlawful spending in universities and colleges.

References

Acker, J. (1990) "Hierarchies, jobs, bodies: a theory of gendered organizations", *Gender and Society*, **4**, pp. 139–58

Adler, N. and Izraeli, D. (eds) (1988) *Women in Management Worldwide* New York: M.E. Sharpe

Aisenberg, N. and Harrington, M. (1988) *Women of Academia: Outsiders in the Sacred Grove* Amherst, Mass.: University of Massachusetts Press

Alban Metcalfe, B. (1984) "Current career concerns of female and male managers and professionals: an analysis of free response comments to a national survey", *Equal Opportunities International*, **3**, pp. 11–18

Alimo-Metcalfe, B. (1993) "Women in management: organizational socialization and assessment practices that prevent career advancement", *International Journal of Selection and Assessment*, **1**, pp. 68–83

Association for University Teachers AUT (1994) "Long hours, little thanks", in Davies and Holloway (1995)

Boulgarides, J. (1984) "A comparison of male and female business managers", *Leadership and Organization Development Journal*, **5**, pp. 27–31

Brooks, A. (1997) *Academic Women* Buckingham: Open University Press

Burris, B. (1996) "Technocracy, patriarchy and management". See Collinson and Hearn (1996), pp. 61–77

Calás, M. and Smircich, L. (1993) "Dangerous liaisons: the 'feminine-in-management' meets globalization", *Business Horizons*, March–April, pp. 71–81

Carpenter, G. (1995) "The relationship between collegiality and patriarchy", in Payne, A.M. and Shoemark, L. (eds) *Women Culture and Universities: a Chilly Climate? Conference Proceedings* Sydney: University of Technology, Sydney Women's Forum, pp. 58–67

Child, J. (1969) *British Management Thought* London: Allen & Unwin

Clark, V., Garner, S.N., Higonnet, M. and Katrak, K.H. (eds) (1996) *Antifeminism in the Academy* New York: Routledge

Clegg, S. and Dunkerley, D. (1980) *Organizations, Class and Control* London: Routledge & Kegan Paul

Cockburn, C. (1990) "Men's power in organisations: 'equal opportunities intervenes'", in Hearn, J. and Morgan, D. (eds) *Men, Masculinities and Social Theory* London: Unwin Hyman, pp. 72–89

Cockburn, C. (1991) *In the Way of Women: Men's Resistance to Sex Equality in Organizations* London: Macmillan

Cohen, E.W. (1965) *The Growth of the British Civil Service, 1780–1939* London: Cassell

Collinson, D.L. and Hearn, J. (1994) "Naming men as men: implications for work, organization and management", *Journal of Gender, Work and Organization*, **1**, 1, pp. 2–22

Collinson, D.L. and Hearn, J. (eds) (1996) *Men as Managers, Managers as Men: Critical Perspectives on Men, Masculinities and Managements* London: Sage

CUCO (1997) *A Report on Policies and Practices on Equal Opportunities in Employment in Universities, Colleges and Higher Education* London: CVCP

Davidson, M. (1989) "Women managers and stress: profiles of vulnerable individuals", *Clinical Psychology Forum*, **22**, pp. 32–4

Davidson, M. and Cooper, C. (1984) "Occupational stress in female managers: a comparative study", *Journal of Management Studies*, **21**, pp. 185–205

Davies, C. and Holloway, P. (1995) "Troubling transformations: gender regimes and organizational culture in the academy". See Morley and Walsh (1995), pp. 7–21

DFEE (1997) *Higher Education in the Learning Society* London: HMSO, 9 vols

de Groot, J. (1997) "After the ivory tower: gender commodification and the 'academic'", *Feminist Review*, **55**, pp. 130–42

Donnell, S.M. and Hall, J. (1980) "Men and women as managers: a significant case of no significant difference", *Organizational Dynamics*, **8**, pp. 60–77

Duke, C. (1997) "Equal opportunities versus elitism", *Journal of Gender, Work and Organization*, **4**, 1, pp. 47–57

Dzeich, B.W. and Weiner, L. (1984) *The Lecherous Professor: Sexual Harassment on Campus* Boston: Beacon Press

Epstein, C.F. (1970) "Encountering the male establishment: sex-status limits on women's careers in the professions", *American Journal of Sociology*, **75**, pp. 965–82

Farish, M., McPake, M., Powney, M. and Weiner, G. (1995) *Equal Opportunities in Colleges and Higher Education: Towards Better Practice* Buckingham: Open University Press

Fay, B. (1975) *Social Theory and Political Practice* London: Allen & Unwin

Ferguson, K. (1984) *The Feminist Critique of Bureaucracy* Philadelphia, Pa.: Temple University Press

Ferrario, M. (1990) *Leadership Style of British Men and Women Managers* MSc thesis, Faculty of Management Sciences, University of Manchester

Flynn, N. (1990) *Public Sector Management* London: Harvester Wheatsheaf

Giddens, A. (1981) *The Class Structure of the Advanced Societies* London: Hutchinson

Ginsberg, E. and Lennox, S. (1996) "Antifeminism in scholarship and publishing". See Clark et al. (1996), pp. 169–99

Gough, I. (1983) *The Political Economy of the Welfare State* London: Macmillan

Hansard Society (1990) *The Report of the Hansard Society Commission on Women at the Top* London: Hansard Society

Harlow, E., Hearn, J. and Parkin, W. (1995) "Gendered noise: organizations and the silence and din of domination". See Itzin and Newman (1995), pp. 89–105

Hearn, J. (1992) *Men in the Public Eye: the Construction and Deconstruction of Private Men and Public Patriarchies* London: Routledge

Hearn, J. (1994) "Changing men and changing managements: social change, social research and social action", in Davidson, M. and Burke, R. (eds) *Women in Management: Current Research Issues* London: Paul Chapman, pp. 192–209

Hearn, J. and Parkin, W. (1983) "Gender and organisations: a selective review and a critique of a neglected area", *Organization Studies*, **4**, pp. 219–42

Hearn, J. and Parkin, W. (1995) *"Sex" at "Work": the Power and Paradox of Organisation Sexuality* (rev. edn) Hemel Hempstead: Prentice Hall/Harvester Wheatsheaf

Higher Education Statistics Agency (1996) *Resources of Higher Education Institutions 1994/95* Cheltenham: HESA

Institute of Management (1995) *National Management Salary Survey* Kingston-on-Thames: Institute of Management

Itzin, C. (1995) "Gender, culture, power and change: a materialist analysis". See Itzin and Newman (1995), pp. 246–72

Itzin, C. and Newman, J. (eds) (1995) *Gender and Organizational Change: Putting Theory into Practice* London: Routledge

Jackson, D. (1990) *Unmasking Masculinity: a Critical Autobiography* London: Unwin Hyman

Jago, A.G. and Vroom, V.H. (1982) "Sex differences in the incidence and evaluation of participative leader behavior", *Journal of Applied Psychology*, **67**, pp. 776–83

Keller, E.F. and Longino, H.E. (eds) (1996) *Feminism and Science* Oxford: Oxford University Press

Lorber, J. (1989) "Trust, loyalty, and the place of women in the informal organization of work", in Freeman, I. (ed.) *Women: a Feminist Perspective* (4th edn) Mountain View, Ca.: Mayfield

Lyotard, J.F. (1984) *The Post-Modern Condition: a Report on Knowledge* Manchester: Manchester University Press

Martin, P.Y. (1996) "Gendering and evaluating dynamics: men, masculinities and managements". See Collinson and Hearn (1996), pp. 186–209

Mills, A. and Tancred, P. (eds) (1992) *Gendering Organizational Analysis* London: Sage

Morley, L. and Walsh, V. (eds) (1995) *Feminist Academics: Creative Agents for Change* London: Taylor & Francis

New Ways to Work (1995) *Balanced Lives: Changing Work Patterns for Men* London: New Ways to Work

Nichols, T. (1970) *Ownership, Control and Ideology* London: Allen and Unwin

Paludi, M.A. and Barickman, R.B. (1991) *Academic and Workplace Harassment: a Resource Manual* Albany, NY: State University of New York Press

Parkes, E. (1981) *Grant for 1981/82 and Guidance for Succeeding Years, Circular Letter 10/81* London: University Grants Committee

Parkin, D. and Maddock, S. (1995) "A gender typology of organizational culture". See Itzin and Newman (1995), pp. 68–80

Pateman, C. (1988) *The Sexual Contract* Cambridge: Polity Press

Pollitt, C. (1990) *Managerialism and the Public Services: the Anglo-American Experience* Oxford: Blackwell

Powell, G. (1988) *Women and Men in Management* Newbury Park, CA: Sage

Powney, J., Hamilton, S. and Weiner, G. (1997) *Higher Education and Equality: a Guide* London: EOC/CRE/CUCO

Prichard, C. (1996) "Managing universities: is it men's work?". See Collinson and Hearn (1996), pp. 227–38

Prichard, C. and Willmott, H. (1997) "Just how managed is the McUniversity?", *Organizational Studies*, **18**, 2, pp. 287–316

Remy, J. (1990) "Patriarchy and fratriarchy as forms of androcracy", in Hearn, J. and Morgan, D. (eds) *Men, Masculinities and Social Theory* London: Unwin Hyman, pp. 43–54

Rendel, M. (1980) "How many women academics 1912–1976?" in Deem, R. (ed.) *Schooling for Women's Work* London: Routledge

Robbins, Lord (Chair) (1963) *Committee on Higher Education Report, Cmnd 2145* London: HMSO

Roper, M. (1993) *Masculinity and the British Organization Man, 1945 to the Present* Oxford: Oxford University Press

Roper, M. (1996) "'Seduction and succession': circuits of homosocial desire in management". See Collinson and Hearn (1996), pp. 210–26

Rose, H. (1994) *Love, Power and Knowledge: Towards a Feminist Transformation of the Sciences* Cambridge: Polity Press

Rose, N. (1987) "Beyond the public/private division: law, power and the family", *Journal of Law and Society*, **14**, pp. 61–76

Rose, N. (1993) "Government, authority and expertise in advanced liberalism", *Economy and Society*, **22**, pp. 283–99

Rosener, J. (1990) "Ways women lead", *Harvard Business Review* November/December, pp. 119–25

Scase, R. and Goffee, R. (1989) *Reluctant Managers* London: Unwin Hyman

Schein, E. (1973) "The relationship between sex-role stereotypes and requisite management characteristics", *Journal of Applied Psychology*, **57**, pp. 95–100

Sinclair, A. (1995) "Sex and the MBA", *Organization*, **2**, pp. 295–319

Thomas, R. (1996) "Gendered cultures and performance appraisal: the experience of women academics", *Gender, Work and Organization*, **3**, pp. 143–55

Vicinus, M. (1985) *Independent Women: Work and Community for Single Women 1850–1920* London: Virago

Vinnicombe, S. (1987) "What exactly are the differences in male and female working styles?", *Women in Management Review*, **3**, pp. 13–21

Walby, S. (1986) *Patriarchy at Work* Oxford: Blackwell

Waters, M. (1989) "Patriarchy and viriarchy: an exploration and reconstruction of concepts of masculine domination", *Sociology*, **23**, pp. 193–211

Waters, M. (1993) "Alternative organisation formations: a typology of polycratic administrative systems", *The Sociological Review*, **41**, pp. 54–81

Whitehead, S. (1998) "Disrupted selves: resistance and identity work in the managerial arena", *Gender and Education*, **10**, 2, pp. 199–215

Whitehead, S. (1999) "From paternalism to entrepreneurialism: the experience of men managers in UK postcompulsory education", *Discourse: Studies in the Cultural Politics of Education*, **20**, 1, in press

Wright, E.O. (1985) *Classes* London: Verso

Young, K. and Spencer, L. (1990) *Women Managers in Local Government: Removing the Barriers* Birmingham: INLOGOV

CHAPTER NINE

Intermanagerial rivalries, organizational restructuring and the transformation of management masculinities

Stella Maile

Introduction

To talk of transforming masculinities is to raise questions about the nature of work and the occupational identities in which it is immersed. When set patterns of employment undergo radical change, occupational identities have to be renegotiated. This is often a highly complex process which, by its very nature, cannot be divorced from broader political and institutional dynamics. Furthermore, changes in the workplace often accompany changes in the private sphere of the home and family. In relation to this, recent literature has underlined the continuing presence of "patriarchal" forms of power both as a distinctive feature and also as necessarily complex in its enmeshment of the private and public spheres (Hearn 1992: 82). Yet, in spite of the complex nature of masculinity, being pivoted on an array of economic, social and cultural processes, it is classically represented as uncomplicated, rational and controlled (see for discussion, Seidler 1994). Management discourse has often played a crucial role in shaping "masculinized" work cultures, characterized by a denial of "feelings" (Swan 1994), or domestic responsibilities and commitments (Yancey Martin 1993). However, even this observation needs to be qualified by reference to the *different types of masculinity* which are present in managerial discourses (Collinson and Hearn 1994, 1996). It is recognized, then, that masculinities are subject to change over time and according to different organizational contexts.

Roper (1994), for example, has traced the historical shift away from the entrepreneurial to the calculative rationality of the money-maker in current managerial discourse. He argues that the distinctiveness of contemporary British management lies in its encouragement of a "rugged individualism" that operates within a broader business/profit environment (Roper 1994: 27). Paralleling this broader culture are transformations in management and managerial forms of masculinity within the public sector. These are, in turn, shaped by an overarching political and institutional environment (Hearn 1992), that influences public-sector restructuring. However, those

145

masculinities, which might be identified with the individualism and drive of the enterprise discourse (Keat and Abercrombie 1992), are mediated by different work histories and professional affiliations, which coexist, possibly, with an earlier social democratic framework (Maile 1995a). Self-evidently, managerial discourse and associated practices are, to this degree, necessarily complex and "fused" in character (Fairclough 1992).

Informed by an understanding of masculinities as fluid and, therefore, potentially transformatory, this chapter examines the gendered consequences of organizational restructuring – specifically, shifts in men managers' perceptions of themselves as men. The research site is a local authority, "Westward District Authority", and the managers interviewed, whose narratives this chapter draws on, were all employed in Environmental Health Services (EHS).[1]

Given the profound restructuring of local authorities, a process which is still occurring, it is timely to examine the impact of restructuring and emerging managerial discourse on men in different managerial positions, with specific reference to their perceptions of gender in the workplace. Initially, though, it is important to locate these processes within the broader political environment of "managerialism". This has significant implications for the transformation of masculinities, given that these have become pivotal in ideological struggles between managers working at different levels of the management hierarchy and within different departments. However, as already stated, the transformation of the public sphere has implications for men's private lives. I argue that these dual experiences are active in the transformation of "masculinity". As such, managers' perceptions of local authority restructuring cannot be examined without reference to the ways in which they incorporate aspects of their private lives, notably perceptions of the domestic world of "home", in their understanding of shifting gender relations in the workplace.

As the research reveals, the increasing presence of women in the various divisions and, specifically, the Women's Group[2] in the Environmental Health Services Directorate of "Westward District Authority" seemed to become a focal point for many men managers' projection of anxiety and hostility towards restructuring. While senior managers wished to explain this simply in terms of raw chauvinism, it is difficult fully to understand reactions to the women's group without careful examination of the impact of managerialism on different divisions. The chapter will therefore be broken down to include (a) the role of politics and new discourses in senior management, (b) the differential impact of managerialism on different divisions and finally (c) their impact on gender relations and how these are mediated by perceptions of local authority policies aimed at the improvement of the position of women under restructuring. I shall be arguing that the latter are intimately related to forms of rationalization and employment insecurity on the part of men. Finally, these factors may be linked to the decline of collectivism in welfare provision and the rise of a more distanced form of management, whose increasing centralization is associated with what female members of staff have dubbed the "new man" manager, in contrast to more traditional, collectivist forms of management and experiences of masculinity. As will be noted, these transformations enter into intermanagerial conflicts as individual managers attempt to secure their positions during a period of heightened insecurity.

The impact of managerialism: politics and new discourses

Management techniques are generally presented as value neutral, based upon pragmatism, sound business sense and "rational" decision-making (Bendix 1963, Child
1969, Thompson and McHugh 1995). They allow for a degree of individual interpretation and personal skill, depending upon particular circumstances and the intuition of individual managers. It is due to common-sense assumptions which equate
good management with skill, technical and practical acumen and an ability to communicate with people that management discourse comes to be placed outside of
politics and within the world of value-neutral work. It is partly due to this that both
the previous Conservative government and the current Labour government have
utilized management discourse to such effect. The Labour government has retained
the previous Conservative government's concern to reduce public expenditure, largely
as a consequence of continuing neo-liberal economic policies and pressure from the
International Monetary Fund. In a similar vein, they adopt a managerialist orientation to welfare cuts by placing a stress upon appropriate management techniques
and styles. However, while the previous government called for tighter management
control of resources, with the treatment of staff as factors of production, this government appeals to common-sense assumptions that surround "people management"
and focuses upon the softer side of human resource management (HRM) with a
consequent emphasis upon employee training and development, teamwork and
self-actualization (see Legge 1995).

At the time this research was being conducted, aspects of managerialism in local
authorities included the use of performance indicators encouraged by the Audit
Commission and the establishment of quasi-markets through the introduction of compulsory competitive tendering and competition between (a) authorities, (b) authority
services and (c) private/voluntary-sector services. It can be argued that compulsory
competitive tendering (CCT) is a classic example of attempts on the part of central
government to introduce quasi-markets into local authorities which thereby reduce
the power base of trades unions. While this has traditionally affected those manual
workers employed in what are termed direct labour organizations (DLOs)   for
example, street cleansing, refuse collection, parks and gardens – in 1990 CCT was
extended to cover professional and semi-professional services, the justification being
that Environmental Health Services employs both types of labour, and includes the
work of street cleansing, engineering and environmental health.

Any examination of intermanagerial tensions will need to recognize, then, that
managers are not a homogenous social group, but are in fact subject to different
organizational and political pressures and ways of working. Managers with different professional backgrounds and employment histories negotiate shifts in public
service in different ways. Managerial masculinities are also bound up with loyalties
to pre-established working patterns and, if these are threatened, they may become
active in the contestation of emerging managerial styles and practices. It is no longer
possible for men to feel assured of their status in the organization as they attempt
to come to grips with senior management directives which undermine both their
gendered, and organizational, status and authority. As such, when I spoke with

147

them, they were entering the painful process of a growing consciousness of their changing surroundings, a process which was challenging and transforming their conceptions of paid work and their sense of themselves as managers and as men. Moreover, as will now be discussed, personal experiences of managerialism in "Westward District Authority" appeared to be aggravated by the decline of traditionally male-dominated professions and occupations – for example, engineering and street cleansing – and the paralleled rise of a female-dominated profession within the Directorate; notably, environmental health.

Environmental Health Services: intermanagerial tensions in "Westward District Authority"

As already argued, what makes managerialism distinctive is its ideological investment in neo-liberal economic policies (Keat and Abercrombie 1992). These emphasize public spending restraints facilitated by the establishment of internal quasi-markets, CCT and the reconceptualization of service-users as "customers". This is mirrored by the deployment of alternative management techniques and metaphors borrowed from the private sector (Flynn 1993) – such as "corporate downsizing" or "streamlining" – processes prominent since the 1980s and 1990s as firms search for both a greater competitive edge and greater shareholder returns.

Consequently, public-sector managerialism is now embedded within this "realist" culture, although pressure comes not from shareholders but trickles down from central government, via councillors and council taxpayers. As Cousins (1987) notes, the growing demands on local authority services to manage within reduced budgets results in the centralization and intensification of management control and work processes. Thus greater emphasis is placed on tightened budgetary control, speedy customer responsiveness, and the forging of new relationships between some local authority services and the private sector. Similarly, tightened budgetary control, coupled with reconceptualizations of administration to management, has resulted in massive restructuring within "Westward District Authority". In addition to senior management delayering, there has been a widening of middle management responsibilities, particularly for middle and front-line management. Chief officer numbers have been reduced and professionals have had to compete for senior management (rather than chief officer posts) in the newly formed directorates (Maile 1995b). Coupled with this is the impact of legislation on professions, particularly legislative influence on the rise or fall of particular services in the context of the new consumerism and the establishment of quasi-markets already mentioned. As an illustration of this, Environmental Health Services, represented by trained environmental health officers (EHOs), used to stand apart from other departments, but has now been retitled Environmental Health Services (EHS) to reflect its broad statutory function of keeping the streets and restaurants of Westward clean and pest free. EHS now employs about fifty EHOs, largely female, who are engaged in monitoring and inspecting food premises, farms, abattoirs, butchers, and so on. More recently, it has taken upon itself a number of related non-statutory functions, including various "Green initiatives" and Health and Safety instruction.

The political currency of EHS has, then, a basically regulative or statutory function, rather than a key municipal agency role. This has provided the rationale for formerly independent departments to be amalgamated under its rubric. These included Cemeteries and Crematoria and Engineering, which along with Policy and Resources comprise the three new divisional structures in EHS. Although, as we shall see, many of these DLO functions have now gone out to a private tender, the client or monitoring role of previous DLO functions remains within the new Directorate under the control of the new EHS Director. The director (who is himself a trained environmental health inspector) had to compete for his post with the previous chief officer of the old Engineering department. However, now that the Director is in post, *he is responsible for a profession which is often at odds with engineering, both professionally and in terms of its political symbolism.* We might also add at this point that there are at least two distinctive masculinities associated with the different professions and work of the new Directorate and also with shifting political priorities of both national and local government. As we shall see, these transformations impact upon new managers' perceptions of women's initiatives and highlight questions of gender within the departments. In terms of intermanagerial tensions, it is apparent that while cleansing and engineering staff have been subject to the greatest scrutiny in terms of restructuring, they, in addition to general support and financial services, have also taken the heaviest toll in terms of reduced working conditions, largely because of their greater contact with the private sector.

It is also notable that, while engineering and cleansing services were scrutinized in terms of ways to cut labour costs by introducing more flexible working practices, EHOs experienced an increase in their numbers, something prioritized in a management document which recognized the increasing work burdens of EHOs. Here again, legislation played a role, for the 1990 Food Safety Act meant that local authorities were given more money to ensure the licensing of food premises and to stipulate training in Food and Safety for new restaurateurs. Although the government has since backtracked and the money has not been forthcoming, due to pressure from food trader lobbying groups (traditional supporters of Tory policy), the director of Westward EHS took advantage of the new legislation and recruited more EHOs for Food and Safety inspections. In addition, EHOs have been subject to a general upgrading to senior officer grade. This upgrading of EHOs is also associated with attempts to reformulate professional occupations along managerial lines. At second officer (middle management) levels, these managerial tasks are subject to common job descriptions. As the report on restructuring states:

> ... this is an indication that the managerial ethos has been properly reflected throughout the new Directorate. Fourth tier managerial posts share many common principles, however they take into consideration the differing nature of the various professional and technical groups whom they will affect.

Added to the greater status accorded to EHO functions in the new structure is the more secure position of EHOs, whose tasks are buffered from the market rationalities that affect cleansing and engineering. This is because the work of environmental health officers is largely regulative and statutory.

As Thompson and McHugh (1995: 180), have pointed out, senior managers often speak of "downsizing" and redundancy programmes in terms of creating flexible "less hierarchical forms where whole layers of middle management have been removed on the back of new, horizontal communication channels and devolution of responsibility to self-managing project teams". Westward District Authority would appear to be quite typical in this respect. However, while EHOs work in self-managed project teams, they are still affected by the targets and output figures recommended by the local Audit Commission which, as several EHOs have noted, involve a stress on *quantitative* rather than qualitative measures, thereby reducing the quality and experience of their work. EHOs are thus no less subject to bureaucratic working practices. The introduction of performance indicators and targets (e.g. how many inspections of premises have taken place in the last month) means that as one manager put it, "although the directorate would like to think of itself as 'post-bureaucratic' it isn't, it's bureaucratic". Moreover, directors often cite the influence of elected politicians and senior management on these bureaucratic ways of working and explain this in terms of everybody wanting to hold on to their own particular power base in the context of restructuring. Thus the two most powerful (Labour) councillors, those for Housing and the Policy and Resources Committee, are seen to represent the new order in terms of introducing more "innovative working practices". These include more rigorous procedures for sacking people if their performance is not good enough; a stricter policy on sickness absences, and so on – and the forthcoming introduction of performance indicators. As I go on to argue, all of these practices are embedded in and symbolic of an emergent management machismo.

Management machismo and ideological contestation of "managerialism"

In addition to the more general concern across local authorities to inject management efficiency into the tighter control of restricted budgets, there is the differential impact of CCT and relationships with the private sector. Moreover, the changing statutory functions of the authority have resulted in the perceived prioritization of environmental health over, say, the engineering profession. These factors have combined to threaten management masculinities which were previously "secured" in now outdated professional practices and work cultures (Ferguson 1984). Many commentators have noted that masculinities can acquire an overtly ideological quality (Hearn 1993), especially when the male employment in which they are invested is threatened either by technology (Cockburn 1983, Baron 1992), or management rationalizations and lay-offs (Yarrow 1992). Masculinities and machismo have been shown, then, to enter into workplace struggles and survival strategies (Willis 1979, Burawoy 1985), and may explain one female member of staff's observation that "there seem to be the old boy managers resisting the 'new man' managers – some of them are in-between". She was referring to the managers of engineering and environmental health respectively.

Management ideology – in so far as this informs conflicts between managers – also has clear implications for perceptions of changing gender relations. This is partly associated with those (senior) managerial agendas which inform women's initiatives under restructuring. As we have seen, although the employment experiences of EHOs and their management is far from secure, intermanagerial tensions occurring in EHS are often associated with the perceived upgrading of EHOs. In "Westward District Authority", intermanagerial tensions surrounding the "victory" of environmental health over engineering is further aggravated by the recruitment of EHOs (albeit at non-managerial level) from a pool of female graduates. Although this was to overcome a shortage in this area of expertise, many men in the Directorate equate this increasing recruitment of women with the new political and managerial ethos, a combination of factors which culminates in their own felt employment insecurity *as men*.

At the political level, the chair for environmental health has been involved in work with women's groups in other organizations, notably the now disbanded Greater London Council (GLC), and is particularly committed to improving their employment experiences. Also, within the culture of HRM, the Directorate is aiming to improve its performance *vis-à-vis* women in management. This is further associated with the council's general wish to gain recognition for its attempt to develop their workforce (part of the *Investors in People* initiative) and their involvement in the *Opportunity 2000* programme, designed to encourage women in management.

It also needs to be recognized that, given that senior managers are directly appointed by the political wing of the authority, they may tend to modify their political views in order to achieve greater career security. One significant means of doing this may be to utilize equal opportunities discourse in their restructuring programmes. The director knows that his performance, both in relation to promoting women into management and green initiatives, will probably have some bearing upon his future with the council, a stance which he sees as compatible with a view of himself as a socialist – a socialism, however, which is more effectively encapsulated by what some identified as the women's movement and the Save the Whale campaign than by what one man ungraciously referred to as the politics of the bin men. It needs to be recognized then, that senior managers are themselves as insecure as any other type of employee, especially when they are also faced with imminent unification with the county authority, restructuring which is likely to result in many members of staff having to reapply for their posts.

Hence, implicated in the transformation of masculinities is the new organizational form in which managers are placed; an environment in which female-dominated professions and "services" are prioritized to reflect new pressures and new political thinking. The emphasis on services (rather than utilities) is further complemented by an equal opportunities strategy in which women's skills and qualities are presented as a positive alternative to male norms and practices. For cleansing managers in particular, masculinized "class awareness" (Nichols 1974), thus becomes a form of both defence and resistance. Manifested in open disdain for council policy, this is a masculinized form of resistance which equates white-collar service work and effete "professionalism" with chattering "middle classes" and their "liberal, wishy-washy notions". As alternative types of masculinized management legitimation, these discourses come to inform many new managers' responses to restructuring, as well as their overt responses to women's issues and organizational practices (Bendix 1963, Child 1969, Merkle 1980).

These legitimatory practices highlight the interplay of agency and structure in management strategy and organizational culture, rather than suggesting a "managerialist position" which argues that managers as individuals are wholly responsible for the instigation and implementation of work processes.

The fact that EHOs are employed by the director of EHS creates some bitterness, largely due to misperceptions concerning improvements in EHOs' employment conditions. *This in itself is a gendered process.* For the reconceptualizations of public service have been shown to be associated with the reduction of manual and male-dominated professional work, with an increasing onus on newer female-dominated professions and restructured management positions, in addition to the monitoring and processing work of general white-collar, administrative work. These transformations are not helped, as far as managers in the older municipal services are concerned, by the establishment of a Women's Group which seems for many to be "adding insult to injury". Men managers often expressed their own need for attention in the context of their increasing vulnerability by asking "Why isn't there a men's group?" However, enmeshed within these political and economic transformations are traditional managerial tensions and the personal injuries which derive from demotion and career opportunity decline in a new, harsher era in which some men can no longer feel secure in employment, or for that matter in terms of what they perceive is expected from them as providers (Tolson 1977). Hence, former functions of EHS, which in previous years were characteristic of municipal socialism (i.e. refuse collection, street sweeping, and so on), although still crucial to public perceptions, have a lowered profile. This reduced profile is associated with the fact that such functions have been incorporated under the rubric of EHS, whereas they were previously part of City Engineers. There are clear tensions here relating to the subordination of engineers to environmental health, tensions which are both gendered as well as being a manifestation of professional struggles for power. One manager put it thus:

> Personally I feel the engineering side has come out second rate, and erm . . .
> I personally don't feel that it is recognized by the Director. Basically the respect value is not there from the engineering side. I don't think the Director appreciates us or what we're doing. I would say that the troops don't appreciate that. He just doesn't know what people are dealing with.

The male managers appeared particularly defensive about the way in which they are being treated by senior management, whose interests prioritize the more political (Authority) goals of strictly environmental issues (Green initiatives, and so on), equal opportunities and front-line services. This prioritization reflects the greater status that environmental health was implicitly given when it took under its rubric the engineering and cleansing department. This has quite clear repercussions for functions or "services" which have a reduced profile in the new structure, particularly in the case of EHS. As the manager in cleansing services stated:

152

You know, he goes on about "front line services". This is his policy priority. Now you can't be more front line than refuse collection. But he's far more interested in recycling issues and green issues than what we're trying to do. Refuse collection doesn't manage itself. We have to empty a 160,000 bins a week – we're issuing out wheel bins, we've always got lots of challenges. I have to deal with resistance from unions over these bins for example and believe you me it's a real headache. The last two or three months he's never said "How's it going?" I might have been up all night and he doesn't care.

Perhaps the Director just fancies his chances with some of the women, something like that. I don't know whether he's a happily married man, or a bit frustrated or what. It's a standing joke around here, that if you're a woman and you're involved in Green issues, then you will be able to get in to see him. The rest of us have to go in the diary.

Another stated:

If he walks the job, he won't walk in our direction. If a group of women were standing down one end of the corridor, he'd walk by me and go straight to them. Now I don't think he's shy . . . I think it's that we just don't interest him.

I get the feeling when I go into my immediate line manager that er . . . he's just as confused as we are. So many things are being done centrally within the Directorate that er . . . things that we might not agree with, we are just being told to get on and do it. It's all just upheaval. And if you want my opinion, if you were to ask me, well I'd say that equal opportunities was quite low down on my list of priorities.

Managers and colleagues view the council's attempts to introduce career break schemes and flexitime as unworldly and effete, given the new targets and budgetary constraints that they are facing. There are conflicting loyalties for engineering managers, because of pressures from Wessex Water,[3] in terms of who managers feel most accountable to, particularly in relation to those council policies that are aiming to enhance the representation of women throughout all managerial and non-managerial grades. Such policies are anathema to the macho image often associated with the engineering profession. As can be seen, masculinist identifications are not an arbitrary process but are tied up with definite material concerns, made more so when confronted with the "real world of the market". Indeed, links can be drawn here between the identification that these engineering managers have with life outside the authority and feminist critiques of the essentially public domain occupied by men.

Men know that women's initiatives coincide and are indeed part of their own employment insecurity, because that is precisely how they are being used in the restructuring programme. For the increasing vocalization of the need for women in management coincides with a shift towards service delivery, particularly the need for a more "humane" and flexible management response to consumer needs or, as is frequently suggested, public pressure. Even so, women working at Westward tend to predominate in non-managerial, support roles and are only slowly being recruited to lower-tier management positions. However, as Roper (1994) has argued, although women are still under-represented at management level, their gradually increasing presence in organizations has implications both for the masculinist identity of management and for what it means to be a manager.

This re-gendering process cannot be dissociated from the perception by many within the authority that women are best suited to the need to control a reduced workforce given their "natural feminine skills", especially since the most fractious elements of the workforce have now been neutralized with the selling-off of Contract Services. In one male manager's words:

> Work practices make it far more encouraging for women now. I suppose in engineering – it is usually male-dominated. But now the work is no longer hands on, telling them what to do; it's much more caring, sharing, dealing with clients.
>
> We've got three or four more women now, working as client officers dealing directly with the contract and they've come from clerical backgrounds because the nature of management tasks has changed. You no longer need to be able to shout for a start. You don't shout at them much now because we're not dealing with manual workers.

Thus in men's eyes women are increasingly associated with male employment insecurity and the rationalizations which are presented in terms of new forms of public service as this draws upon previous gender divisions. This point was exemplified in a number of men manager's comments:

> When five members of staff had to go in the shake-up it was five men! I gave some references for some of these men, but they kept me out of the interviews because they had passed me over for promotion earlier on. Anyway I said "you're not gonna expect me to get involved in all these interviews and pay me less" . . . but the men got a rough ride in the interviews, because they are manual workers and they're not very good at interviews . . . management don't seem to appoint for practical skills anymore, it's all what they say in interviews.
>
> Basically the Directorate is going pro-women, giving them time off to talk about themselves, their careers, their job opportunities. Oh yes, with the establishment of that Women's Group they're bringing in what you might call the "he" and the "she" now (grimace). But I'm waiting for men's liberation. I honestly believe, I think they're taking unfair advantage (pause) I need to be careful in what I say here.

In a similar vein, engineering managers bemoan the loss of a masculine group identity; a process exacerbated now that much of their work, particularly sewerage-pipe work, is being undertaken by a cheaper private company. This loss of status that engineers are coping with within the Environmental Health Services Directorate is made more poignant by the self-effacing, whispered comment on the part of one engineer, who said:

> Please don't feel that I'm blowing our own trumpet here, but do you know, we guys in the engineering unit had the best reputation in the whole of Britain for designing and laying sewerage pipes. We all shared the same goal here, we were the best . . . and it's all about to be blown asunder.

Organizational restructuring, and the gendered managerial discourse which it relies upon, is often quite subtle in the ways in which it differentially positions women and men (Maile 1995a). Although current rhetoric favours, ostensibly, women's career development and "female friendly" management styles, women actually remain under-represented in positions of authority and are as subject to labour intensification and stress associated with managerialism as anybody else in the authority (Collinson and Hearn 1996). However, as we have seen, for many men, women's initiatives are singled out as a key determinant of their personal experience of employment insecurity. Ironically, the decline of collective working and the rise of individualism and insecurity have come to be associated in many men's minds solely with the implementation of equal opportunities policies and women's initiatives in the workplace.

The masculinity of these managers appears to be bound up with a sense of collective responsibility and collective skill. Although this can be interpreted as a masculinized form of caring, for the large part, it ultimately pivots upon the exclusion of women. As such, attempts to hold on to male power are bound up with an earlier, masculinized, political consensus that informs municipal welfare provision. Women's continuing under-representation in management positions may thus be accounted for by these masculinized forms of resistance to the more obviously individualistic forms of management for which women are often blamed. This amounts to a defence of the (male) camaraderie and sense of esteem attached to the collectivism of an earlier period of management in male-dominated areas of work: a time when men felt safe.

Consequently, resistance becomes caught up in a preoccupation with management styles and identities, rather than broader management rationalities. As Alvesson and Willmott (1992: 7) note, subordinates tend to be more critical of management techniques and styles than they do the social division of labour. This observation becomes even more significant in the political context of managerialism within local government. Far from subordinates (in this case, subordinate managers) becoming radicalized by their increasing employment insecurity and a perception of declining public services, managers tend to vent their spleen by making reference to the director's "frosty" management style, with "him barricading himself behind heavy doors". The new, centralized management is symbolized in EHS by the director's office which, not long after his appointment, was girded by doors which blocked out the view of any staff who might have peered at him through the old glass doors. What staff seem to want, above all else, is a solid entrepreneurial approach in which the director "walks the job". As several engineering managers noted:

I don't think the Director puts himself about enough. If you were in his position wouldn't you want to try to get around the office ... every now and then? That never does happen and the troops don't appreciate it. This morale business is a complex issue, but he doesn't help. It is something very easily rectified.

Although management is often regarded as involving a particularly distanced form of masculinity, this is not borne out by interviews with managers with different work histories and responsibilities, and subject to different forms of control. Masculinity is rooted in broader political and social environments. It became identified with "reason" and control within the context of the Enlightenment thinking, and subsequently influenced classical management theories (Ferguson 1984, Hearn and Parkin 1987, Seidler 1991). Similarly, "masculinity" may be incorporated into new political and managerial discourses, although the effectiveness of this will depend upon individual agency and the subjective internalization and interpretation of dominant discourses.

For all the rhetoric of empowerment and flexibility which characterizes modern management discourse, lower-tier managers responsible for the allocation of work in pressured organizational settings are increasingly disenchanted by threats to more collective styles of management and loyalties associated with an earlier period:

I hold a corporate view. If a colleague is in trouble, I'll help out because I regard it as a team effort. I have found lately that I am a voice in the wilderness because people, especially EH, just want to look after their own team. I don't think that is right.

Although the managers in Contract Services are far from sympathetic to "the workers", while adopting a management style which, as a cleansing client manager noted, "had to have a bit of steel in it", it is clear that the working-class culture of men managers on either side of cleansing is part and parcel of the distrust that they have for a new organizational structure which favours "the green men up there". The difficulties that senior management have with individual cleansing client managers are associated with the continuing loyalties which cleansing client managers and officers have to the old director of Contract Services. It is interesting to note here that the area director for the new private contractor for street cleaning and refuse collection is the former director of Contract Services! People on both the client and contractor side, hitherto formally employed under Contract Services, had experienced many years working with the director and, in remembering the "good old days when you could have a laugh with nobody taking offence", maintain loyalties to him. As one such manager recalled:

When I worked for John it was such a good management team. Anybody could say if they disagreed with him and it was OK. I came across this article on management styles once and I said 'ere John, have a look at that and he read it, and he thought it was great. Anyway we decided that John

156

was a charismatic type, Terry was a resource man and Dave a company man . . . I was a completer–finisher and a bit of an ideas man as well. Anyway, we worked well together. Then CCT blew it all apart and because I was a completer–finisher I was thought best for the client side of things.

Although men may attempt to understand their demotion in terms of newer forms of managerial discourse and managerial identities, as the above quote highlights, often the protection of masculinity and management positions occurs through the use of older management styles. In this research context it is, arguably, associated with various attempts to hold on to the greater status that engineering had before the introduction of the private-sector rationality and the incorporation of engineers under Environmental Health Services. A female engineer stated that in her division, "the men just love the old Scientific Management approach and don't want things to change because they've got a vested interest in it". Other women highlighted the degree to which these alternative management styles were caught up in the conflict between "new order" and "old order" or, as another female member of staff put it, "the old boy" and "new man" managers, who will adopt different positions for their own benefits. This is most pronounced between engineering and EHOs, with Financial and Support Services taking a kind of middle ground between the two, while continuing to favour men over women in their recruitment of women into management posts. Again, although males in engineering and cleansing services appear to view things as "going too much the other way", EHOs complain of the lack of room for manoeuvre in terms of changing management strategies or styles, because of the overall atmosphere of pressure and fear.

Masculinity, collectivist forms of caring and the private/public sphere

We have already seen how the insecurity of male managers can be understood in relation to (a) their own perceptions of gender in restructuring and (b) their own experiences of masculinity and changing demands upon them as men. In this section, I discuss in more detail the kinds of concerns that men expressed on both an individual level (through interviews) and in discussion groups. The overall aim here is to demonstrate that it is necessary to distinguish between men's responses to women's issues in the immediate context of workplace restructuring, and perceptions of women's issues as informed by personal (i.e. domestic) relations with women. As the research reveals, there was a marked difference in response to questions of changing gender relations when male managers were given the space to talk about their own insecurities as influenced by both their public and private lives.

In the context of management discussions, the engineering managers (particularly professional engineers) and men who were former managers of the DLO, were often openly hostile in discussions on "women's issues", and women's initiatives. It is important here to recognize the sense of solidarity that men express and also the masculinized collectivist forms of caring and loyalty that may partially offset the new masculine individualism. I would argue that this collectivist identity is as much

157

bound up with a political stance on welfare provision as it is with masculinity. When these men are defensive of their former ways of working, they are also defensive of the part that they considered that they formerly played in "doing some good for society" and of having a distinct role and function outside the home. A recurrent theme in the interviews was the overwhelming power that wives and mothers have in the home, and the consequent need to escape to work in order to assert authority. Even those men who support women's initiatives talked of the need for a man to be in control, i.e. to be "the boss" at work, and for the woman to be the boss in the home. For managers who are experiencing demotion in terms of authority and status in restructuring, these existing perceptions of more traditional gender relations acquire a particularly negative connotation, especially given their concerns about retiring or becoming unemployed. As we shall see, this was a significant theme in discussions around the issue of retirement. Importantly, the increasing perception of threat to this collectivist masculinity has implications for their responses to initiatives which are designed to enhance the position of women in the Directorate.

During the course of group discussion, there was often something extremely infantile about the men's responses to me as a woman researcher. They often expressed anger towards me for raising certain issues and used offensive body language (pointing fingers and so on) to convey their hostility. For those who appeared to be supportive of women's issues, there was some indication that they wanted approval – looking to me as group facilitator for some form of acknowledgement. Similarly, some encountered almost as much hostility when they attempted to express some level of identification with females. The atmosphere of the discussion intensified when one man, nearing retirement age, and with many years of experience in the forces, stood up to quote his grandmother (who had brought him up after the Second World War):

> I remember when I was a nipper, my grandmother saying, life might be hard for you Jack, but women have it the hardest of all and never forget it, and I never did and she was a fantastic woman, strong and independent and managed everything.

He then proceeded to talk about the responsibility that men have for women's general condition and for the need for men to think about their own behaviour, particularly in organizations which are undergoing change.

The psychoanalytical dimensions of these processes – the tendency for men to both elevate and denigrate women (i.e. the "good" and the "bad" mother), who also thereby come to embody something "other" in the harsh environment of restructuring – have to some degree been discussed by Roper (1994) and Collinson and Hearn (1996). It could be argued that the space in which men can feel assured of nurturance, support or encouragement is diminishing. This is most clearly apparent in anxieties that the men expressed over retirement or personal relationships – a feeling that they would get under their women's feet, that they would themselves be subject to the authority of the wife in the wife's domain. This is illustrated by frequent references to the observation that "men come to work to dominate". However, for many men in the organization, coming to work is not simply about domination, it is also about needing to be needed by "society", something which in this case is bound up with an earlier public service ethos. The two often fused in discussions about home life.

Concerns about early retirement for the older men, or finding another job for the younger men, were pronounced in discussions and highlighted the anxieties that were repeatedly expressed over changing expectations and role adjustment:

> I went through my forties thinking I'll probably work until my late fifties and then all of a sudden, bang, I've turned fifty and I face the prospect of being out of work next year. There is a strong emotional side to that. I mean, I've been in employment all my life. Am I now going to sit back, go home and read books, wash up, do the crossword and make the beds and wait for death? What am I going to do with my life? Will I be able to find more work? I feel I need to find more work, because I need to make a contribution to society. I came into Local Government as an engineer because partly, even as a young man, the notion of doing work for society was appealing, doing work out in society, and I have felt that, so I've got a need to feel part of society. I have a need to feel wanted, the need to be needed by society possibly.

The implementation of a women's group is, for many men, simply adding insult to injury, especially given their concerns about having to enter into the "woman's domain" (i.e. the home) when they retire at a far younger age than they had expected. In this sense, for these men, the woman's domain would appear to be extending itself into their traditional sphere of "society", thereby leaving them no "masculine space". Older men, who had been working in the authority for about twenty-five years, repeatedly spoke of being worried about being in the "woman's domain" once they retired. They often drew on what they remembered of retired fathers or uncles when they were kids:

> My uncle retired when he was about sixty and he was unbearable, he didn't last very long because he could not cope in his wife's space. He then went back to the office, I think for about a year and he was a new man and then when that finished again . . . he didn't survive. I've come to the conclusion that you've got to prepare yourself with this. I'm sitting down with my wife now, discussing what we will do when I retire. We need the personnel department to do something for the men who are going through all this.

For younger men who had recently entered employment in the authority, these concerns were not so apparent: they talked instead of the importance of flexible employment practices for them and for females. Some already had experience of jointly contributing to household income and were not afraid of the impact of equal opportunities and women's initiatives on their own employment. As already mentioned, masculinity is multiple and contingent (Brittan 1989), and enters into differences between men as well as accounting for conflicting personal orientations to work and home. Within the group discussion there was an underlying conflict between the younger and older men, a division which appeared to signify two markedly different forms of masculinity.[4] The younger members seemed frustrated with the incapacity of older men (who, incidentally, are their bosses) to understand that the changes are positive and readily to embrace them. It might be the case that this reflects a dynamic much discussed in psychoanalytical approaches to gender relations in which patriarchy as an order of power and control mediates relations between men as well as women. However, for most men, young and older, there was a general question mark over how they might be expected to behave given what they experienced as conflicting expectations of them, both within work and also between family and work.

Most men stated that they "just didn't know how to behave any more", one explaining the new gender-sensitive work practices in terms of "having to watch your P's and Q's, be careful what you say, sort of thing". Another stated that he felt in danger if he simply admired an outfit that a woman was wearing and couldn't understand why that should be. This narrative is often associated with men's self-perceptions as "lovers of women"; women being regarded in a more positive light than their male colleagues often because they can "talk to them" or simply because they have more style, flair and imagination than men – especially, in this case, men in the local authority.

Women, of course, often complained to me of the degree to which they have to listen to the personal problems of men who would then attempt to exploit their good nature and take advantage of their so-called status as friend. But when men managers were asked if this way of behaving might actually be detrimental to women's initiatives and development, they often said that it was, but that they were not sure in which way. All the men interviewed individually were asked if their communication with women was any different to that with men in the organization. I asked them this question as an indirect way of getting to their more firmly rooted assumptions, and to avoid glib PC responses which women from the women's group had complained of. Interestingly, the responses tended to highlight the problems that men encounter in relation to their sexuality and their tendency to be attracted to women in the organization (for discussion, see Hearn et al. 1989). This, rather than female employment capacity or assumptions about their work, was often stressed by men, who said things such as:

> I do find it difficult to ignore my attraction for a woman, especially if she is well dressed and friendly and I know that on one level this shouldn't matter, but then I am only human and maybe we should simply accept this as part and parcel of human nature.
>
> It is difficult to work with people who you are attracted to or who you are not attracted to and they are attracted to you. For me these are the gender issues.

Men often expressed feelings of guilt for not being aware enough. One senior manager was surprised when one of his newly appointed female managers complained to him of his undermining body language and tone of voice when he spoke to her. He talked to me about it, perturbed and defensive but clearly frustrated with the disjunction between his desire to be aware and the constraints of his earlier training and prejudices, saying "I told her, 'look don't blame me for all the ills you women suffer, I know I make mistakes, but I'm only human and I'm trying . . . you'll just have to teach me'".

Another spoke of

> . . . getting dragged over the coals because I saw a woman leaning over the photocopier and her breasts were very attractively placed on the glass and I said "Wow you look a lovely picture" and she reported me. I didn't mean anything by it, I certainly didn't mean to hurt her feelings or anything. I mean, how do you behave? I meant it as a compliment.

This response to the erotic posture of the woman over the photocopier – of desiring women for their sexuality – was linked to, but conflicted with, the desire to find a female partner who was an equal, who had her own career, somebody who was not *dependent* – "I'd prefer a utopian equal partnership but I've yet to find anybody. All the emotional baggage that people carry around."

It is also interesting to highlight the links between this sexualized perception of women and responses to the women's group. Often, the women's group was considered an arena in which women could discuss their various hormonal, menstrual and mothering problems to gain support from each other. As one man manager observed:

> Well it gives women a bit of space to talk about the things they couldn't do in mixed company. I suppose things like health issues, menstrual cycles . . . childcare etc., I don't see why else there should be a women's group, the issues should generally be management issues.

When probed beyond their superficial resistance to the women's group and women's general career progression, it was often these anxieties that were uncovered, anxieties which once expressed seemed to begin to clear the way for a more positive discussion of gender at work. Once the problems of their female colleagues and co-workers were illustrated to them – specifically, problems of sexism and sexual harassment – thoughts about female members of their own families often seemed to help the men to think more constructively about what could be happening to women in the workplace. They often expressed what some might argue to be politically dubious, paternalistic and patriarchal, masculinized forms of caring; men caring for each other as workmates with common concerns. However, once men were allowed to talk about their own concerns in the context of restructuring, they tended then to extend this "caring paternalism" into discussions about what they perceived to be their own potentially damaging attitudes towards female members of staff. This awareness crystallized somewhat when I informed these men of the grievances that women in the organization had expressed to me, specifically in relation to continuing sexism and lack of career advancement. Consequently, the new managers often expressed a wish to "protect" or defend women, in so doing heavily individualizing women's problems. This protection of women is associated in some cases with the protection of "friends" and "workmates". It is also bound up in an indirect fashion with the need to protect wives and daughters, often as men see it, from certain aspects of their own behaviour.

As the research progressed, what became increasingly clear was the confusion that men expressed in relation to responses to women's initiatives (seen here as a central aspect of the centralization of senior management control over their own work) and the feelings of remorse which stemmed from a perception of women's grievances as a symptom of "being hurt". Men often identified with women as workers, which is not surprising, given the increasing perception of their presence in the labour market. However, because of the unease felt by many men middle managers with regard to the potential of women's initiatives to displace them in the new managerialism, rather ironically this perception tended to be fed by drawing upon their experiences of women at home. This may be associated with an attempt to humanize work relations in a way that is not possible in what is otherwise experienced as a fragile and harsh working environment. How could they possibly be responsible for a female member of staff's unhappiness? After all, they would be the first to encourage wives or daughters to go for a career, to "break out of the mould". As one manager stated when describing his daughter to me:

> I mean she's got far more about her than my son. *I'd do anything to encourage her* [my emphasis] she's the one who will come home from school and get down to her work. She's the one who likes sport, not him. And I'm really proud of her and my wife. My wife doesn't have a career or any job out-side the home, but I know that she would make an excellent manager. She tells me straight what needs doing about the house and garden, she doesn't pull any punches. Oh no, I don't feel I have any prejudices about women working.

Conclusion

This chapter has shown that, in the context of restructuring, managers as employees and as men bring into the management process their own specifically gendered experiences, as these have become embedded in traditional organizational cultures, work practices and management discourses. In addition, the utilization of "mascu-linity" as an ideological construct tends to be elliptical in organizational conflict, becoming differentially and often implicitly expressed according to responsibilities within specific divisions. The deployability and fluidity of masculinity in ideological processes is also related to the differences – notably professional and hierarchical differences (Hearn 1992: 153) – which exist between men in organizational restruc-turing. In the context of this research, these differences in orientation can be seen as related to the restructuring of Environmental Health Services and the relationship of divisional managers in a new local authority Directorate. Thus intermanagerial tensions and the masculinities which they manifest are, I would argue, simultaneously political, ideological and material.

Contrary to recent feminist organizational theory, or to the individualized concept of "organizational asset exploitation" (Wright 1985, Savage et al. 1992) as a way of analyzing gender dynamics, overtly masculinized management legitimation can be seen to be associated with a recognition of the enmeshment of women's initiatives with the increasing centralization of senior management control. Male managers in traditionally male-dominated professions or types of work such as engineering might be expected to express a hostile orientation to women's initiatives, simply because of the "male culture" with which they are familiar and which they subsequently feel the need to defend. However, one cannot ignore the impact of their tenuous position in the restructuring exercise – in particular, in this research, these men managers' subordination to EHOs under the amalgamated Directorate. Finally, there are clearly different responses by men to "women's issues" and women's initiatives, differences which become apparent when men managers feel able to openly express their deeply felt concerns and anxieties, rooted, as these now are, in the transformation that is occurring in previous masculine spaces.

Acknowledgements

I thank David Griffiths and Steve Whitehead for helpful comments and advice on earlier drafts.

Notes

1. This recently completed research utilized in-depth, repeated interviews, and focus groups, quantitative methods designed to provide some space for the men managers interviewed openly to express and critically to reflect upon the kinds of negative feelings and assumptions which they might make about women in the organization. As the research reveals, in the main, such views tended to be expressed informally outside the hearing of those senior managers committed to promoting women in the organization.

2. The women's group, supported by the newly appointed director, was formed with a primary objective of encouraging women to apply for and enter management positions within the newly created Directorate. It is important to note that many women in low-grade clerical positions were reluctant to become fully involved in the women's group because of their perception that (a) it was primarily a senior management initiative and attendance appeared to be compulsory and (b) that it was steeped in "middle-class", feminist, politics of women who were out of touch with the experiences and feelings of the average woman employee. Interestingly, as time progressed and as alternative women decided to "own" and be responsible for running it, the women's group became much more proactive in striving for extending basic childcare facilities provided by the council, and raising health and safety issues. Appealing to a more broadly based practical need, the women's group has been successful in achieving their aims.

3. In the context of the client/contractor split, engineers became accountable to what were, in effect, two employers – the authority as client and Wessex Water, the contractor. While engineers were formally employed by Westward City Council, they had to engage in some work for Wessex Water which, driven by the bottom line of healthy profit, forced the men to work to extremely stringent deadlines and financial constraints. As such, any talk within the Directorate about the pursuit of more enlightened management styles appeared utopian to say the least.

4. See Thompson (1994) for a discussion on men, masculinity and ageing.

References

Alvesson, M. and Willmott, H. (eds) (1992) *Critical Management Studies* London: Sage

Baron, A. (1992) "Technology and the crisis of masculinity: the gendering of work and skill in the US printing industry, 1850–1920". See Sturdy et al. (1992), pp. 67–96

Bendix, R. (1963) *Work and Authority in Industry* New York: Harper & Row

Brittan, A. (1989) *Masculinity and Power* Oxford: Blackwell

Burawoy, M. (1985) *The Politics of Production* London: Verso

Child, J. (1969) *British Management Thought* London: Allen & Unwin

Cockburn, C. (1983) *Brothers: Male Dominance and Technological Change* London: Pluto Press

Collinson, D. and Hearn, J. (1994) "Naming men as men: implications for work, organization and management", *Journal of Gender, Work and Organization*, **1**, 1, pp. 2–22

Collinson, D. and Hearn, J. (eds) (1996) *Men as Managers, Managers as Men: Critical Perspectives on Men, Masculinities and Managements* London: Sage

Cousins, C. (1987) *Controlling Social Welfare: a Sociology of State Welfare Work and Organizations* Brighton: Wheatsheaf

Fairclough, N. (1992) *Discourse and Social Change* Cambridge: Polity Press

Ferguson, K. (1984) *The Feminist Case against Bureaucracy* Philadelphia: Temple University Press

Flynn, N. (1993) *Public Sector Management* Hemel Hempstead: Harvester Wheatsheaf

Hearn, J. (1992) *Men in the Public Eye: the Construction and Deconstruction of Private Men and Public Patriarchies* London: Routledge

Hearn, J. (1993) "Emotive subjects: organizational men, organizational masculinities and the construction of emotions", in Fineman, S. (ed.) *Emotion in Organizations* London: Sage

Hearn, J. and Parkin, W. (1987) *"Sex" at "Work": the Power and Paradox of Organization Sexuality* Brighton: Harvester Wheatsheaf

Hearn, J., Sheppard, D., Tancred-Sheriff, P. and Burrell, G. (eds) (1989) *The Sexuality of Organization* London: Sage

Keat, R. and Abercrombie, N. (eds) (1992) *Enterprise Culture* London: Routledge & Kegan Paul

Legge, K. (1995) *Human Resource Management* Basingstoke: Macmillan

Maile, S. (1995a) "Gendered managerial discourse", *Journal of Gender, Work and Organization*, **22**, 2, pp. 76–87

Maile, S. (1995b) "Managerial discourse and the restructuring of a district authority", *Sociological Review*, **43**, 4, pp. 720–42

Merkle, J.A. (1980) *Management and Ideology* London: University of California Press

Nichols, T. (1974) "Labourism and class consciousness: the class ideology of some northern foremen", *Sociological Review*, **22**, 4, pp. 483–502

Roper, M. (1994) *Masculinity and the British Organization Man since 1945* Oxford: Oxford University Press

Savage, M., Barlow, J., Dickens, P. and Fielding, T. (1992) *Property, Bureaucracy and Culture: Middle Class Formation in Contemporary Britain* London: Routledge

Seidler, V.J. (1991) *Recreating Sexual Politics: Men, Feminism and Politics* London: Routledge & Kegan Paul

Seidler, V.J. (1994) *Unreasonable Men: Masculinity and Social Theory* New York: Routledge

Sturdy, A., Knights, D. and Willmott, H. (eds) (1992) *Skill and Consent: Contemporary Studies in the Labour Process* London: Routledge & Kegan Paul

Swan, E. (1994) "Managing emotion", in Tanton, M. (ed.) *Women in Management: Developing a Presence* London: Routledge

Thompson, E.H. Jr (ed.) (1994) *Older Men's Lives* London: Sage

Thompson, P. and McHugh, D. (1995) *Work Organization: a Critical Introduction* (2nd edn) Basingstoke: Macmillan

Tolson, A. (1977) *The Limits of Masculinity: Male Identity and Women's Liberation* London: Tavistock

Willis, P. (1979) "Shop-floor culture, masculinity and the wage form", in Clark, J. (ed.) *Working Class Culture: Studies in Theory and History* London: Hutchinson

Wright, E.O. (1985) *The Debate on Classes* London: Verso

Yancey Martin, P. (1993) Feminist practice in organizations: implications for management", in Fagenson, E.A. (ed.) *Women in Management: Trends, Issues, and Challenges in Managerial Diversity* London: Sage

Yarrow, M. (1992) "Class and gender in the developing consciousness of Appalachian coalminers". See Sturdy et al. (1992), pp. 25–66

CHAPTER TEN

A personal encounter: exploring the masculinity of management through action research

John Clark

Diverse though feminist and profeminist debates on gender and organization are, all ultimately confront the vexed question of men, masculinities and change. In short, can men managers (as the dominant gender grouping) critically reflect on their (gendered) practices, thus weakening or disabling what Ozga and Walker (ch. 7, this volume) describe as the patriarchal power relations of the workplace? Moreover, what tensions, contradictions and ambiguities arise from such a personal/political action? In seeking to illuminate some of the issues and possibilities that emerge from self-examination of masculine subjectivity, this chapter draws on my experiences and reflections as a man manager in higher education. The setting in which the research is located is one of public-sector change, (inter)departmental conflict and new managerialism. The chapter raises questions as to men managers' potential to undertake critical self-examination and reflexivity, and in so doing assist the facilitation of positive and ethical organizational transformation.

The account of events which follows is extracted from a series of research engagements that ultimately contributed to a larger project. In this, action inquiry was utilized both as a guide to my own interventions, notably in respect of gender and conflict, and as a methodological base from which to interrogate and understand organizational dynamics. A central research question was "How can action research help middle managers to manage their own development in times of organizational change in new organizational forms?" The fieldwork for the larger project was undertaken with groups of managers in a further education college and on a Masters of Business Administration (MBA) course. In both cases, participants were using action inquiry to help them as they managed change. One of my reasons for adopting action inquiry was to give me first-hand experience that paralleled the work of these managers in other organizational settings. In all instances a detailed narrative, or "thick description" (Geertz 1993) was written in order to capture a degree of authenticity.

Action inquiry is a qualitative research methodology developed by Torbert (1987, 1991) and Torbert and Fisher (1992), and has its roots in action research, which Easterby-Smith et al. introduce thus:

> It assumes that any social phenomena are continually changing. Action research and the researcher are then seen as part of this change process itself. The following two features are normally part of action research projects:
>
> 1　a belief that the best way of learning about an organisation or belief system is through attempting to change it, and this therefore should to some extent be the objective of the action researcher;
>
> 2　the belief that those people most likely to be affected by, or involved in implementing, these changes should as far as possible become involved in the research process itself. (Easterby-Smith et al. 1991: 33–4)

From this starting point, Torbert argues for an action inquiry in which the researcher develops high levels of reflexivity and self-awareness while in the midst of intervening (see Reason 1988, 1994). A section below examines the research method in more detail. Overall, my intention is to suggest a strategy that might address the issues that Collinson and Hearn (1994: 3) draw attention to: "Men in organisations often seem extraordinarily unaware of, ignorant about and even antagonistic to any critical appraisal of the gendered nature of their actions and their consequences."

In adopting action inquiry as such a strategy a number of ethical and personal dilemmas faced me, and I place an emphasis on these because they seem to go to the heart of what it means to inquire as a man. I propose to throw light on two aspects of men in management: first, how the task of interrogating masculinities in organizations might be pursued and, secondly, what has surfaced in one person's work on this task. The chapter exemplifies the strategies that managers might adopt if they wish to examine their daily practices and the impact of gender upon these. It contributes then to the body of work: ". . . needed that critically examine the conditions, processes and consequences through which the power and status of men and masculinities are reproduced within organizational and managerial practices" (Collinson and Hearn 1994: 18).

An examination of my own efforts to make sense of my experience through these practices is intended to suggest ways in which men, as they manage in changing organizations, can enhance their self-awareness, reflect critically upon their actions, and through these processes initiate different working relationships with each other and with women in organizations. The use of action inquiry to address these issues might then subvert traditional male-dominated organizational cultures (see Marshall 1995: 300–12) and thus generate more equitable alternatives.

Having utilized action inquiry to interpret the organizational dynamics presented by way of research vignettes, the chapter proceeds to draw on Foucault's work on the "technologies of the self" to evaluate this model of research, my efforts to inquire chiming with his remarks that "For me intellectual work is related to what you would call aestheticism, meaning transforming yourself" (1988a: 14). The subject that was attempting such a self-transformation was, for Foucault, struggling within a broader social context. Similarly, organizations are not discrete entities but are subject also to externalities and the dynamics of intersubjectivities. In attempting to behave differently as a man during organizational change, public-sector men/ managers may use action inquiry, and in so doing, they may face dilemmas similar to those examined below. An inevitable question is, then, what might drive men to scrutinize their practice as managers and experiment with new strategies? Alas, very little perhaps. On this occasion, my efforts were a response to the challenges from female colleagues to face up to what they experienced as male power plays. My willingness to engage with this challenge, rather than rejecting it out of hand, came through my own immersion in the practices of action inquiry, which I saw as a means of improving the quality of my management. These practices provided the discipline that channelled my efforts into understanding the significance of gender in my experiences of management and organizational life. In many public-sector organizations, men will be under pressure to examine their approach to manage- ment through broader organizational pressures, such as training and management development schemes, or quality improvement programmes, or as a result of efforts to transform their organizations through restructuring. I suggest action inquiry to be a useful tool in carrying out such individual and institutional transformations.

Central to this notion of individual transformation is, of course, the concept of identity. My understanding of identity is, following Foucault (1988a), one which places emphasis on fluidity. For, as will be outlined below, action inquiry demands reflective practices on the part of the inquirer, thus incorporating the notion of the inquirer's identity as being continually in the process of formation: "Like all identities, masculinity is to be conceived of as multi-layered, fluid, and always in process ... It is contingent and shifting not least in the lifetime of individuals" (Kerfoot and Knights 1996: 84).

The chapter is structured in the following way: an account of the conflict, an introduction to action inquiry as a research tool, a series of vignettes that illustrate research dilemmas that I experienced and a reflection on Foucault's work on the self and its implications for interrogating masculinities.

Change, conflict and a critical event

In the early 1990s, I was working in a university business school as a lecturer in management. In response to the Research Assessment Exercise, the university was reviewing its strategy for developing its research base. Following pressures to improve our research standing, a review within the organization about how best to organize for research was initiated. The broader context within which the university was restructuring was a higher education system in a period of transformation; debated in detail, for example, by Parker and Jary (1995) and Pritchard and Willmott (1997). Similarly, across the whole HE sector, staff movement between universities came to imitate the football transfer market, as universities sought to "reposition" themselves. Academic staff with good track records of research and publication moved between universities, sometimes becoming professors – often, in the process, building larger research empires. In return, the newly acquired staff improved the institution's research ratings, this higher rating being rewarded by additional government funding.

In addition, universities were experiencing pressure to recruit more students. Some institutional identities were in transition in the aftermath of the creation of the "new" universities, with the threat that some might be designated teaching institutions while others would hold to a research mission. Within universities, practices drawn from the world of commercial corporations, such as performance reviews of staff, became more commonplace; "mission statements" were prepared and entered the organizational discourse.

Such change happened to an extent in my workplace, but there was also an effort to create organizational structures that would enhance research output and quality from existing staff. The efforts to reshape to these ends led to the local conflict described below. While minor, I have characterized this as a critical event in several respects: it generated strong emotions amongst staff; it was a moment when decisions about collaborative work between men and women would be made; it was important in terms of the future research work in the department and not least, the future financial well-being of the department.

This chapter examines my personal experience as a male action inquirer rather than the nuts and bolts of the conflict itself. What then follows is an outline of the event. This is brief, so that attention can be maintained on the process of using action inquiry to reflect on the gendered aspects of the conflict. From the outset, I would stress that the dispute under focus would be familiar to many of us in employment, and not out of the ordinary in any public-, or indeed private-, sector organization. Events began to unfold following a period during which rumblings between staff suggested that something was amiss. However, the real efforts made to tackle the ensuing difficulties led to an explosion of emotion rather than the intended consensual resolution. For some participants, the exchanges were a helpful letting off of steam; for others, however, a more bruising experience. For some, events threw light on organizational processes; others were left baffled as to the nature of the conflict. As with many organizational conflicts, no single account could do justice to the varied experiences of the participants and the little I have written here would be challenged as partial by my colleagues.

Two sides were engaged in this event, one side composed mainly of women, and the other mainly of men. This gendered polarization in the department arose from a research centre with a focus on equal opportunities in business, which was mainly staffed by women, and a second group which was working on the topic of management, mainly staffed by men. Along with a colleague, I was managing the development of the research centre focusing upon management. The conflict arose as the management group began to include gender issues in its remit. The equal opportunities group responded by proposing a merger as a sensible means of harnessing staff energies, skills and knowledge. Although there were overlaps in interests and potential for collaboration, the differences were such that a territorial struggle ensued. Discussions between men and women staff culminated in a heated meeting that divided in a transparent manner on gender lines. The outcome did not facilitate co-operation between the two groups in the short term and they continued to work separately on their agendas.

Across the organization, however, boundaries between the two groups were flexible and several of the staff involved had connections with both. The management group had been working informally with shared responsibilities and so my involvement was as a peer rather than a manager. The initial memo from the equal opportunities group proposing a merger had infuriated me. It struck me as a piece of organizational imperialism, and my initial response was to oppose this move. However, after my initial reaction I took stock, sensing the positive intentions behind the proposal but also realizing the potential for a ritualistic and unproductive dispute. At this point, I decided to use an action inquiry approach to reflect on my own involvement and to guide my interventions in the organizational processes. My reasoning was that action inquiry might offer me a way of engaging differently in events. I was hopeful that by taking this stance the exchanges would become more productive for all parties. As well as using action inquiry to make sense of organizational conflict and in terms of wider research, I had an interest in examining my own responses as a man. Although my experience is presented in the form of a series of vignettes and not in the conventional narrative form, I accept that it is open to the criticism of Kerfoot and Knights as being in the tradition of:

> Accounts of organizational encounters (that) become tales of organizational heroism, of targets met, meetings conquered and moments of weakness, failure or despair retold and reconstructed as personal triumphs over adversity, hopelessness or social impotence. Masculine subjects thus constitute the organizational and managerial world as a series of discrete challenges, in order to rise above them. (Kerfoot and Knights 1996: 91)

With this caveat in mind, I will proceed to describe action inquiry and the various ways in which it came to be used during the events in question.

Intervening and sense-making with action inquiry

Action inquiry is a form of action research developed by Torbert (1987, 1991) and Torbert and Fisher (1992), and is linked closely with the action science of Argyris et al. (1985) and Schon (1990, 1991). In this chapter the term "action inquiry" is used for the sake of consistency, but the practice of my research draws on both models. Torbert outlines a process in which "Action inquiry is used to describe this kind of leadership – that simultaneously learns about the developing situation, accomplishes whatever task appears to have priority, and invites a reframing or restructuring of the task if necessary" (Torbert 1987: 160).

The possibility of making sense of organizational events and taking action at the same time offers a model for critical research that can be practised by managers in organizations – in theory, improving the quality of their actions and producing a stance essential for the development of the learning organization. I was not directly managing these events but participating in them as a peer. Nonetheless, the goals of learning, acting and collaborating were ones I sought to adopt. To realize these aims, I attempted to develop a sensitivity to and awareness of what was happening: "'Consciousness' in the midst of action" (Torbert 1991: 221; italics in original).

170

My efforts in this regard included interviews, correspondence and conversations with colleagues about what was happening, reflecting on my experiences with other researchers, and keeping a research journal that recorded events and my experiences of them. The notion of collaboration as integral to team-working, and conflict management was important for me here, for individuals were seeking ways of working together, and the ability to handle and recognize differences would be vitally important. By adopting an action inquiry stance and talking with colleagues about how it might be practised, I hoped that my interventions would be "to good effect".

Argyris et al. point to the Frankfurt School as a source of inspiration in its encouragement of a "critical theory . . . that seeks to unite knowledge and action, theory and practice" and make the case for an action science that ". . . stimulate(s) critical reflection among human agents, so that they might more freely choose whether and how to transform their world" (1985: 71). Casey also acknowledges the influence of the Frankfurt School, but her research engagement is without ". . . a pretension on my part that my research is catalytic or 'action' oriented toward change in the site under study. That is neither my task, nor my business" (Casey 1995: 199).

Her model of critical ethnography contrasts sharply with action inquiry. The latter accepts that each research encounter is also a social episode and then attempts to build a research practice around this principle. Action research has traditionally had a strong appeal to practitioners; for example, managers, teachers and change consultants who want to make sense of their work without relying on the interpretations of academic researchers. This marks a clear boundary between it and the ethnographic fieldwork, on which Casey comments that:

> Each of my interviewees constructed a narrative about their experiences of their work, and about themselves. I, in turn, have interpreted these narratives in a way that I believe makes deeper theoretical sense of their collective world. This is the privileged assertion of the academic researcher. (Casey 1995: 203)

In stepping on to the territory of the practitioner and beyond the academic framework of ethnography and more orthodox scientific methodologies, with their accepted reference points for objectivity, rigour, quality and validity, action inquiry is vulnerable to criticisms of subjectivity and partiality. Reason comments that "One of the major difficulties of action science rests in the defensiveness of human beings, their ability to produce self-fulfilling and self-sealing systems of action and justification, often with patterns of escalating error" (Reason 1994: 330).

Similarly, the cautionary words with which Casey frames her research outcomes are applicable to this work:

> There is no illusion that my selection of data and that which I have constructed and interpreted as knowledge is either objective or definitive. Critical theorists eschew certainties and absolutes, but endeavour to practice systematic reflexivity and to construct rational analyses and interpretations. A claim to validity and reliability is thereby justified. (Casey 1995: 203)

During this conflict I wanted to participate in a knowing, albeit subjective, way that enabled me to be both clearer about my actions and able to make choices about my responses. At several key moments I hesitated, did not react spontaneously but instead forced myself to consider or generate alternative courses of action. By acting in this deliberate manner, I was hoping to get to a point at which choices were available; partly generated by my own self-reflexivity and heightened awareness.

However, as the chapter proceeds to discuss, some of these moments of reflection are also gendered dilemmas. Unhappily, much of the theorizing of action research is gender-blind. Therefore, nested in my efforts to analyze the masculine nature of my responses to the conflict was also an intention to examine action inquiry as a gendered research process. For example, initially I noticed my anger and rush to engage in a "turf war"; responses that I recognized as being a familiar part of my masculine repertoire. Critical self-reflection on my part shifted my actions so that an aggressive response was modified. I stepped on to less familiar territory, made efforts to acknowledge the problems likely to arise from conflict and tried to open up a dialogue. Aware of the gendered nature of my subjectivity and experience, I was attempting to use action inquiry to reconstitute my masculine subjectivity (for discussion, see Middleton 1992), towards a more facilitating and sensitive practice. Yet, at the same time, action inquiry appeared ". . . to be advocating an updated version of a Western and masculine 'rugged individualism'" (Reason 1994: 335). Therefore, I needed to examine with caution the ways in which I might be using this as a vehicle to exercise power in the conflict. This meant that my use of the research approach needed to be scrutinized as closely as my actions, thus problematizing any attempt to "transform my world" (Argyris et al. 1985) heroically.[1]

Nevertheless, in this engagement I did wish to make a difference. Action science's insistence on a high degree of self-reflection meant that I had to address issues in my practice, but it did not prescribe solutions. Rather, I was provided with a means of validating and disconfirming assumptions that I was making about my behaviour as a man/manager. In the exchanges between staff in this inquiry, my interventions in the large meeting and with individuals were efforts to reflect on our work together in order to develop a capacity for double-loop learning. The model of learning that I have been guided by in these practices is summarized thus by Argyris:

> The mainstream epistemology of practice focuses on means–ends rationality. Failure to achieve the intended ends leads to a reexamination of means and a search for a more effective means. The action science epistemology of practice focuses on framing or problem-setting, as well as on means–ends reasoning or problem-solving. Failure to achieve intended consequences may, given this model, lead to a reflection on the original frame and the setting of a different problem. We will refer to the first approach as single loop learning and to the second as double loop learning. (Argyris et al. 1985: 53)

Single-loop learning would happen as I scrutinized my interventions in order to make them more effective. Double-loop learning would arise if I could examine and improve the action inquiry model that I was using as a research tool. In this case, the shift of frame occurred as I came to understand the way in which my masculinity shaped the inquiry process. In terms of how I was collaborating with male and female colleagues, this examination would also surface gaps between my espoused theory of action and the theory-in-use. Again, in Argyris's framework:

> There are two kinds of theories of action. Espoused theories are those that an individual claims to follow. Theories-in-use are those that can be inferred from action. (Argyris et al. 1985: 81–2)

By creating dialogues with my colleagues, with others outside the organization and through the inner dialogues of research journals, I sought to point to the gaps between my theory-in-use and my espoused theory, with a view to narrowing them.

These research strategies had, then, an impact in various ways, and in the following section a series of dilemmas that I encountered are sketched out and reflected upon.

Inquiry and intervention dilemmas

During the conflict I intervened in different ways, conducting inquiries by talking to individuals involved, contributing in the large meeting and reflecting on the inquiry through journal-keeping and PhD supervision sessions. I kept notes on each of these, and what follows in the boxes are some of the dilemmas that surfaced during this period. Apart from illuminating the intersubjective dynamics of organizational conflict and change, each vignette also suggests difficulties for researching as a man. No easy remedies or resolutions are proposed, but each is followed by a reflection.

Where does the inquiry end and real life begin?

Bumping into Susan at the drinks part in the common room was a surprise as we had difficulty in finding time in our diaries to meet for an interview about recent events. The conversation inevitably moved on to these events and we discussed several of the themes that I wanted to talk about. In a vigorous manner, Susan criticized several colleagues for their behaviour in the run-up to the meeting and for the way in which they consistently "carved up" the women. Their behaviour was never challenged. In practice, the department turned a blind eye to it and even rewarded people for their actions sometimes. As the conversation continued, I became increasingly puzzled to know what there would be left to talk about next week, whether the informality of this encounter meant this was off-the-record, and would it somehow be a more authentic account of matters than I would be likely to get in a more formal exchange.

There were the familiar set piece engagements in this inquiry – a staff meeting and series of interviews. At the same time, working in the organization meant that I encountered colleagues and occasions on which exchanges over issues related to the inquiry occurred informally. These were located in the interstices of organizational life – part of the informal side that keeps organizations working. Often, these exchanges were as illuminating of organizational processes as the formal exchanges.

Action inquirers will necessarily have continual access to such material: How should it be handled? Does it have to be bracketed off, held in research logs to guide further interventions? Does its exclusion leave research accounts short of the whole truth, and does its inclusion require a code of ethics that alerts all of my colleagues that anything they say or do may be used in my inquiries? What price am I willing to pay, in terms of my relationships at work, by taking up an action inquiry stance that is all encompassing and potentially all revealing? All research writing is read in particular ways by different members of its audience: work on gender by a man that transgresses the boundaries between the formal and informal may be judged to be a manipulative power play.

Where do my loyalties lie?

At the end of a major meeting about possible collaboration between the two groups, there was a brief review of what had happened . . .

It was strange to be sitting with this group of men after the meeting. The conflict in the last hour and the force of the criticisms made about our activities produced a strong bond amongst us – a sense that we had survived the onslaught. Yet a few days earlier I would have seen myself as likely to be aligned with the work and style of the women researchers. The divisions that arose in the heated meeting were as limited as the subsequent alliances. Yet the events appeared to produce "either/or" choices and demand that I put my feet firmly in one camp or another – having a foot in both was no longer an option at this moment.

"Whose side are you on?" was a question that was put to me explicitly and implicitly many times during this conflict. By working with a group of men from the outset, my position was apparently established. Indeed, the initial exchanges appeared to locate all colleagues in one camp or the other. The polarization in the large staff meeting and the incident described above indicate the ways in which the conflict affected staff – for some participants, it generated "tribal" feelings not previously held, and for others it fostered nascent group loyalties. Commentaries on the nature of my allies or the qualities of the opposing camp were a regular feature of interviews and conversations. This was especially problematic, as my espoused position was one which opposed discrimination on grounds of gender. I saw myself as wishing to oppose the stereotypes of male behaviour – dominance and power plays, careerism, and insensitivity to the emotional life of organizations. Development of an awareness of the ways in which I was being cast in a particular role by others, and the processes by which I took on the characteristics of these identities, became a key theme of the inquiry. Thus, reflecting on events I would initially assume limited choices on my own behaviour – I had to be a member of one group or another. However, further reflection revealed the option of refusing this choice and meant that I could elect to maintain connections with both. In this, as in many organizational conflicts, gender issues were evidently leading myself and other participants to initially assume set positions and alliances with same-sex colleagues. My awareness of this pattern, and in part the reasons behind it, were facilitated by action inquiry.

Which parts of my experience do I bring to this inquiry?

> *I spent several hours that evening completing an account of the events so far and finished with the intention of polishing it off the next morning. I awake dreaming. Several people from the previous evening's writing feature in the dream and I write down as much as I can remember of it. What am I to make of this? Parts of the dream seem to connect to events – the location, the characters, the problems of shifting identity – but other parts seem unconnected and enigmatic to say the least. Returning to my word processor later in the morning I am puzzled over whether and how to place this dream in the research account. What does it indicate about my unconscious concerns over the inquiry and how am I to process the content and associations?*

Action inquiry makes the case for collaboration amongst inquiry participants and for the action inquirer to consider him or herself as wholly engaged in the process. From a holistic point of view, one would consider actions, thoughts and feelings when inquiring. Inquiring with a desire to be rigorous and to ensure validity requires a means of working with unconscious elements, such as dreams. As a man, the preservation of privacy, the maintenance of firm boundaries between the public and personal, and the primacy of acting and thinking over feeling are significant codes of masculine conduct (for elaboration, see Seidler 1994, Hearn 1992). An exploration of these gendered ways of being, as part of the reflective process, may be integral to action inquiry, but do I really have to tell others about this?

How do I keep action and inquiry in balance?

> *At one point towards the end of the interview, Jackie asked me what I was going to do about the management research group. Taken aback by this question, I realized that for the last month, in my preoccupation with talking to colleagues to make sense of matters I had given little thought to what I planned to do. The inquiry had been helping me to understand the organizational processes and was shifting my grasp of matters, but none of this had crystallized into a specific intervention that would make a difference. Does this imply a failure on my part to sustain both action and inquiry, or is it OK to work with a period of inquiry and reflection as preparation for further action? Am I judging myself too harshly and is my changing understanding of events part of the action?*

As an approach to management education, action inquiry proposes a synthesis of managing and researching – of acting and inquiring. Doing this work, I had a "natural" tendency to the dualism that keeps these activities separate. I was not line managing staff in this event and this made it more feasible to initiate inquiries in a less threatening manner. At the same time, I had a management role in respect of the research centre; this made others suspicious of my motives and actions. Yet the self-reflection and growing awareness of the ways in which gender issues were being enacted shifted my view of matters and were in themselves action on my map of the world. In talking to women, I acquired a stronger sense of the way in which they experienced themselves as marginal and vulnerable in the organization. Finally, the challenge implicit in the question put by Jackie made me wonder to what extent I was holding back from some forms of engagement in the conflict, thus making myself less potent.

Am I betraying colleagues by presenting this paper?

> *Preparing a paper on this work for a conference, I looked at the early proposal for the paper and at my field notes, and then realized with increasing dismay that I was deeply reluctant to send off a raw narrative of the conflict. As a piece of knowledge-production it seemed correct to send off a thick description for discussion amongst other management researchers. It matched several of the conference themes – the management of difference, a critical stance, etc. And yet there was no way in which I could comfortably talk about these matters in such detail. It was not just squeamishness about how far my methodology was sound or whether I wished to be subject to criticism. It was that I would feel it an act of treachery.*

A primary purpose of the whole inquiry was to make a difference within my own working life. To do this has meant exploring the darker side of organizational life. Does this become, then, the "washing of dirty linen in public", an act of organizational treachery? To gain a fuller picture of events, I have worked closely with colleagues to produce as high a level of disclosure as possible while observing people in action in a range of circumstances. This was done in the context of a local inquiry, often with an assumed or explicit confidentiality and with no talk at the time of a wider audience. Do I wish to publish and be damned, or return to colleagues to negotiate over what can and cannot be said? As previously stated, the inquiry is a part of a larger research project and my responsibilities towards this have created loyalties to a wider research community. The need to pay my dues to this group was part of my decision to prepare the paper, posing me the paradox of speaking my truth to add to this field of knowledge, but risk betraying organization and colleagues.

All of this happens in an organizational context

> *The meeting started with my female colleague outlining how good working relationships might develop between women and men, and concluded with an appeal for a discussion that would produce co-operation between the two groups. Ten minutes after this, the battle lines were being drawn, as members of each group defined their territory. Co-operation came to imply the sub-suming of one group's work within the other's and the emergence of the newer group was seen as indicative of changing organizational priorities that would undermine the work of the older group. Shocked at the rapidity with which the meeting had taken a particular direction, I pointed to the parallels between the power plays of this meeting and how they reflected those political games played by senior managers in the organization. My comments made, the meeting continued in much the same fashion.*

It becomes apparent that using action inquiry during these events is counter-cultural. I am also recognizing that there are significant, if symbolic, issues at stake. For example, resources for research, the careers of individuals and the balance of power between men and women were themes in play. Many of the participants – both men and women – saw the organization as having a male culture, and the women's research group were important in challenging this. My involvement arose from a desire to work differently from the dominant culture, but I was threatened by what I saw as the women's counter-culture. For me, "Why bother?" and "How on earth to make a difference?" were two recurring questions. Staying calm and regarding events as an "experiment-in-practice" was one way of responding, but it led to a coping posture rather than an energizing one. Noticing my interventions being swept away by the forces produced in men/women conflicts was disheartening, and made more so by the vulnerability of my adopting an eccentric, non-traditional, stance. Not wishing to take up the power practices of the dominant male culture by attacking the women's ways of acquiring power – which I see here as imitating that dominant male culture – leaves me marginalized in an organizational space, with little influence on events.

These vignettes do not of course, provide a full narrative of the inquiry, but throw light on some aspects of my own experience of inquiring. In the following sections, I want to work towards some double-loop learning by examining my experience of using action inquiry in the context of Foucault's "technologies of the self".

The care of the self

The above material suggests some of the themes that arose during this research. In disciplining my self during this research I have drawn on the concept of critical subjectivity (Reason 1988), and on action inquiry practices (Torbert 1991). Both Reason and Torbert's projects embrace a modernist technology of self that aligns closely with Giddens' work (1991) on self, identity and late modernity. This includes a number of elements: the self as a reflexive project, self-reflexivity as a continuous and all-pervasive project, an explicit narrative of the self, an awareness of bodily responses, risk taking as part of the project, the importance of being "true to one-self", one's life course as a series of "passages" and the self as a reference point for validity (pp. 75–80). I now want to stand outside this frame and reflect more broadly on the question "What is the nature of the discipline that I brought to bear on my self during this sense-making?" I want to comment on the practices of "becoming a subject" adopted here and to consider aspects of action inquiry as a process of "caring for oneself". The ways in which the self became constituted as a subject was a focus for the later writing of Foucault (1988a, b, 1990, 1992). He examined:

> . . . technologies of the self, which permit individuals to effect by their own means or with the help of others, a certain number of operations on their bodies and souls, thoughts, conduct and way of being so as to transform themselves and attain a certain perfection of happiness, purity, wisdom, perfection or immortality. (Foucault 1988b: 18)

For Foucault, the work on the care of the self was to complement his earlier work on domination, power and knowledge/truth. It was an effort to break with the framework that portrayed societies as strong disciplinary processes and individuals as docile, thereby holding limited possibilities for social and personal change. His exploration of the care of the self was to reveal the complex, often hidden, connections between broader social forces and the subject. Action inquiry has, as one of its goals, the transformation of organizational life and must similarly address the interconnections between the subject and processes of political domination. One of my goals in this situation was to effect a change in the processes of organizational life, and another was to examine the ways in which I was developing and changing during this process. A feature of Foucault's earlier work, that was and remained important for me, is contained in his idea of "the arts of existence":

> What I mean by this phrase are those intentional and voluntary rules by which men not only set themselves rules of conduct, but also seek to transform themselves, to change themselves in their singular being, and to make their life into an *oeuvre* that carries certain aesthetic values and meets certain stylistic criteria. These "arts of existence", these "techniques of the self", no doubt lost some of their importance and autonomy when they were assimilated into the exercise of priestly power of early Christianity, and later, into educative, medical, and psychological types of practices. (Foucault 1992: 11)

The assertion in the last sentence spoke directly to me. It prompted me to draw on Foucault's work on Graeco-Roman practices. I wanted to examine my own practice of action inquiry as a technology of the self, to see if in Foucauldian terms anything had been lost – to look at the effect of this loss on my practice, and to look at ways of constructing new practice in the light of this. My aim was to stand outside the frame within which I was fashioning my own "technology of self" so that I might be able to reflect on how I was reflecting on this work.

What is it that Foucault considers to have been lost? His central argument is that the shift from the guidance "Take care of yourself" to "Know thyself" was critical (see Townley 1995). The Graeco-Roman technologies of self were based on the former, which held the possibility of a moral system determined by the individual. The Christian tradition held to the latter injunction, because a moral order originating with the individual was inconceivable:

> We find it difficult to base rigorous morality and austere principles on the precept that we should give ourselves more care than anything else in the world. We are more inclined to see taking care of ourselves as an immorality, as a means of escape from all possible rules. We inherit the traditions of Christian morality which makes self-renunciation the condition for salvation. To know oneself was paradoxically the way to self-renunciation. (Foucault 1988b: 22)

The Graeco-Roman practices that were associated with care of the self included retreats into the country, writing letters to friends, keeping notebooks, meditating, remembering rules of conduct, abstinence, practical tests and the interpretation of dreams. These activities could be personal, but also social with groups, students who were tutored in these techniques and the use by some families of advisers:

> People resort to many different formulas. One can set aside a few moments, in the evening or morning, for introspection, for examining what needs to be done, for memorizing certain useful principles, for reflecting on the day that has gone by. (Foucault 1990: 50)

The aim of these practices was a self-examination that took stock of whether or not one had done things correctly. The outcome would be the sound administration of the self. Foucault contrasts these practices of self-formation with those of self-awareness. He argues that the Christian tradition is ousting the Graeco-Roman practices and thus influencing modern strategies for self-examination. In the strategies for self-awareness there emerges "a morality of asceticism, (which) insists that the self is that which one can reject" (Foucault 1988b: 22). This regime is one that is more judgemental of wrong-doing, carries punitive consequences, scrutinizes the self for faults and deep feelings, and assumes bad intentions. The source of moral order is in the external world and the confessional qualities of these practices brings the individual to an acceptance of this authority. This finds its ultimate expression in monastic life: "Here obedience is complete control of behaviour by the master, not a final autonomous state. It is a sacrifice of the self, of the subject's own will. This is the new technology of the self" (Foucault 1988b: 45).

For Foucault, the practice of psychoanalysis is part of this tradition of self-examination and the confessional self (see Hutton 1988, Mahon 1992) and as such contributes to the process of subjectification of the individual in line with society's codes of conduct. It is a process of normalization rather than one of emancipation.

Critical subjectivity and action inquiry as alternative technologies of the self

Critical subjectivity is conceptualized within the psychodynamic framework and, for example, encourages practitioners to achieve high-quality self-awareness to avert the problems of "unaware projection" and "consensus collusion" (Reason 1994: 327). Thus it carries with it the judgemental dimensions of self-awareness and, as the following passage indicates, carries these through to the next level of reflecting upon the practice of critical subjectivity, which:

> ... means that the method is open to all the ways in which human beings fool themselves and each other in their perceptions of the world, through faulty epistemology, cultural bias, character defense, political partisanship, spiritual impoverishment, and so on. (Reason, 1994: 327)

In action inquiry, Torbert proposes that the manager will operate with high levels of self-awareness and proposes a hierarchical model of development (1991: 47). For example, at the stage of "diplomat" the manager is characterized as a person "who observes protocol; avoids inner and outer conflict; works to group standard; speaks in clichés, platitudes . . .". As with critical subjectivity, this model chimes closely with a judgemental process of subjectivization, in which the person discovers errors in their practices.

What, then, characterizes action inquiry as a technology of the self? First, there is great value placed on engagement with the world, which is seen as integral to the process of learning and critical self-reflection. Secondly, the action inquirer is encouraged to reflect on the experience of managing, but the reflection is seen as an accompaniment to action, rather than requiring withdrawal for contemplation. Thus action inquiry leads to an extensive and intensive examination of felt and lived experience. Importantly, it includes those aspects of organizational and personal life that might lie outside other research forms; for example, those "interstitial spaces" described by Hearn and Parkin (1987). These might be "physical spaces, such as corridors, staircases, lifts, kitchens, passageways, entrance ways, 'cubby holes', anywhere that people 'bump into' each other . . . or they may also occur in time . . . tea breaks, lunchtimes, and drinks (one for the road) as well as the more occasional office party, Christmas 'do' . . ." (Hearn and Parkin 1987: 96). In terms of my inner world, it meant that I considered, for example, my dream life as a potential source of research data. The scope and the complexity of these engagements is perhaps a good match for the broad canvas on which the self is constituted and of the multi-faceted nature of any self in the process of constitution.

To comment on the limitations of action inquiry, it is worth noting that the emphasis on action and on thinking may be at the expense of feelings. Thus, the approach may be attractive to men/managers because of an active and reflective emphasis that serves to reinforce a masculine tendency to develop only some aspects of the self, while disengaging from others. It may be attractive as another way of becoming a powerful change agent, simply reinforcing conventional expectations of male dominance and potency, rather than challenging them. McNay, for example, has commented that Foucault is asserting "a conventional notion of sovereign self, which in turn rests on an unexamined fantasy of male agency" (McNay 1994: 149). Similarly, the male manager as hero of organizational life is a key theme of management writing (see Collinson and Hearn 1996). Action inquiry holds this potential too, although the demands of engagement with others and continual returning to an examination of one's actions and motives would subject this to frequent scrutiny. In the final section, I consider the nature of this scrutiny and the extent to which it should be considered an interrogatory, if not obligatory, process.

Interrogations and the care of the self

Action inquiry has helped me to make sense of myself as a man participating in this conflict. I have seen that it can be holistic and serious and yet playful, risky and pleasurable. The process of action inquiry has, however, been at some remove from an "interrogation" of myself as a man. This has been a source of curiosity for me, for as in my own and in others' writing, the notion of interrogation features regularly. To play with the notion of interrogation for a few moments draws attention to other ways of caring for the self. There is a firmness to an interrogation that suggests that the focus of the interrogation is likely to be evasive, choosing to keep some information back and giving it up only under pressure. An interrogation seems appropriate in the context of gender relations and organizations where men hold power; the resonances with police or military questioning, where opposition and resistance will be present, ring true. In such instances, questioning will be difficult and possibly painful. Would interrogations have been appropriate in this case? For Foucault, the early practices of care of the self would not have tolerated this form of interrogation, because of the importance of taking pleasure in oneself. Foucault quotes Seneca's comments on the purpose of finding time to reflect on one's past actions:

> There is a part of our time that is sacred and set apart, put beyond the reach of all human mishaps, and removed from the dominion of fear, by no attack of disease; this can neither be troubled nor snatched away – it is an everlasting and unanxious possession. (Foucault 1990: 66)

In this case "the individual who has finally succeeded in gaining access to himself is, for himself, an object of pleasure" (Foucault 1990: 66). Despite the huge transformations in context and purpose, the care of the self and the constitution of oneself as a man might benefit from being charged with a degree of the pleasure that would surely be driven out by an interrogation.

Towards research strategies that enhance awareness and encourage a critical examination of emerging masculinities?

My response to women making their voice heard, seeking changed, more equitable working relationships, and my engagement in the subsequent conflict, touched some deep personal chords. Action inquiry helped me to recognize some of these; for example, the maintenance of boundaries in my outer and inner world, the concerns around loyalties and (gendered) allegiances. These may be preoccupations that influence other men/managers' behaviour in periods of conflict and change; although it is recognized that, within the public sector, the current pace and scale of change will militate somewhat against the reflective practices outlined here. Pressures to make decisions and act with little time for consultation contribute to men, and women, enacting patterns of masculine behaviour imposed on them by their local organizational cultures and society. Paradoxically, and ironically, the act of will demanded to confront these forces will be familiar to many male managers as they enact dominant cultures – but rarely, I would argue, in the service of such a subversive end. The reflective practice of action inquiry can facilitate an awareness of different choices, thus encouraging changes in attitudes and, hopefully, more successful interventions as men's work as managers is further explored. However, slips into self-justification will be a part of this process too, although the collaborative dimension of action inquiry insists on a continuing dialogue with colleagues to encourage an awareness of such pitfalls. Also, as a "technology of the self", action inquiry has characteristics of the Christian traditions and, with its interrogatory tone, provides a model of self-awareness that is, I suggest, less life enhancing than an approach that embraces self-formation.

Note

1. My reading here of Argyris's phrase "transform their world" is that it refers to the internal world of the action scientist, although his focus was also upon a potent change agent that influences the world of organizations.

References

Argyris, C., Putnam, R. and McLain Smith, D. (1985) *Action Science* San Francisco: Jossey-Bass

Casey, C. (1995) *Work, Self and Society* London: Routledge

Collinson, D.L. and Hearn, J. (eds) (1996) *Men as Managers, Managers as Men: Critical Perspectives on Men, Masculinities and Managements* London: Sage

Collinson, D.L. and Hearn, J. (1994) "Naming men as men: implications for work, organization and management", *Journal of Gender, Work and Organization*, **1**, 1, pp. 2–22

Easterby-Smith, M., Thorpe, R. and Lowe, A. (1991) *Management Research: an Introduction* London: Sage

Foucault, M. (1988a) *Politics, Philosophy, Culture: Interviews and Other Writings 1977–84* Kritzman, L. (ed.) London: Routledge

Foucault, M. (1988b) "Technologies of the self". See Martin et al. (1988), pp. 16–49

Foucault, M. (1990) *The History of Sexuality* (Vol. 3) *The Care of the Self* London: Penguin

Foucault, M. (1992) *The History of Sexuality* (Vol. 2) *The Use of Pleasure* London: Penguin

Geertz, C. (1993) *The Interpretation of Cultures* London: Fontana

Giddens, A. (1991) *Modernity and Self-identity* Cambridge: Polity Press

Hearn, J. (1992) *Men in the Public Eye: the Construction and Deconstruction of Private Men and Public Patriarchies* London: Routledge

Hearn, J. and Parkin, W. (1987) *"Sex" at "Work"* Brighton: Wheatsheaf

Hutton, P.H. (1988) "Foucault, Freud and the technologies of the self". See Martin et al. (1988), pp. 121–45

Kerfoot, D. and Knights, D. (1996) "'The best is yet to come?': the quest for embodiment in managerial work", in Collinson, D.L. and Hearn, J. (eds) *Men as Managers, Managers as Men* London: Sage

McNay, L. (1994) *Foucault* Cambridge: Blackwell

Mahon, M. (1992) *Foucault's Nietzschean Genealogy* Albany, NY: State University of New York Press

Marshall, J. (1995) *Women Managers Moving On* London: Routledge

Martin, L.H., Gutman, H. and Hutton, P.H. (eds) (1988) *Technologies of the Self* London: Tavistock

Middleton, P. (1992) *The Inward Gaze: Masculinity and Subjectivity in Modern Culture* London: Routledge

Parker, M. and Jary, D. (1995) "The McUniversity: organization, management and academic subjectivity", *Organization*, **2**, 2, pp. 319–38

Pritchard, C. and Willmott, H. (1997) "Just how managed is the McUniversity?", *Organization Studies*, **18**, 2, pp. 287–316

Reason, P. (ed.) (1988) *Human Inquiry in Action* London: Sage

Reason, P. (1994) "Three approaches to participative inquiry", in Denzin, N.K. and Guba, Y.S. (eds) *Handbook of Qualitative Research* London: Sage

Schon, D. (1990) *Educating the Reflective Practitioner* San Francisco: Jossey-Bass

Schon, D. (1991) *The Reflective Practitioner* Aldershot: Avebury

Seidler, V.J. (1994) *Rediscovering the Self* London: Routledge

Torbert, W. (1987) *Managing the Corporate Dream* Illinois: Dow Jones–Irwin

Torbert, W. (1991) *The Power of Balance* London: Sage

Torbert, W. and Fisher, D. (1992) "Autobiographical awareness as a catalyst for managerial and organisational learning", *MEAD*, **23**, 3 (special issue), pp. 184–98

Townley, B. (1995) "'Know thyself': self-awareness, self-formation and managing", *Organization*, **2**, 2, pp. 271–90

CHAPTER ELEVEN

The organization of intimacy: managerialism, masculinity and the masculine subject

Deborah Kerfoot

Introduction

The purpose of this chapter is to explore the linkages between masculinity, the activities of management and intimacy. Intimacy is here discussed as emotional connection with another: expressed otherwise as the "play" form of human inter-action. My concern is with the "feel" or embodied experience of oneself in relation to another. This is distinguished from, for example, such intimacies as might be experienced – no less real for those involved – as physical or as sexualized forms of intimacy. In drawing this distinction between intimacies, my concern is not to chart a typology of intimacy, or to delineate a hierarchical order of "rank" within which one might classify such experiences. Nor is the question one that overlooks the oppressive aspects of those forms of sexualized intimacy, organizational or other-wise, now discussed under the umbrella debates surrounding sexual harassment (for a summary and discussion, see Brewis and Grey 1994). The issue is rather one of illuminating, and thence problematizing, what I regard as a form of intimacy that much contemporary management practice would seek to bring about. Instrumental in its desire to capture the subtleties and nuances of social relations for organiza-tional ends, this intimacy is constitutive of a mode of expressing human interaction in given settings. Simultaneously, it provides the means by which other alternative possibilities of intimacy are discounted, displaced or marginalized. My concern here is to shed light on certain of these aspects of intimacy; the alternative possibilities for intimacy which are largely absent in business and management practice.

The site for the discussion is contemporary organizational life, and more particu-larly the practices of management now in ascendancy in many settings, both public and private sector alike. Drawing on Bologh (1990), I discuss intimacy not as a fixed, essential property of individuals, their interactions or of organizations, but as a range of possibilities produced in and facilitated by social encounters. Likewise, following Connell (1993), masculinity is held to be "an aspect of institutions and is produced

184

in institutional life" (1993: 602). Connell's contention on masculinity forces us to recognize the organizational location of masculinity, as a part of what has elsewhere been referred to as the "public sphere" and its constitution in everyday settings. Alluding to debates on the separation of the public and private sphere, writers elsewhere have sought to discuss masculinity in ways that force a critical engagement with the categories of public and private (e.g. Hearn 1992) and question the seemingly unproblematic existence of a dualism that at once both creates a separation of spheres, and reinscribes precisely the self-same behaviours and practices that it purports to explore (for discussion, see Kerfoot and Knights 1994). In this regard, the intention here in this chapter is further to underline the problematic nature of this dualism in aligning with those writers who would "transcend the opposition between these spheres by reformulating the relationship between them" (Benjamin 1986: 78). My own attraction to the critical analysis of masculinity in part resonates with a number of writers, male and female, whose experience of "being managed" by others in the widest sense; of observing management; and of researching, teaching and engaging with managers over a period of many years, is one that has aroused a personal and academic curiosity as to masculinity and the nature of managerial work and organization. Of particular interest is the frenetic and seemingly highly labour-intensive character of much activity with which the behaviours and practices of masculinity are "acted out", so to speak.

In the desire for order, security of identity and stability, those for whom masculinity resonates most loudly appear to be so preoccupied with "fixing" the world around them and others in it as to detract from the possibilities of other forms of engagement. As a result, in its concern to achieve a fixity in social relations and quash the "uncontrollable" elements of everyday existence, masculinity expends considerable energy in the drive for success, and overlooks the possibilities for other forms of interaction. Yet even this success in conquering the insecurity that is itself both a condition and consequence of "the social" and of masculinity, can only ever be so momentary and superficial, such that its achievement requires constant validation. The puzzle then, is one of uncovering – and thence unravelling – an account of the attractions (often but not exclusively to many men in particular, at different times, places and spaces in their lives) of masculine forms of engagement, and why its "achievement" should be so valued and so highly prized.

More than this, however, the chapter holds masculinity to be an aspect of identity, always fluid and always in process, in that masculinity is an element of human subjectivity and identity. For the discussion that surrounds masculinity is no mere casual excursion around the question of "why bother?" This is to recognize the political dimension to debates on masculinity and acknowledge the relations of hierarchy and social and economic inequality that can be both an outcome of masculine practices in given contexts and the conditions of possibility for the maintenance of gender inequality in particular. In this regard, and by way of recognizing the problematic and contested nature of even the very term "masculinity", I develop work begun elsewhere on the concept of the *masculine subject* (Kerfoot and Whitehead 1998). Such discussion is largely underpinned by the work of Foucault (1977, 1988) and other writers, whose theoretical insights on subjectivity and identity have furthered the discussion of the dynamic relationships between discourse and subject, and the interconnections between power and resistance.

Masculinity and the masculine subject

Although not specifically directed to a discussion of the gendered aspects of human interaction or of gender subjectivity, Foucault's understanding of subjectivity and identity, as the ongoing process within which subjects strive to gain security of identity, presents the possibility of advancing the theoretical discussion of masculinity and of intimacy. From such a perspective, men and women as organizational (and other) subjects are active in and embedded within relations of power and resistance: such relations themselves are at once both a condition and a consequence of the multiplicity of discourses and subject positions made available by discourse.

Plainly, the organizational locale is but one site for construction and reconstruction of masculinity amongst many; the home and domestic relationships, for example. Rather than see masculinity as a "fixed" outcome of biological or other configurations, this is to understand masculinity as actively produced in given settings and in specific moments. The purpose of the chapter, then, is to illuminate one such setting – one such configuration of moments – in the constitution of masculinity and its productive possibilities in terms of intimacy. Moreover, the term "masculine subject" enables us to avoid the dualism of masculinity and femininity into which much of the discussion of gender differences has been collapsed (for development, see Kerfoot and Knights 1994). The concept of the masculine subject recognizes that both men and women can be masculine, although masculinity, in whatever manifestation, can be conventionally conceived as elevated and privileged as a range of behaviours for many men. Masculinity exists merely as a way of being, most often but not exclusively for men, in which men express what it is "to be a man" at any one time and in whatever location.

In their (frequently unfulfilled) desire for emotional intimacy with the opposite sex, many women sustain an alternative formulation of the possibilities for intimacy as other than concerned with purposive ends (also Gilligan 1982). Concerned first and foremost to merely "be" in the moment, these encounters are grounded in a conception of human interaction as serendipitous and immediate in the largest sense, without obvious purpose other than the experience of the shared connection so generated. Part of the frustration experienced by these women stems from the contrast between this desire of experience and connectedness for its own sake, and that preoccupied with specific ends, such as is offered most frequently by the men in and around their lives. This can result in tensions and anxieties, for women and men, borne of often competing and seemingly unbreachable perspectives on intimacy and its possibilities; an outcome of which is that non-instrumental formulations of intimacy collapse in the face of an unwilling or unknowing partner, and emotional intimacy recedes ever further.

In whichever manifestation, masculinity or, more particularly, what is here referred to as the masculine subject, can be seen to be concerned – first and foremost – to control the possibilities within which human interaction might take shape. Even in everyday conversation, for example, it is often "revealed" by many women of their male partners that such men are unforthcoming in terms of being comfortable with the connections between people and events in daily life, and similarly disquieted by the possibilities for emotional intimacy that these encounters might offer. Unconcerned with the narratives of social intercourse for other than purely purposive ends, such men are stereotypically characterized by their womenfolk as "wooden", or so distanced from their partners and those around them that no spontaneous interaction can take place (see also Duncombe and Marsden 1995). Spontaneity is significant in that, not least for many women, what "counts" in relations is described as the ability to connect with others in terms of "the feel" or immediate shared emotional experience of any situation. At one and the same time as these women are disconnected from their male partners, they connect with one another if only in their discomfort and dissatisfaction with the men around them. They forge linkages borne of shared experience in a form of tie that binds one to another, if only for the momentary common experience of frustration or dissatisfaction as to their lot.

For masculine subjects, the experience of spontaneity is as threatening as it is precarious and destabilizing. For spontaneity, by definition, comes without a pre-ordered "script" which might otherwise govern and direct the encounter: while the notion of an unscripted encounter is self-evidently threatening to those subjects whose very *raison d'être* is the control of uncertainty and of the uncertainty generated by their own inability to respond in situations. In managing the uncertainty and unpredictability that is inherent in encounters with others, many men stereotypically find recourse to conventionally masculine behaviours as a means of evading or avoiding social interaction that is evidently uncomfortable. It is uncomfortable in that, because of the emotional intimacy so desired by many women, such intimacy, by its very nature, requires that the men respond authentically. For in order for the moment to be experienced as genuine, and thereby unscripted, emotional intimacy requires merely responding to the other, rather than drawing on a knowledge of *how to* respond. To script the encounter in order to provide the means by which it might be managed is at one and the same time to "lose the moment" and for emotional intimacy to evaporate. Masculinity thus gives the appearance of providing masculine subjects with the knowledge of how to respond, and of how to manage – rather than experience – intimate situations. In consequence, emotional intimacy remains ever on the horizon for masculine subjects, who are ever guarding against its possibility.

In seeking to control the uncertainty that might be generated by emotional intimacy, many men – consciously or otherwise – reach for conventional practices and behaviours of stereotypical masculine behaviours: masculinity thereby becomes a means of rendering social relations manageable, thus avoiding the emotional intimacy that is so threatening. Emotional intimacy is threatening in that it necessitates "letting go" of the script that fashions the responses of masculine subjects, and requires that they reveal aspects of themselves as vulnerable; vulnerable since the reactions of others can never be totally predicted or controlled. Ever concerned with their own and others' judgements of themselves as to their competence at being "on top of" situations, masculine subjects must at all times labour at being masculine and to conceal or downplay personal fears and weaknesses that stimulate a questioning of this competence (Kerfoot and Knights 1996). Moreover, since emotional intimacy occurs "in the moment", its experiences as transient as they are unique, such intimacies are further uncomfortable for masculine subjects (also Seidler 1989, 1992). Since they can never be fully replicated, emotional intimacies necessitate responses that are neither amenable to instrumental control nor capable of being "learned" in advance. Emotional intimacy is thus doubly precarious for masculine subjects, leaving them bereft of the means to initiate non-instrumental forms of engagement, and unable fully to experience or comprehend the intimacy offered by others. Regarded with suspicion, doubt or outright hostility, emotional intimacy acquires the status of a "no-man's land" for masculine subjects who are unwilling or unable to let go of the barriers that protect them from the threat of their own vulnerability and its consequences.

Similarly, in the organizational arena, many women, and those men who are less than successful at replicating its behaviours and central tenets, are marginalized by masculine-dominated management practices. For such management practices are concerned, at all times, to control the unpredictability of social interaction and render it "safe" within the confines of a pre-designated script such as is offered by "modern" management practice. Partly as a result, many women and some men find a discontinuity between the ideals of a shared and mutually supportive working environment coupled with meaningful work, and the harsh reality of organizations and managements that are increasingly dominated by bottom-line accounting principles. In the shifting cultures of many work organizations, public and private sector alike, they find they are no longer able to risk revealing aspects of themselves as otherwise frail human beings for fear of being interpreted as uncommitted, unproductive, inactive or "weak". For such subjects, the experience of managerial and other work is one of dislocation, and a continual sense of being at odds with their environment and the working practices that surround them.

Whether male or female, many managers now find themselves faced with organizational cultures that are dominated by regimes of management practice that are, likewise, increasingly instrumental in their search for success. This form of management and of masculinity is intensely goal-driven, often in the pursuit of abstract targets and objectives, and is purposive-rational in its orientation towards others (for elaboration, see Kerfoot and Knights 1993). All social intercourse and interaction is subjected to a yardstick of its degree of utility to the larger goals of the organization and to the designs of senior management. Thus, contemporary management practice appears to have a "natural home" and an immediate resonance for masculinity, and for those masculine subjects who are drawn into its discourses and behavioural displays. Moreover, in so doing, masculine subjects at once both reconfirm themselves as masculine in such activities at one and the same time as reconstituting the very discourse with which they engage.

In this regard, masculinity exists merely as a way of being, yet one that is privileged in organizational (as other) sites. A masculine mode of engaging with the organizational world is one in which all encounters and events become potential arenas for instrumental control. Characterized by the pursuit of control of all social relations, this masculinity is elevated in the discourses and practices of management as *the* way of relating to the world and to other persons. Moreover, the dominance of this mode of being in the activities of managing and organizing is such that all persons, regardless of their sex, must "become" masculine, if only in order to succeed as a manager or to achieve any seniority or credibility (for elaboration, see Kerfoot and Knights 1998). In "becoming" masculine in this way, managers must adopt those behaviours and practices required of them in order to be masculine, or at very least give the appearance of so doing.

This masculine mode of engaging with the world and with the activities of management is further attractive in that it suggests a way of "handling" the precarious and uncertain nature of many areas of management work as well as "managing" – in a very immediate corporeal sense – some of the more distasteful activities involved in contemporary management, often disguised under the euphemisms of "managing change", "downsizing", "restructuring" and "outplacing". An additional point here relates to the anxiety and insecurity of managerial work and of identity. For the discourses of masculinity and of management suggest a solution to the experience of insecurity and anxiety, and of the precarious nature of identity. Masculinity and management are thereby further seductive in their possibility for reconciling the tensions of being a man and a manager. Accepting that masculinity is always precarious, contingent and multiple, the argument here is that masculine subjects are active participants in the conditions of the reproduction of masculinity. They breathe life into the discourses and practices of masculinity and of management such that, for many managers, "being a manager" and "being masculine" are near synonymous. The following section explores further the argument on management and intimacy.

Managerial discourses and intimacy

The effects of "marketization" on management practice and the shift of emphasis towards greater and more productive interaction between consumers and organizational members in both the public and private sectors is now clearly documented (for a summary, see Davies and Kirkpatrick 1995; see also Fuller and Smith 1991, du Gay 1996). Buttressed by the discourse of "the market", the past 10–15 years has seen managerial practices in many public-sector sites turning to the potential of management and staff to "add value" in social encounters (Keat et al. 1994), most notably with clients, customers or end-users, but also with fellow organizational employees of all persuasions. In referring to the emergence of the narratives of entrepeneurialism and the "enterprise culture", a number of commentators have noted the ways in which the language and practices of the market have formed a managerial paradigm governing all internal as well as external social relationships. du Gay and Salaman (1992: 624) refer to it thus:

> In this sense enterprise refers to a series of techniques for restructuring the internal world of the organization along market lines in order to anticipate and satisfy the needs of the enterprising sovereign consumer, and thus ensure business success.

As an aspect of the attempt to garner commitment to what has been referred to as the "cult[ure] of the consumer" (du Gay and Salaman 1992), many organizations are increasingly concerned to focus attention on the delivery of service quality to their client base, and with the larger programmes of management that might facilitate improved commitment, both to organization goals in general and to the specificities of the required behaviours thought to bring them about (for discussion, see Wilkinson and Willmott 1995). In the case of managerial discourses such as human resource management (HRM) for example, the expectation on the part of those practitioners, gurus and advocates who might further its advance, HRM is often presented as a means of similarly "releasing untapped reserves of labour-resourcefulness by facilitating employee responsibility commitment and involvement" (Keenoy 1990: 4). More than this, HRM, in whatever its incarnation (for a discussion and a critique, see Keenoy 1997) centres on capturing the creative and productive potential of social encounters for the ends of the organization. Even in those arenas that are previously unaccustomed to its languages and techniques, the public sector in particular, the drive to "hammer home" the messages of customer orientation and focus on the client as consumer of goods and services has left few aspects of organizational life untouched (Ogbonna 1992, Willmott 1993). For those subordinates subjected to its dictates, HRM requires that social encounters be henceforth transformed – albeit not unproblematically – in such a fashion as to better facilitate the link between the organization and its client base.

Similarly, with a focus on "customer service" and "quality", the phenomenon of total quality management (TQM) in service and other industries seeks to rein in the productive potential of sales and service encounters in such a manner as to suggest that "the customer is king" (Tuckmann 1994). The links between TQM and HRM as both forms of managerial rhetoric and organizational practice have been fully explored by many critical and other writers (for a reprise, see Wilkinson and Willmott 1995). In brief, such linkages commonly centre on ceding a degree of responsibility and accountability to workforces that are hitherto unaccustomed to these practices. More than this, and in the search for such responsibility and "quality" of service, staffs are required routinely to nuance their behaviours according to the supposed dictates of the client. In aiming to align embodied behavioural displays with the requirements of each customer, organizational members must tailor their presentation of self so as to create at least the appearance of a momentary intimacy between themselves and the client (Fuller and Smith 1991). For a period, however brief, the employee is called upon to metamorphose him- or herself into whatever is required, in a succession of transient encounters across what is often a wide-ranging client base. In order for the service to be perceived as "real" by the client, staffs must draw upon a range of social skills and embodied behaviours, often tacitly held (for discussion, see Sturdy 1998). For in giving at least the appearance of effortlessly shifting between modes of display, an objective is to harness the larger knowledge base of the employee as a human being in the call to make embodied social skill a productive element of such organizationally "efficient" – and thus profitable – social encounters (Ogbonna and Wilkinson 1990).

Plainly, whether clients experience this element of the transaction as genuine depends on an unacknowledged and unspoken "feel" on the part of employees for the situation at hand. The difference between success and failure in the transaction can rest precisely on employees' ability to create at least the illusion of intimacy from which – in, for example, the case of sales or service encounters – trust might be generated. At one level, however much staff are exposed to the idea(l)s of immersing and rearticulating those very intimate (*sic*) aspects of self within the everyday practices of the organization, they are clearly capable of resisting and reinterpreting managerial designs to re-engineer their interactions with others (Sturdy 1998). Indeed, the core of the debate for commentators concerned with organizational resistance has turned precisely on such matters as the ambivalence and scepticism of employees in resisting managerial designs at cultural control (for a reprise, see Thompson and Ackroyd 1995). Yet, as du Gay and Salaman (1992: 630) express it:

> . . . even if people do not take enterprise seriously, even if they keep a certain cynical distance from its claims, they are still reproducing it through their involvement in everyday practices through which enterprise is reinscribed.

Enterprise arguably revolves not merely on the culture of the consumer but the means by which employees, in the private and public sectors alike, are to deliver the goods that would facilitate its achievement. As I have discussed above, such mechanisms involve the "capture" for purposive ends of the social skills and potentiality for intimacy that such skills entail.

Regardless of the degree of success or otherwise of this project to "govern the soul" (with due respect to Rose 1989) of organizational members and in the debates that surround it, the "synthetic sociability" at the heart of new managerial discourses is at once both panacea and problem for managements. It is panacea in that discourses such as quality management and HRM appear, on the surface at least, to proffer solutions to the uncertainty generated by contemporary managerial work and, in particular, the organizational ills of flagging profit margins, increased competition and the high fixed costs of labour in both private- and public-sector organizations. The notion that staffs themselves might hold "the key" to greater efficiency and profitability is clearly a seductive proposition to senior managements that are long accustomed to regarding their workforce as little more than a "necessary evil", in spite of the invocations of their own personnel departments. It is a problem in that, at one and the same time as organizational subordinates are required to "discover" the potential for the organization of their embodied social skills, managements must, likewise, become acquainted with and accustomed to displaying the very same embodied human behaviours that they require of their employees. The burgeoning demand for social skills and "emotional awareness" training packages for managers and for the larger feminization of management (for discussion and evaluation, see Calás and Smircich 1993) can be seen as exemplifying this trend for modern managers to "get in touch with" the skills and abilities long buried by the day-to-day practice of hierarchical management and the unquestioning autonomy exemplified in maxims such as management's "right to manage".

191

That managers might explore their own contribution to the process of humanizing organizational life creates the conditions for the furtherance of their own uncertainty (for development, see Kerfoot and Knights 1996): uncertainty since, while calling for the emotional awareness of staff in the execution of their duties, management are, at one and the same time, forced to recognize their own role in revealing aspects of themselves as otherwise frail human beings. Calls to humanize managerial work arguably rest on the desire to create at least the appearance of intimacy in the relationships between managerial and other staff, if only in so far as such intimacy might itself be amenable to instrumental control (Kerfoot and Knights 1993, 1996). In another context, Peters and Waterman (1982) speculate upon the conditions within which such narratives of organizational intimacy might take hold. In their oft-quoted text on so-called "excellent" companies in America, they refer to the phenomenon – albeit uncritically and merely as an aside – in one large corporation, discussing the conditions for its resonance with staffs as follows:

> Companies like 3M have become a sort of community centre for employees, as opposed to a place of work. We have employee clubs, intramural sports, travel clubs and a choral group. This has happened because the community in which people live has become so mobile, it is no longer an outlet for the individual. The schools are no longer the social centre for the family. The churches have lost their drawing power as social family centers. With the breakdown of these traditional structures, certain companies have filled the void. They have become sort of mother institutions. (Peters and Waterman 1982: 261)

Although the authors overemphasize the degree to which corporations can substitute for other structures and exaggerate the extent to which social ties have been eroded – as opposed to reconfigured – elsewhere in society, Peters and Waterman nonetheless allude to the conditions of possibility for organizations to be reinscribed as arenas for intimate relations. This point is no mere broad-brush argument such that one steady state is unproblematically supplanted by another; organizations have, like as not, always been arenas for the constitution of intimacy of all persuasions (Burrell 1984). Rather, the point at issue in this chapter surrounds the degree to which intimacy, or more particularly its constitution as a means of instrumentality in organizational relationships, has achieved such significance in contemporary managerial practices.

Flowing from this discussion of the ontology of intimacy in organization and its connections with masculinity and the masculine subject, the larger question concerns the alternative possibilities for intimacy that are displaced within masculine-dominated management practices. Accepting that this displacement is never total, absolute nor achieved, since other intimacies of a non-instrumental nature continually "seep out" in the interstices of organizational life despite managerial efforts to contain them, the question can be expressed as follows. What other possibilities are there for intimacy and for an intimacy that is non-instrumental in its orientation? Having outlined the argument that surrounds the masculine subject, its link with purposive-rational masculinity and of the form of intimacy that is its expression, the following section explores Bologh's conception of erotic love in developing the discussion of emotional intimacy as one alternative possibility.

On intimacy

Bologh (1990) charts the emergence of a narrative of intimacy in the work of Weber and in his elaboration of the notion of "sociability". In producing a scholarly critique of his work, her purpose is to develop a discussion of the concept that she refers to as "erotic love" as a form of sociability. Bologh holds this (feminist) alternative to be in parallel with Weber's patriarchal understanding. Briefly, it is argued that Weber's discussion of sociability is grounded in a conception of social relations as fundamentally coercive in their character. Here, sociability is defined as:

> . . . a relationship in which the presence of one makes a pleasurable differ-
> ence to, *affects*, the other. [. . .] Sociable relationships may be more or less
> pleasurable, more or less affecting, more or less stimulating. As such all
> sociable relationships are erotic relationships. I mean this not necessarily in
> the narrow sense relating to sexual intercourse but in the broad sense of
> social intercourse that includes all kinds of mutual pleasuring, mutual stimu-
> lation and mutual empowering. (Bologh 1990: 213; emphasis in original)

Recognizing that all cultures, societies and groupings need some means of balancing the coercive nature of individual self-expression with the need for human contact and social involvement, sociability is said to provide the mechanism by which a reconciliation of this fundamental paradox might be achieved. Since individual self-expression requires, to varying degrees, imposing oneself upon the other as recipient of this expression, a willingness on the part of the other person is required in order to facilitate the encounter. The encounter becomes successful only in so far as each respects the rules of social interaction, such that both parties comprehend the manner by which the interaction can take shape, so to speak. At the same time as imposing him/herself upon another, sociability requires that he/she *takes care* for the reaction and feelings of the recipient; hence the aspect of mutuality bound up with sociability. Introducing notions of "caring" for the other and their feelings separates *caring about* someone in the larger sense of a disembodied or detached manner (similar to the way in which many readers of the quality Press in developed Western nations could be said "to care about" the disenfranchised poor they read of in so-called Third World countries) from *caring for* them. This takes the discussion beyond the level of its most simple human concern for the general good of another. For in "caring for" the other in social encounters, Bologh's conception of sociability requires that the parties concerned should care for the other as *an embodied human subject*.

Thus, care and caring for a person force us to consider a practical dimension to sociable behaviour and to erotic love as sociability more directly. This practical dimension is no mere matter of "good form" (Simmel 1950), or simply deploying a kind of etiquette or tact in order to facilitate the encounter by means of certain rules. It calls upon persons to recognize, value and acknowledge the subjectivity of the other, however problematic this may be, even within the terms of the encounter itself. It requires that participants "take the trouble" to care, with all that this entails, rather than feigning the appearance of care, however well-intentioned such feignings. For in feigning care and the appearance of care, often expressed commonsensically as "going through the motions", the instrumental orientation of the relationship becomes immediately evident, even within the boundaries and behaviours described by good form.

Furthermore, it is argued that Weber sets up a polarized view of the possibilities for human interaction by virtue of the very means by which sociability is conceived in Weberian theorizing. Thus a dualism is created wherein:

> ... all self-expression which involves imposition is one side of sociable action; concern for and receptiveness to the other's response is the other side. Weber sees this two-sided nature of sociable action in dualistic terms: one either expresses, struggles or opposes or one submits, complies, appeases. [. . .] [Weber] seems to recognise only interests and conflicts of interest. (Bologh 1990: 216)

In the context of management and organizational practices, one can easily discern the modern trend to "befriend" the client, patient, student or customer as instances of simulating care in numerous management programmes. From corporate practices such as the ubiquitous name badges, worn by staffs across innumerable public and private organizations for example, through "personalized service" in hospitals, transport, taxation, education, policing, finance and services, staffs are required routinely to reproduce the manner and demeanour that is suggestive of caring for the client to hand. Similarly, when senior managements "take the trouble" to display their commitment to staffs, it is often a parody – couched in and accompanied by a kind of "we" language that renders the exercise so self-evidently synthetic to lower-hierarchy staffs and at odds with their daily experience of life in often fraught and insecure working environments. This intimacy, born of instrumentality, and enforced by management, finds clear resonances for masculinity and for masculine subjects. But for management and masculine subjects, "taking the trouble" is both "troublesome" in that it requires investments of time, energy and resources for an unknown – that is, unquantifiable – return, and "troubling" in terms of their very subjectivity and identity.

As such, the distinction between instrumental intimacy and emotional intimacy lies at the heart of Bologh's conception of erotic love as sociability. For erotic love as sociability rests on each party recognizing the subjectivity of the other as embodied being; subjectivity not as a fixed property of persons, but varying and variable within the context of time, place and discursive constitution. Erotic love as sociability requires then, that each is "attuned" to and, in tune with, the embodied subjectivity of the other – always shifting and in motion – doubly reinforcing its link with the practical aspects of care and underscoring the effort that is required to engage in emotionally intimate encounters. Furthermore, this is to introduce the concept of play and play-fulness in subject positions, to overturn conventional relations grounded in hierarchy and inequality, such as that between layers of management and between manage-ments and staffs or between spouses in (unequal) patriarchal relationships, and to challenge the instrumental intimacy that is their condition and consequence.

In contrast to Weber, whom she regards as sustaining instrumentality in his account of social life, Bologh offers the possibility of a form of relationship defined not by fixed or pre-ordered relations of who is "in charge", whether patriarchially defined or otherwise. The conditions for emotional intimacy rest primarily on each party being neither subject nor object in the relationship. Emotional intimacy describes:

> . . . a relationship of subject–object to subject–object, sometimes stressing the subjectivity of self or other and at other times the objectivity of self or other. [. . .] each relates to the uniqueness of the other as spirited body, embodied spirit. The particularity of the other does *matter*, does make a difference. (ibid.: 226; emphasis in original)

Emotional intimacy exists only in so far as each party respects and recognizes the other to the point of moving between these subject/object positions according to the demands of the relationship, however fleeting, in any one moment or location. This is to conceive of social relationships and of emotional intimacy as fluid and always in process. Where one party, either by "accident" or design of managerial or patri-archal relation, requires command of the relationship or calls upon the formalities of a fixed hierarchy in order to script the encounter, then the possibilities for emotional intimacy dissolve.

Clearly paralleling developments in the arena of workplace practices, where the emphasis on social encounters and their productive potential is plainly to the fore, relationships of erotic sociability are likewise said to: "stimulate creativity; or, as Weber himself relates, [. . .] erotic interest is 'valuable as a creative power'" (ibid.: 213).

In the call for intimacy amongst organizational members, and between employ-ees and consumers in the front line of business, management is at one and the same time faced with the paradox that is an outcome of its own practices. In requiring subordinates to "be intimate" with others in an authentic way, management at once seeks to generate the conditions within which employees might "tap" the creative and productive power thought to improve service levels and commitment. At the same time as requiring this authenticity in subordinates, however, management is concerned to shield itself from the revelations of discovery, such as might be uncovered were they themselves to be "authentic", in whatever form. For, in so doing, managerial practices provide masculine subjects with an opportunity to "hide behind" hierarchy and formal relations, not only reducing the possibilities for the emotional intimacy that is so threatening, but also further concealing their own instrumentality. Since the activities and practices of both management and masculinity are grounded in hierarchy, not least in terms of symbolic, material and social rewards, this provides masculine subjects with a near-impenetrable barrier that their formal positions offer. The activities of management thus acquire significance as a series of designs and mechanisms for distancing oneself from others and for avoiding and evading such intimacies as may be otherwise "unleashed". As Bologh contends:

> ... the more that formalities predominate, the less that personal self-disclosure occurs and the more superficial the relationship remains. [. . .] Because intimacy breaks down the barriers that formality provides, intimacy promotes vulnerability. Intimacy can be dangerous; one's trust can be betrayed, one's weaknesses exploited, and one's esteem or desire unreciprocated. In other words, one can be hurt and humiliated. On the other hand, intimacy can be protective and intensely pleasurable. Trust can be met with care, vulnerability and tenderness, exposure with recognition and affirmation, esteem and desire reciprocated. In other words, one can be nurtured affirmed and exalted. Because erotic love involves more or less intense desire as well as exposure and disclosure, erotic love involves the greatest personal risk but also the greatest possibility of communion. Hence erotic love can produce the most intense agony and ecstasy. (ibid.: 217)

In this regard, management and masculinity appear as a form of deception: deception in that, most notably in capitalist market environments and organizations, the activities of management serve to conceal the "real" (unequal) nature of employment relationships, where the primary benefits accrue to employers rather than employees. While giving the appearance of care for employees and lower-hierarchy managers, most notably in paternalistic styles of managing, senior managements deny or downplay the expression of any alternative reality in their subordinates, other than that which is officially sanctioned, controlled or "protected" by managements themselves, such as employee newsletters, team briefings, quality circles and the like. But, above all else, management and masculinity provide masculine subjects with the ultimate in self-deception. For in their attempts to control their environment, to distance themselves from others and control the perceptions of those around them, masculine subjects live out the belief in a mode of engaging with the social world as grounded in instrumentality and control. But this narrative of self as self-deception can only ever be contradictory; for it denies the linkages with others that are its very condition. In other words, not only are the discourses of management and masculinity internally contradictory in their attempts to refuse and refute the links between persons, but the lived experience of masculine subjects is frequently one of tension, anxiety and daily contradiction in the struggle, however "well managed" or internalized, to sustain what it is to be "successful" as a manager and as masculine.

Concerned to maintain and reinforce their protective barriers for fear of the disclosure that might be humiliating or exploitative, masculine subjects further deny the possibility of removing such barriers, since to do so would be regarded as immediately giving a power advantage to the other. In refusing their own vulnerability, to others and themselves, masculine subjects thereby live out the consequences of a narrow and otherwise foreshortened range of possibilities for human interaction. Their impoverishment is twofold: in the concern to maintain control, masculine subjects disavow the possibility of relationships and forms of intimacy that are non-instrumental, relationships "that are desired *because they are pleasurable and valuable in themselves*" (ibid.: 216, emphasis added). Masculine subjects are further impoverished by the fear of "letting go" in their engagements with others. Masculine subjects can find confirmation of themselves only in the control that they exercise over events, situations and over others, however unfulfilling its experience:

> . . . the more a person needs and desires recognition and response from another without being able to recognise and respond to the needs and desires of the other, the more susceptible the person is to flattery and manipulation of indiscriminate others and the less able to find satisfaction and enhanced pleasure. Consequently, the more the person will need to engage continually in external exploits and turn to external rewards as a source of pleasure and recognition in an unending search for pleasures and satisfactions that ultimately fail to please and satisfy. (ibid.: 229)

Conclusion

This chapter has sought to explore the links between masculinity, management and intimacy. In particular, I have elaborated certain of the conditions within which intimacy is constituted and expressed in contemporary organizations. Referring to these conditions, I have examined two forms of intimacy, defined here as instrumental and emotional intimacy. My contention is that both masculinity and management deny the ambiguity, fluidity and alternative possibilities of human interaction other than that which is grounded in instrumental intimacy. In this regard, masculine subjects, in seeking to deny the subjectivity of the other, thereby fix and limit human possibilities in such a fashion as to offer the greatest propensity for instrumental control. But this control can never be fully achieved, nor ever fully realized; hence the precarious nature of masculine subjectivity. Moreover, this instrumentality that is a condition and consequence of management and masculine subjectivity *requires*, for its continuance, the repression of the other in social relations. Masculine subjects thereby deny the possibility for "play" within social relations – of shifting between subject positions – for masculinity and management necessitate that the other is subordinated to self. Masculine subjectivity is equally unreflexive and unreflective in its unwillingness, or sheer inability, to challenge the conditions of its own perpetuation, however self-destructive or impoverishing the consequence.

The notion of play and playfulness corresponds to Irigaray's (1980) notion of "jouissance", defined as the multiplicity of corporeal, sexual and bodily pleasures, and the pleasure in its largest sense of embodied engagement with others. Here, social relationships are valued for the possibilities that they offer for connection and play and for moving between subject/object positions. My own experience of organizational life in paid work, almost universally based in masculine-orientated and numerically male-dominated public-sector working environments over a period of 20 years, similarly corresponds to and resonates with the notion of play in subject

197

positions. As a woman in a predominantly male and predominantly masculine field of work, I am intrigued and engaged by the possibilities for playfulness in organizations and by the subversive potential of play in organizations. This is not some argument in support of organizational or managerial anarchy but, rather, it is a challenge to the conventional ordering of social relations that would stimulate the conditions for alternative possibilities to emerge; for example, a form of management and organization that is non-hierarchical – one that is other than repressive in its expression and consequences.

Much in the manner of a child's skipping game, emotional intimacy presents a range of possibilities for subject/object positions: social encounters are thus characterized by movement – the to and fro – as participants in the social encounter move within and between subject/object positioning in playful fashion. This playful attitude to relationships stands in contrast to the discourses and practices of masculinity. In their representation of intimacy as amenable to instrumental control, such discourses are founded upon a denial of the very conditions that could make such alternative subjectivities possible. Unable to "give of themselves", masculine subjects and masculine subjectivity at one and the same time attempt to retain control of the organizational sites wherein such masculinity is reproduced and remain unreflective of the conditions of their own masculinity and its constitution.

Recognizing that contemporary organizations increasingly seek to "conjour up" intimate moments, in an albeit synthetic manner, for the larger purposes of the organization, I have argued that managerial and masculine practices displace and deny alternative non-instrumental expressions of intimacy and their possibilities for organizational subjects. Outlining Bologh's conception of erotic love as sociability, I have argued that her analysis enables the elaboration of one such alternative expression, that of emotional intimacy.

References

Benjamin, J. (1986) "A desire of one's own", in de Lauretis, T. (ed.) *Feminist Studies/Critical Studies* Bloomington: Indiana University Press

Bologh, R.W. (1990) *Love or Greatness: Max Weber and Masculine Thinking – a Feminist Inquiry* London: Unwin Hyman

Brewis, J. and Grey, C. (1994) "Re-eroticizing the organization: an exegesis and critique", *Journal of Gender, Work and Organization*, **1**, 2, pp. 67–82

Burrell, G. (1984) "Sex and organization analysis", *Organizational Studies*, **5**, 2, pp. 97–118

Calás, M. and Smircich, L. (1993) "Dangerous liaisons: the 'feminine-in-management' meets 'globalization'", *Business Horizons* March/April, pp. 71–81

Connell, R.W. (1993) "The big picture: masculinities in recent world history", *Theory and Society*, **22**, pp. 597–623

Davies, A. and Kirkpatrick, I. (1995) "Face to face with the 'sovereign consumer'", *Sociological Review*, **43**, 4, pp. 782–808

du Gay, P. (1996) *Consumption and Identity at Work* London: Sage

du Gay, P. and Salaman, G. (1992) "The cult(ure) of the consumer", *Journal of Management Studies*, **29**, 5, pp. 615–33

Duncombe, J. and Marsden, D. (1995) "'Workaholics' and 'whinging women': theorising intimacy and emotion work – the last frontier of gender inequality", *Sociological Review*, **43**, pp. 150–69

Foucault, M. (1977) *Discipline and Punish: the Birth of the Prison* Trans. A. Sheridan London: Tavistock

Foucault, M. (1988) "Power and sex", in Gordon, C. (ed.) *Power/Knowledge: Selected Interviews and Other Writings 1972–1977 by Michel Foucault* London: Harvester Wheatsheaf

Fuller, L. and Smith, V. (1991) "Consumers' reports: management by customers in a changing economy", *Work, Employment and Society*, **5**, 1, pp. 1–16

Gilligan, C. (1982) *In a Different Voice* Cambridge, Mass.: Harvard University Press

Hearn, J. (1992) *Men in the Public Eye: the Construction and Deconstruction of Private Men and Public Patriarchies* London: Routledge

Irigaray, L. (1980) "When our lips speak together", *Signs*, **6**, 1, pp. 69–79

Keat, R., Abercrombie, N. and Whiteley, N. (eds) (1994) *The Authority of the Consumer* London: Routledge

Keenoy, T. (1990) "HRM and work values in Britain", paper presented to the International Society for the Study of Work and Organizational Values, 19–22 August, Prague

Keenoy, T. (1997) "Review article: HRMism and the languages of re-presentation", *Journal of Management Studies*, **34**, 5, pp. 825–41

Kerfoot, D. and Knights, D. (1993) "Management, masculinity and manipulation: from paternalism to corporate strategy in financial services in Britain", *Journal of Management Studies*, **30**, 4, pp. 659–79

Kerfoot, D. and Knights, D. (1994) "Into the realm of the fearful: power, identity and the gender problematic", in Radtke, L. and Stam, H. (eds) *Power/Gender* New York: Sage

Kerfoot, D. and Knights, D. (1996) "The best is yet to come: the quest for embodiment in managerial work", in Collinson, D. and Hearn, J. (eds) *Men as Managers, Managers as Men* London: Sage

Kerfoot, D. and Knights, D. (1998) "Managing masculinity in contemporary organizational life: a 'man' agerial project", *Organization*, **5**, 1, pp. 7–26

Kerfoot, D. and Whitehead, S. (1998) "'Boys own' stuff: masculinity and the management of further education", *Sociological Review*, **46**, 3, 436–57

Ogbonna, E. (1992) "Organizational culture and HRM: dilemmas and contradictions", in Blyton, P. and Turnbull, P. (eds) *Reassessing Human Resource Management* London: Sage

Ogbonna, E. and Wilkinson, B. (1990) "Corporate strategy and corporate culture: the view from the checkout", *Personnel Review*, **19**, 4, pp. 9–15

Peters, T. and Waterman, R. (1982) *In Search of Excellence* New York: Harper & Row

Rose, N. (1989) *Governing the Soul: the Social Shaping of the Private Self* London: Routledge

Seidler, V. (1989) *Rediscovering Masculinity: Reason, Language and Sexuality* London: Routledge

Seidler, V. (1992) "Rejection, vulnerability and friendship", in Nardi, P. (ed.) *Men's Friendships* Newbury Park, Calif.: Sage

Simmel, G. (1950) *The Sociology of Georg Simmel* Wolff, K.H. (ed.) New York: The Free Press

Sturdy, A. (1998) "Customer care in a consumer society", *Organization*, **5**, 1, pp. 27–53

Thompson, P. and Ackroyd, S. (1995) "All quiet on the workplace front", *Sociology*, **29**, 4, pp. 615–33

Tuckmann, A. (1994) "The yellow brick road: TQM and the restructuring of organizational culture", *Organizational Studies*, **15**, 5, pp. 727–51

Wilkinson, A. and Willmott, H. (eds) (1995) *Making Quality Critical* London: Routledge

Willmott, H. (1993) "Strength is ignorance; slavery is freedom: managing culture in modern organizations", *Journal of Management Studies*, **30**, 4, pp. 515–52

CHAPTER TWELVE

"Man" management: ironies of modern management in an "old" university

Deborah Kerfoot & David Knights

Introduction

As the broad economic transformations of the post-industrialized era gather pace, so the requirement for contemporary organizations to become ever more "flexible" and responsive to the demands of diverse and fast-changing markets has increased. The collapse of large-scale bureaucratic hierarchies and the consequent restructuring, decentralization and delayering of managerial jobs has been accompanied by new forms of work and new practices of managerial control. Whether it be in the guise of the "flexible firm" (Atkinson 1984), "flexible specialization" (Piore and Sabel 1984), total quality management (TQM) (Deming 1986), business process reengineering (Hammer and Champy 1993) or the "virtual organization" (Chesbrough and Teece 1996), this emergent managerial phenomenon has found a resonance across numerous private-sector sites. Concomitant with the dissolution of rigid vertical lines of control, new so-called "leaner" structures have emerged, informed and framed by the specialisms and discourses of this "new managerialism". Drawing on the rhetoric of empowerment, participation, trust and mutuality (Kerfoot and Knights 1995), the modern organization increasingly invests its survival and productive potential in the legions of project groups, multi-function work groups and forms of team-working that characterize the "flexible" corporation.

Thus traditional forms of managerial control and supervision are rendered problematic. Managers who are unable to respond "positively" to the new turn of emphasis in organizations are quickly marginalized, to be replaced by those who are more "socially skilled" in human engagement (Kerfoot and Knights 1996). What is being demanded of new managers is that they do not protect themselves simply through the formal hierarchy and institutional relations. As a consequence, their vulnerability as human beings can show through; aspects of identity and subjectivity that were concealed by earlier bureaucratic regimes are fully exposed. As our research vignette clearly indicates, this transformation in organizational processes has major implications for the ways in which inequality, discrimination and gendered power are reproduced in organizations and in management. This is not to argue that gender as a dimension of power and inequality disappears but, rather, that "new management" and the structures of "new organization" place some difficulties in its way that could threaten the untroubled continuity of patriarchal power relations at work.

Recognizing the above-mentioned organizational transformations to be endemic across the private sector, this chapter has two aims. Taking the form of a research note and empirical vignette, the chapter signals that, in contrast to the private sector, much of the public sector, and in particular higher education (HE), is "light years" behind many of these organizational and managerial developments. A second aim is to identify one set of gendered subjectivities thus problematized in the public sector as a consequence of men manager's continued investment in what are by now increasingly problematic, masculinist ways of managing. In engaging this debate, we utilize the concept of the *masculine subject*, elaborated in the previous chapter (see also Kerfoot and Whitehead 1998). In so doing, we acknowledge the multiplicity of masculinities; their relationship to spatial and temporal situations; and the discursivity of masculinity as an investment of identity in privileged ways of being a man in a multitude of settings. From this perspective, masculinity, as other gender identities, is precarious; subject to slippage between multiple subject positions (Mouffe 1992). Moreover, masculinity requires the constant approbation and gaze of acceptance by others. Recognizing such, gender and gender differences are seen to be dynamic processes, where masculinity is an *outcome* or product of social processes as opposed to an *amount* that one person may possess. The masculine subject is, then, that person who invests a sense of being in masculine discourses; those languages, practices and symbols that speak to stereotypical ways of being a man, and which are subsequently dominant or hegemonic in various sites across the social field.

While accepting that masculinity is always in flux, bound up in contradiction and uncertainty, we nevertheless recognize that much of managerial discourse has privileged those men and women who are adept at reproducing its central tenets. Characterized by purposive rational instrumentality and disengaged forms of human interaction, we see this form of masculinity to be reproduced in the organizational and managerial practices of our empirical site, UK higher education. Furthermore, in respect of organizational life, this "identity work" of masculine subjects has been acted out in arenas in which men dominate numerically and ideologies of masculinism (Brittan 1989) similarly inform the organizational culture (see also Cheng 1996). This chapter draws on intensive participant and non-participant observation research material from the HE sector, together with extensive documentary material, extracts of which are reproduced here. Our purpose is to provide a partial insight into the patriarchal traditions and masculine preoccupations of the hierarchical control that continues to dominate UK universities behind the "smokescreen" of liberal ideology and democractic procedure.

After articulating our views on the problems of masculinity as it affects corporate activity in the "age of the consumer", the chapter describes a brief vignette to illustrate what we consider to be the limited "progress" of gender liberation – and education – in HE. Due to the commercially and professionally sensitive nature of the data, the empirical material is made anonymous and pseudonyms are given to the various protagonists and their institutions. The chapter concludes by posing the question of whether "New Management/New Organization" could have unintended radical consequences for gender relations at work that are of far greater significance than a century of feminist discourse.

Masculinity and new management

As we have indicated, new management finds its most obvious reification in a discourse of consensus and "relaxed authority". However, the underlying impetus for such transformatory movements is far from benign: for in the attempt to render staff more creative with respect to their customers and each other, managements' primary goal is clearly the improvement of underlying output and profit margins. Moreover, the increased emphasis on social relations as a commercial resource does not only involve those working at the interface of customer engagement; managers at all levels are equally involved. Consequently, many managers are no longer able to continue "managing at a distance" (Cooper 1992), and are, thereby, confronted with all the associated weaknesses and vulnerabilities that such exposure entails. Under the increasingly "outdated" or unfashionable conventional managerial practices of earlier bureaucratic regimes, such exposure, of course, would have been both risky and inappropriate. Consequently, much of managerial labour came to privilege the disengaged and disembodied (masculine) subject. As a way of "being" in the organization, this served to reinforce an image of self as unemotional, rational and stoic – always in control, no matter what.

Thus, what is now increasingly put under tension by new management is managers' sense of themselves as powerful, potent and absolutist agents in a status-driven arena. This is not to suggest that gender as a dimension of power and inequality disappears, but that new management has the potential to disrupt and disturb the *dominant* forms of masculinity which have hitherto characterized managerial labour, particularly in the industrial era (Kerfoot and Knights 1996, see also Roper 1994). As was discussed in the previous chapter (Kerfoot, Ch. 11, this volume), self-estranged and disembodied forms of masculinity – notable in, for example, paternalism and crude expressions of fraternalism – are clearly incompatible with an equitable, emotional and "intimate" form of human engagement; for they are a form of intersubjective communication that acts as a mask to conceal the masculine subject rather than expose it to the scrutiny and judgement of others, especially with respect to social skills.

This is the precise reason why "managing at a distance" proves so alluring for the masculine subject. For while the mask is in place, reified through the well practised and sophisticated performance of the subject, the flaws and cracks in the emotional and intimate capacities of masculine subjectivity remain hidden (see Kerfoot and Whitehead 1998). For those managers who are preoccupied with the instrumental control of others, everyday social interaction is difficult to engage in, at least with any sense of well-being or sincerity. For, traditionally, a masculine performance relied only on executing the "technical" requirements of the office, role or function.

The masculine subject, dominated by the discourses and practices of masculinity, now finds itself in an invidious situation. For having invested much time, emotional energy and identity work in the attempts to render others manipulable for self and instrumental purposes, the masculine subject now faces the prospect of having its once-valued traits potentially condemned as "unproductive" in the new regime. Thus those managers who are unable to appropriate this expertise become themselves victims of what is euphemistically described as the "delayering" process.

While the notion of egalitarian partnerships and equality in the new organization can be dismissed as merely another rhetorical device to seduce employees, albeit into complying with, rather than committing themselves to, the demands of the organization, their significance for managers should not be underestimated. For as social skills packages for managers proliferate, so can be seen an accelerating trend in modern management towards the "added value" to be had from consensual social relationships in organizations. However, their incidence in the public sector is less evident. Moreover, it is within the ivory towers of academia where some of the most stringent critics of new management reside, rendering its introduction into HE problematic.

As suggested elsewhere, masculinity often concerns some reference to physical presence, competitive strength and sexual prowess (Kerfoot and Knights 1993: 660), and is frequently expressed in situations of "male bonding", such as sporting events or pub crawls, where intimacy is simulated through ribaldry, rivalry and rowdiness. In management circles, as the following vignette describes, masculinity manifests itself less crudely, but nonetheless equally vividly and virulently.

Masculinity at work: a case of education

This vignette concerns the development of a research centre that met with strong opposition partly because of a conflict between several of the participants, ostensibly about principles, procedure and academic values but equally interpreted through the lens of masculinity. Two of the participants – the director and deputy director of the Centre for the Study of Strategy, Consumption and Distribution (CSCD) – had, over a period of approximately five years, promoted a research activity through large amounts of private and public funding, and were about to expand further by establishing a new research centre (with an initial £0.25 million of private funding, but with the prospect of this multiplying at an exponential rate if successful). At first, there was acceptance of the proposals within the department, and co-operation and support (including a small start-up grant for an administrative appointment) from the university. It has to be acknowledged, at the outset, that the two founders of the new centre (the director and the deputy director of the CSCD), which was to be named the Centre for the Education of Sex in Schools (CESS), were themselves driven by their own masculinity to demonstrate their entrepreneurial, as well as academic, proficiency.

However, they soon came up against an equally virulent and driven masculinity on the part of a number of senior academics, who sought to constrain activities that they perceived to be running out of control and, perhaps more importantly, bypassing the department in securing support from senior ranks in the university. A new head of department sought to question the legitimacy of the arrangements through which the activities had been organized by his predecessor, not realizing that these arrangements had been agreed legally at the highest level within the university. His attempt through an internal committee to stop the arrangements, after which he was overruled by the registrar, set the scene for a battle of masculinities; for this setback only made the head of department more determined to find ways of stopping the developments in their tracks. It also provided the space for the director and deputy director of CSCD to rub his nose in the error, and thereby give him further reason to attack as the best form of defence.

Little did he realize at this time that, despite further overrulings and setbacks in relation to attempting to undermine the arrangements for running the CSCD, an opportunity would fall into his lap, in the form of a classic masculine conflict that had arisen between the deputy director and another professor (Kevin) in the department. Both of these were co-supervisors on a research project run by the director of CSCD, which had been funded externally to research sex education in schools. The conflict occurred when the deputy director instructed a researcher on the project to attend and represent him on an external committee that was seeking to promote sex education in schools. The following E-mail from Kevin was sent, and this was followed by a response from Bill that was extremely aggressive, and by one from Brian asking for a meeting between the three, so that the researchers could be given clear guidelines. The E-mails are quoted in full (including the aggressive use of capitals) to avoid any danger of reinterpreting them, but the names and identities of persons and bodies are disguised:

15th May

Dear Brian and Bill

I saw Janet and John this lunch time and went through the document they had produced on the research issues, plus comments from Brian. . . . So I am happy that they are making a good start here.

However, there is one issue which I need to raise now, so that we get our boundaries agreed between this XXX project and the work that Janet and John are contracted to under [its auspices], and the activities of the Centre for the Study of Consumption and Distribution (CSCD) and the Centre for the Education of Sex in Schools (CESS). When we were talking, Janet mentioned that she was going to London for the meeting of the Sex Education Group (SEG) tomorrow, and so I assumed that she was going in the role we agreed at our last (and in fact first) joint meeting, i.e. that she would go purely as an observer, since the lines between the research and the activities of the Centre needed to be clearly drawn, from the outset. However, it sounded to me that she was now being asked to take a rather different, and far more active role, as if she were going to act on behalf of, or as a representative of the Centre for the Education of Sex in Schools

(CESS) on the Sex Education Group (SEG) body. When she told me that there was a document to which she was being asked to speak, I felt that I had to request her to let me have a sight of it, since this seemed to be a very different role that she was being presented with than the one than I thought we had agreed. Obviously since I have been away for the past week I could not expect to have been consulted about this before now, but now I was back I did want to be sure that any thing she was to do would not in any sense jeopardise the XXX project, or her position *vis-à-vis* future potential interested parties (or indeed research subjects).

When I saw the document (this is a fax to the chairman of the Sex Education Group) of 8th May I can only say that my reaction was one of extreme concern. No doubt for the best of motives, the lines of separation seem completely blurred, and if, as I understand it, Janet had been required to SPEAK to this document, in my view her role as an independent researcher in an independent research project would have been seriously compromised. I am not using these words lightly here. But specifically, I find it misleading to describe the sex education project to outsiders as having been "developed together with the document 'Licensing Sex Education'". In my understanding this project took shape because Brian and I began to discuss issues of mutual concern, *re* problems in the understanding of sex and sexuality and problems in pedagogy, problems which coincided in the kind of area that we then decided on. I have not even read "Licensing Sex Education", so even if that was part of the background to your inputs to the project, I find it hard to accept the characterisation that it was "developed together with" that research project. And certainly while we might recognise many inputs, I find it a real hostage to fortune to describe this sex education project in terms that only associate it with that particular piece of CSCD research. It also means that the project is given a particular slant to this group, which I see as unfortunate, at this early stage, in being associated with schooling and education, when much of our discussions have been so far about NOT making that connection in the way we go about our work. So again it seems to me quite the wrong message to send out to a group which is precisely looking at that area. Indeed we kept rehearsing the point (I thought) that we wanted to differentiate ourselves from the Sex Education Group agenda over PRECISELY that issue, both in terms of how they might see us, and in terms of any wider public. This to me again sends a diametrically wrong message about the research, and so of course about the position of Janet as a researcher on the research.

That brings me to the point that really disturbs me: the "Proposal" that our project would benefit from being extended, and the statement that we are WILLING to extend the project. I want it quite clear that I at least have not been consulted about extending the project, and that since I was out of the country, I would have expected to be consulted on my return, or at least to have been copied with such a suggestion. I also want it clear that I am NOT IN THE LEAST at this moment willing to extend this project via money from the Sex Education Group, as seems to be suggested in the Proposal. I again thought we had an agreement at our meeting that this research needed to be kept clear from all compromise in terms of its funding sources, and from the characterisation given of the Sex Education Group by Bill at the meeting, I did not come away with the impression that they would be a source we would be keen to approach. IF they are, then let us talk about it. But please do not again put forward a Proposal which, as in the case of this one, clearly has major implications for the Sex Education project without at least involving me in some level of discussion. For me there is a line of principle here: this project is a joint project. It is not a CSCD project in the usual sense, but jointly headed up and therefore requires joint agreement. Again, please correct me if I am wrong on this. If you do think I am wrong, then I think we need to have a serious discussion about just where the lines are to be drawn between this research and the activities of the CSCD and CESS. Terms such as "we" are very dangerous in documents such as this, since we need to be aware of who "we" are.

I actually do agree with one thing in the document, which is the point about our "wholly independent position, without reliance on any particular source of funding". I think I made the point to Brian at least, maybe to all, that it was perhaps beneficial that the national retailer had decided not to support the project because that did guarantee its independence. That is how I want to keep it, and I hope you do too. I am sorry to make my points at such length, but perhaps you will understand that this is a measure of my concern. Perhaps I should just reiterate the things that I, in my personal capacity, think we should clarify, in so far as we have not done so yet. These are in other words my views for discussion.

First, that the research should from now on be clearly identified something separate from other CSCD activities, (i) since it is separately funded, by the XXX, as a theoretically-informed study, and therefore we would want in terms of the XXX and our relations with them, if nothing else, to make this separation not only clear, but seen to be clear; and (ii) because the direct objective of the research is with the public not the schools as such, so that in terms of its substantive research and the presentation of that content it needs to be differentiated from other activities.

Second, if it is after discussion agreed that this is the kind of separation that we want for the project, then we should ensure that Janet and John as the researchers on it are given some kind of ring-fencing from the activities of the Centre as such. I do not want to suggest that they cannot do things that are helpful and supportive to the Centre, indeed that is why I agreed at our meeting that it could be useful, in terms of the research, for Janet or John to attend meetings of SEG. But I thought it was also clear, in the context of that discussion, that the first priority was not to put them in any compromised situation *vis-à-vis* the XXX project.

I am afraid that I feel that this is, though for good and well-intentioned reasons, what could all too possibly happen tomorrow. Since we have not had any opportunity to discuss or clarify the boundaries between activities, I have therefore felt that it would be invidious to put Janet in a potentially compromising position as between the objectives of the XXX project and the concerns of the Sex Education Group. I have therefore instructed her that she is not to engage in any advocacy position of any kind tomorrow, except in so far as promoting the XXX project as one which is new and different and one in which we would welcome interest and support. But I have told her that we cannot at this stage do more: neither encourage them to consider funding us, nor encourage them to get directly involved in our activities.

So she will, for tomorrow, be going as an observer. She will not, on my instructions, speak to the paper faxed on 8th May: indeed at this point, until we have had a chance to discuss the situation, she will distance herself from it in every respect except in underlining the point about our commitment to independence as a school generally, and in this project in particular. Indeed, since I understand that her trip is to be paid out of the XXX budget, she cannot, in my view, do otherwise than attend in that capacity. And I hope it is understood that I am very happy that, in that capacity, she does attend. Indeed, I look forward to her briefing on her return.

Kevin

Having heard something from Brian of what was in Kevin's E-mail before receiving it, both as a forwarded E-mail from Brian and directly from Kevin, Bill replied as follows:

17th May

Kevin

I suggest we have a meeting about your totally over the top E-mail with Brian. And before that meeting may I suggest that you reflect on your message and consider on whose coat-tails you are actually very fortunate to be hanging!! We can say more about this when we meet, since it is hardly the action of a team player to write notes like this, when we are just a tel. call away.

It may also be a good idea to check your facts with others before launching into such extreme print. Janet was not asked to SPEAK (incidentally it is bad form to SHOUT at someone by E-mail in this way) to any proposal and she was clearly attending the meeting as a stand in for BD/me, not as a researcher. Did she also show you the earlier fax to the Chairman of SEG? Or did you think to check with me whether you (or she) had got it wrong? If I write any more I shall also be guilty of your practice, but I don't have your tel. number at home, nor access to get it, otherwise I would have called to make these points, and others, verbally. My experience, perhaps not yours, is that it's usually much more effective to talk.

My number is yyy and Brian's is zzz and we were both available on Monday. Try calling and talking rather than memos, you will probably find it a lot more constructive. Look forward to your call.

Regards

Bill Brown

The response from Kevin was equally aggressive: clearly, the two were by this time locked in a battle for masculine pre-eminence and both sought to invoke the support of Brian as both director of the CSCD and as the head of the XXX project. Bill did this through informal means – either face-to-face or via telephone conversations – whereas Kevin sought to secure a formal meeting that excluded Bill, as can be seen from the E-mail below. But, first, here is Kevin's reply to Bill:

Dear Bill

I haven't seen Brian's response yet. So I can only tell you how I feel as an immediate reaction to yours. My previous E-mail was written very coolly, with all the benefit of the doubt that I could offer under the circumstances, and offering plenty of avenues for anyone who was prepared to reflect on what had happened in the week that Janet had been employed, and just ask a few questions of themselves about how she might feel about being put in a potentially invidious position where she appeared to be serving two masters. Unfortunately you don't seem to have picked up on that. Maybe you will now.

Don't come the coattails stuff with me ever again. I will overlook it on this occasion, but I suggest you think next time before putting your keyboard in gear. And don't come the "team player" line, without first acknowledging that you had put Janet in an invidious position. We only become team players when we know what team we are on. My team is the XXX project, and Janet's team is the XXX project.

Do you think yours were the actions of a team player on the XXX project? I'd really appreciate the answer to that question, along with answers to the other ones that I did have the courtesy to ask in my E-mail. But I think you'd better realise that the reason that I wrote the E-mail was to head off what I could only see as a potentially disastrous situation for that project, and to take Janet out of a difficult situation. Until you see that, there's absolutely no point in a meeting for team-building, since I don't know what team you're on. By the way, I do check my facts. And I have seen an earlier fax to the Chairman of the Sex Education Group (SEG). And I am now aware of earlier missives back and forth, all of which suggest that I am not the only one to feel the gentle breath of your dulcet tones. However, we have not had anything from you yet about the facts of what took place the week I was away, except that you have revealed one "fact", in remarking that Janet was to attend as a stand-in for BD/you, not as a researcher. That is

PRECISELY (Is that "shouting" to you?? It's meant as emphasis, from me) what we discussed at the prior meeting, where we agreed that if she went as a stand-in for you, she would be doing so in her capacity as a member of the XXX team. Which is precisely what the problem was, as soon as you started redefining her mission in the way indicated by this "fact". She couldn't DO BOTH. So somebody had to step in. Which had to be me.

So, I look forward to hearing some more "facts" from you, instead of receiving another E-mail like this one. Then maybe we can have a meeting. But not until, I would humbly suggest.

Kevin

One more thing. It may interest you to know that, once I knew the situation, I asked Helen whether Brian was in, and was told he wasn't. Since some-one needed to sort Janet's situation out on behalf of the project, that needed therefore to be me, since it clearly couldn't be you. OK? Next time, before sounding off at others about team-work and consultation, try keeping them in the picture yourself in the first place. Just an E-mail or voicemail would have done, at any point during the week I was away. Or perhaps it didn't seem relevant to you because after all, as you might very reasonably point out, I'm not on the team.

Brian also responded after this by suggesting that the three met to discuss the problems:

Dear Kevin

I think there are misunderstandings and inappropriate action recorded in this E-mail which we will need to meet to clear up. It does no good and is not fair to be giving researchers conflicting instructions.

Brian

and Kevin responded as follows:

15th May

Dear Brian

I quite agree. And I'm afraid you're piggy in the middle here. I appreciate the beautifully ambiguous nature of your comment, and I do not like coun-termanding other people. But as I presume your comment is acknowledg-ing, Bill had managed in four days to put Janet in an impossible position, because what he had done was go directly against what was agreed at our joint meeting. So while there were no doubt misunderstandings all round the shop, let there be no doubt where the inappropriate action originated, whatever you may feel about the appropriateness of my action thereafter.

Kevin

PS I would prefer you to keep the rest of this totally to yourself, and perhaps it is something that you and I should meet to discuss. First, if you personally feel that I am on your coattails over this research, then I would prefer that you tell me so. Certainly that isn't how I envisaged it. Though, let me hasten to add that I am fully aware that without doubt you put in all the work in winning the award, something which I have not hesitated to say to people, either. But we'd better clear that up. Currently I'm letting it pass as a cheap shot, but cheap shots can fester if they're not resolved.

Second, you need to be aware that Janet was very distressed on Monday, whatever Bill may think about his moves over the previous few days. She felt that she had been put in a position where she was being asked to speak for CESS, and in her view she had been asked, or even slightly stronger than asked, to take a strongly uncompromising negotiating line, which was simply neither her brief as a researcher nor in line with her personal style. That is why I felt I had to write a very clear message, and at great length. We are one week into this project and this kind of thing happens?? What is it going to be like if things go on like that? I find, in those circumstances, that my first responsibility is to the people in the firing line, who are doing the work, who are not in this instance Bill. Janet is a really outstanding researcher, who also fortunately is very tough. I am sure she will be able to hold her end up from here on out. But she really, in my personal view, didn't need the kind of pressure which Bill, manifestly, from his fax of the 8th had put her under. So we needed to have a showdown right away, and get the ground rules clear. Unfortunately, judging by Bill's E-mail to me, he's a million miles from being prepared to acknowledge any fault let alone any change in his way of operating. And I'm not prepared to see the research or our key researchers compromised from here on out. We need them, in my view: and more than that, with them, we can deliver some really super research. But we and they need this sort of crap like a hole in the head.

So, maybe you and I should talk. Or maybe you should just respond to me by E-mail first, not just about Bill's pique, but the whole wider scenario, not just of last week and this week, but how we get back on track from here on out.

Kevin

Had it not been the case that Kevin had on two previous occasions conflicted with Brian – first, about the presence of Bill at a meeting to discuss the project and, secondly, in relation to the appointment of staff – Brian may have agreed to a private meeting. But this was quite clearly a case of Kevin seeking to secure Brian's support so as to win his case against Bill. Brian refused to engage in any further production of E-mails other than those specifically written to arrange the dates of a meeting, not privately between him and Kevin, but between all three of the supervisors on the project. Hopefully, once the situation had been resolved, he anticipated asking the researchers to join the meeting. Having failed to get Brian to take sides, Kevin reluctantly agreed to a meeting between all three. When the meeting eventually took place, Kevin appeared to have already decided that the game was lost, since in response to the question from Brian as to why he didn't telephone him at home as he had done on numerous previous occasions, he refused to say anything other than "I rang your secretary and she said you weren't in." This he repeated several times in an increasingly contorted and emotional fashion. After a highly strained period of interaction, Kevin declared his resignation from the project.

The first round of the battle for masculine pre-eminence appeared to have been won comfortably by Bill, but things were not going to rest there and, some short time afterwards, a third party told Brian that Kevin was determined to get back at Bill. Without going into the detail, Kevin, assisted by the head of the department, eventually managed to get a committee to throw out the Centre for the Education of Sex in Schools (CESS), which then created a conflict that ran completely out of control and ended with a number of people losing credibility.

Discussion and conclusion

It is unlikely that the department in question ever intended to press the conflict so far as to lose all of the funding that was already committed from the private sector, nor to create a situation that was irretrievable. But there are a number of conclusions that may be drawn from the episode that are of relevance for this chapter. First, it is clear that a masculine struggle for pre-eminence was instrumental in influencing, if not creating, the events that unfolded. Significantly, it was possible to communicate in great detail through electronic mail, but when confronted with one another in the flesh, so to speak, all communication broke down. All of the participants were determined to "win" in some way or other: compromise became a sign of weakness and not admissible if masculine identity was to be sustained.

Secondly, the episode reveals how little this university (but perhaps most) have changed in relation to the "New Management/New Organization" demands for adaptation, creativity, entrepreneurialism, flexibility and innovation, despite very often being the source of new thinking and ideas that eventually have helped to transform practices in the private sector. If, as was suggested in the introduction, "New Management/New Organization" poses a threat to the dominant discourses of masculinity, the university sector may be almost immune to this impact on their practices and procedures. This is all the more bizarre, given that feminist ideas have also been drawn from, and had a strong influence upon, academic discourse, especially among women social scientists, philosophers and literary theorists. Consequently, universities will perhaps remain a backwater as far as the erosion of masculine power and patriarchy is concerned. This may well be so until the profession – certainly at the most senior professorial and vice-chancellor levels – is populated by larger numbers of women: but, even then, the change cannot be guaranteed, because of masculine mimesis by many ambitious women. For both masculinity and management practice sustain a transformation of *all* relations into forms of instrumental control. They reflect and reinforce this instrumental control by virtue of the pressures to produce, distribute and compete in the market place – something with which the university sector has only recently had to cope because of externally imposed research assessment exercises, pressed upon them by central government (Harley and Lowe 1998).

We have been concerned in this chapter to argue that, even though feminism and radical thinking have historically been sustained and supported by the intellectual and political ideas of academics, the workplace organization and management of much of the British university sector remains traditional and conservative. Consequently, in so far as there is a challenge to gendered power in this arena, it remains at the level of intellectual discourse and ideology, rather than at the point of production and practice. By contrast, in areas of the private sector there is far less of an intellectual challenge to gendered discourses and yet perhaps more of a transformative impact that stems from practical changes in the workplace.

Are universities, and other public-sector organizations, so far behind on the practical front of transforming gender relations at work, simply because they have not yet adopted, or are legitimately sceptical of, the new managerial practices? In recognizing, and thence privileging, the creativity and innovative potential in human encounters, modern management innovations draw on an understanding of social interaction that is stereotypically associated with women and "the feminine". One might speculate on the degree to which an unintended consequence of such practices would lead to a fundamental questioning of masculinity in management, organization and subjectivity. Such critical reflection on the very business of management itself holds a key to creating the conditions within which an alternative means of managing can emerge – one that is grounded in non-instrumental modes of relating to others.

Yet the same process of critical reflection is required of those masculine subjects whose very subjectivity and identity has, in certain respects, been the condition and consequence of contemporary means of managing. This change calls upon masculine subjects similarly to reflect on the conditions and possibilities of their own existence and, for many men in particular, to unburden themselves of the mask that is masculinity. Such self-reflection is no less problematic, for masculine subjects are then required to examine critically their own mode of relating to others and to the world around them. However, it offers the potential to embrace non-instrumental modes of human engagement, and a far broader, and arguably richer, range of life experiences than is promoted by the discourses and practices of masculinity.

References

Atkinson, J. (1984) "Manpower strategies for flexible organizations", *Personnel Management*, August

Brittan, A. (1989) *Masculinity and Power* Oxford: Blackwell

Cheng, C. (1996) *Masculinities in Organizations* Thousand Oaks, Calif.: Sage

Chesbrough, H.W. and Teece, D.J. (1996) "When is virtual virtuous? Organising for innovation", *Harvard Business Review*, **74**, 1

Cooper, R. (1992) "Formal organization and representation: remote control, displacement and abbreviation", in Reed, M. and Hughes, M. (eds) *Rethinking Organization: New Directions in Organization Theory and Analysis* London: Sage, pp. 254–72

Deming, W.E. (1986) *Out of the Crisis* Cambridge: Cambridge University Press

Hammer, M. and Champy, J. (1993) *Reengineering the Corporation: a Manifesto for Business Revolution* London: Nicholas Brealey

Harley, S. and Lowe, P. (1998) "Academics divided: the research assessment exercise and the academic labour process", paper presented to the 16th Annual Labour Process Conference, University of Manchester, 6–9 April

Kerfoot, D. and Knights, D. (1993) "Management, masculinity and manipulation: from paternalism to corporate strategy in financial services in Britain", *Journal of Management Studies*, **30**, 4, pp. 659–79

Kerfoot, D. and Knights, D. (1995) "The organisation(s) of social division: constructing identities in managerial work", paper given to the 12th European Group on Organisation Studies (EGOS) Colloquium, Istanbul, Turkey, 6–8 July

Kerfoot, D. and Knights, D. (1996) " 'The best is yet to come': searching for embodiment in managerial work", in Collinson, D. and Hearn, J. (eds) *Men as Managers, Managers as Men* London: Sage

Kerfoot, D. and Whitehead, S. (1998) " 'Boys own' stuff: masculinity and the management of further education", *Sociological Review*, **46**, 3, pp. 436–57

Mouffe, C. (1992) "Feminism, citizenship and radical democratic politics", in Butler, J. and Scott, W.S. (eds) *Feminists Theorize the Political* New York: Routledge

Piore, M.J. and Sabel, C. (1984) *The Second Industrial Divide* New York: Basic Books

Roper, M. (1994) *Masculinity and the British Organization Man since 1945* Oxford: Oxford University Press

CHAPTER THIRTEEN

Masculine/managerial masks and the "other" subject

Roy Moodley

Introduction

When critical studies on men and masculinities first emerged, they posited a "crisis of masculinities" which focused chiefly on family relationships, the structure of social mobility and social organization of work (Kimmel 1986, Brod 1987). This was the continuation of an investigation begun by feminist scholarship, which would lead to some understanding of the epistemological and ontological terrains of the categories "men" and "masculinities". In the past decade, this exploration has not only confined itself to the study of gender relations (Kimmel 1986; Brod 1987; Connell 1987; Hearn 1987, 1992; Kaufman 1987; Chapman and Rutherford 1988; Brittan 1989; Kimmel and Messner 1989; Seidler 1989, 1994; Middleton 1992; Morgan 1992; Harris 1995), but has also entered work organization cultures (Cockburn 1985, Hearn and Parkin 1987, Collinson 1992, Kvande and Rasmussen 1994, Gherardi 1995), particularly managerial discourses and management practices (Kerfoot and Knights 1993, Collinson and Hearn 1994, 1996). Since management itself has long been synonymous with masculinity (Ozga 1993), it is vital that a critical analysis of the behaviours and actions of men (women) managers is undertaken in the study of work, organizations and management.

Traditional gender roles and stereotypes are still pervasive and persistent in contemporary organizations (Collinson and Hearn 1994, Nicholson and West 1996), despite overwhelming attempts at "feminization" (Fondas 1997) of organizational cultures. For women, even the traditional employee–employer psychological contracts (Schein 1965) which lay at the foundation of "acceptable" employment relations, sometimes overshadowing gender inequalities, are being violated as a result of restructuring, downsizing and demographic diversity (Morrison and Robinson 1997). The "glass ceiling", as both material actuality and signifier, has been exposed through critical gender enquiry. Although glass ceilings give the impression of transparency and fluidity, they nevertheless have remained concretely fixed across most organizational sites, sustained, moreover, by new management practices and managerial discourses. Kerfoot and Knights (1993: 661), in suggesting that "particular forms of masculinity are sustained, reproduced and privileged in work and within management practices" emphasize this relationship, and in so doing point to where the interrogation might be brought to bear on the oppressive practices that mitigate against any democratic practice in the workplace.

However, locating "man"-agement dysfunction and situating it within critical theory is less complicated and abstract than the "face-to-face" (face-to-mask or mask-to-mask) interactions that evolve daily in the workplace. In order to contribute to an understanding of men (women) managers' inter- and intrapersonal relations, I have employed the metaphor of the "mask" critically to interrogate some of the received ideas about men and masculinities in organizational settings. Therefore, I have attempted, through the form(ulation) of multiple masculinities and their displacement as managerial masks, to show that particular dominant forms of masculinity are sustained and (re)produced in the "man"-agement of the "other". I suggest that traditional and contemporary management practices have legitimized these dominant actions and behaviours, while at the same time rewarding the suppression of those qualities which are often attributed to being feminine or humanistic.

The metaphor of the "mask" in this chapter draws attention to the inherent contingency in gender and (organizational) power that circulates through the discourse of masculinities. The symbolism of the "mask" and its power of illusion offers the opportunity to confront the epistemologies of gender and sexual identities, especially with the "other": women, ethnic minorities, the dis-abled, and gay men and lesbians. Moreover, if we situate these "other" representations and men, in contemporary and often capitalist management practices we begin to see the complexities, discomforts, distresses and dis-eases experienced in the formation of individual and organizational identities. Working outside the polarized gender space of masculinity and femininity, and by finding a hybrid space – a "third space", the "mask'ed" space – I attempt to show the interrelationship between acknowledged manifestations of negative masculinity, management practices and the "other" subject.

The chapter explores the idea that contemporary man-agement practices through the dis-play of multiple mask(ulinities) – hegemonic, compassionate, contrary to "mission(ary) and equal opportunity philosophies" – are still subjecting the "other" to oppressive practices and organizational hierarchies. It seems that when the masculine/managerial masks slip, they reveal forms of dominant and hegemonic masculinities that deny the subjectivity of the "other". Bhabha (1994: 62) suggests that:

> the disavowal of the Other always exacerbates the edge of identification revealing that dangerous place where identity and aggressivity are twinned . . . creating a tension of meaning and being.

The subsequent representations at these hybrid spaces "mock the spirit of the mask" (Bhabha 1994) and perpetuate "otherness". For men (women) managers who indulge at this level of aggressivity: some may either sublimate and control their feelings as a momentary coping mechanism; others may internalize the stereotypical representations and become "dis-eased" (for discussion, see, for example, Gilman 1985); yet other man-agers may fear and hate women and the other "others" (see, for example, Jukes 1993).

Finally, in autobiographical notes, I hope to illustrate how the traditions of the personal, political and sociocultural "normal self" can be at odds with the aggressive, modernist, globalized entrepreneurial philosophy that is now influencing transformations in the workplace. I hope to (un)mask this theatre of masculinity and management by drawing on my own experience as the "other" in public-sector management; particularly as "the black 'other'" in a masculine/managerial "mask" in a further education college.

Universalizing masculinities

A comprehensive understanding of the constitution of masculinity, like patriarchy, may not be possible to attain or sustain in any rational or logical form, given its history and origins (see Brod 1994). Kandiyoti (1991) suggests that most of the debate on patriarchy, although diverse, has:

> ... remained centred on the effects of industrial and postindustrial capitalism on gender relations, with relatively fewer attempts to establish linkages within a broader comparative perspective ... [to] ... reveal the intimate inner workings of different gender arrangements. (pp. 25-7)

The concept of masculinity in Western epistemological theory appears to be a convenient creation to make tangible some of the many human actions and interactions, some of which are perceived to be absent in "women" and thus required to be represented elsewhere. Whether it is a formulation arising from the sociopolitical dialectic of the male–female or male–male axes, it is, nevertheless, a desirable location in which to find a resolution to the inequalities of male gender practices in all spheres of human functioning. In other words, the construction of a specific schema becomes necessary, to incorporate an evolving epistemology of particular human behaviours and actions, generally attributed to the phenotypically male species represented in concepts such as a "thing", an icon, an epoch, a collective consciousness, an urban space and a geopolitical metaphor. In our need to locate this unrepresented "thing" an inscription becomes possible – masculinities (Weeks 1985; Brod 1987, 1994; Connell 1987; Hearn 1987) – and its function – masculinism (Brittan 1989: 4; Kerfoot and Knights 1993; Collier 1995: 6–7).

The epistemological speculations of "masculinity" have covered a wide spectrum: from a position where it reveals a transhistorical and archetypal masculinity (see, for example, Fitzgerald 1995), to a tentatively defined "empty category" which becomes filled with expectations, stereotypes and projections (Frosh 1994).[1] In the middle-ground lies a host of varying stratifications that attempt to define masculinity as "a discourse, a power structure, a psychic economy, a history, an ideology, an identity, a behaviour, a value system, an aesthetic even" (Middleton 1992: 152). For Knights and Murray (1994: 113), masculinity is a socially constructed way of seeing and being, changing itself over time and space within the same society; depending, for example, on class or "race", geographical location, forms of power and sexual orientation. In other words, "there are no essential 'persons', 'selves', 'psyches', 'senses' ... these are all the products of definite conditions of formation, specific technologies of the 'self'" (Hearn 1992: 208).

A single epistemological trajectory of seeing masculinity as the other side of the "same coin" of femininity can sometimes manifest itself into universalizing a human relations science. Such polarized perceptions can be avoided if we take cognizance of Brennan's (1992) concept that femininity is found in both men and women, while at the same time keeping in mind that "masculinity ... is precariously achieved by the rejection of femininity ..." (Weeks 1985: 190), or Kimmel's (1994: 127) assertion that "masculine identity is born in the renunciation of the feminine". Whatever the variations by "race", class, age, ethnicity or sexual orientation, being a man means "not being like women" (Kimmel 1994: 126). The notion that masculinity has become an object, a receptacle or repository on to which everything that is not "feminine" gets projected, has been articulated, although not as yet sufficiently theorized. Historizing masculinities in a singular, binary and dualist way, in which the hierarchical positions of men are interpreted through the themes of domination, subordination and death, appears to resolve a part of the problematic of gender. This sort of dualism, says Ferguson (1993: 36), in *The Man Question*, "enables patriarchy to exist, the opposition of male/masculine and female/feminine, is reproduced and maintained". The replacement of men with women on this plane can lead to just a repositioning of the margins at the male ordered centre, thus not only reinforcing phallocentric discourses but also subverting the feminist enterprise of wanting gender justice.

The interrogation of patriarchy, masculinities and men by feminism, black consciousness philosophies, dis-ability texts and queer theory have been challenging the practice and transforming the conceptual ideas of men as man-agers in public and private spaces. These texts also collectively call into question the historical and moral "truths" which articulate the human condition beyond Western epistemologies of human development, but not without contradictions. For example, the interrogation by feminist theory, especially French feminist theory, seems to have achieved a fair degree of exposure and critique on dominant forms of masculinity, but in so doing has also offered contradictory and conflicting views on male sexuality and masculinity in general to the extent that everything male could be understood as the "bad object" (Seidler 1994). Seidler suggests that a pervasive "social constructionist" view is misguided in asserting that there is something "wrong", "defective" or "inadequate" in masculinity itself and that men can only be accepted if they forsake their masculinity. Whatever the complexities of the politics of gender and sexual identities, feminism and feminist theories, through their radical attempts at rewriting our cultural, historical and social texts, have not only created new forms of knowing but have reformulated the text-ualizations of the individual and collective unconscious.

The experience of multiple masculinity as: "sets of practices which in varying degrees contribute to the maintaince and reproduction of patriarchial systems" (Morgan 1992: 70), a "homosocial enactment" (Kimmel 1994), a "psychosocial dialectic" (Herdt 1982) or a psychocultural complex, while remaining elusive and ambiguous, is constructed by known spaces – cultural boundaries, specific geopolitical conditions and socio-economic environments. It is also within religiocultural, sociohistorical and geopolitical consciousness that men's split selves have maintained dominance and existence, occasionally (re)creating hegemonic masculinities (Connell 1987). Issacs and Poole (1996: 41) suggest that "masculinity is not the possession or non-possession of certain traits". They also cite Ramazanoglu (1992: 342), who comments that "the differences between men are greatly complicated by class, sexuality, 'race' and ethnicity and their inter-connections". Clearly, all of the above conceptions of masculinity "allow for diversity" and "not simply a given or provided for by biology but is something 'constructed' within particular social relationships" (Seidler 1994: 116).

It is clear that there is no natural selection theory that predisposes "man as man-ager", not even by default, through a masculine chromosome defect. Moreover, neither is there a universal masculine management "gene pool" waiting to be "inseminated" through corporate organizational or capitalist market culture. Indeed, even global national cultures themselves have a leaning towards being "masculine" or "feminine". For example, Hofstede's (1996: 256) research on national cultures (50 countries) on the masculinity versus femininity dimension found that the most masculine country was Japan and that the Nordic countries were most feminine, with all the others "in-between". He argues that "the naive assumption that management is the same or is becoming the same around the world is not tenable in view of these demonstrated difference in national cultures". Schein et al. (1996: 39), also remind us that "research supports the view that 'think manager – think male' is a global phenomena, especially among males . . . despite the many historical and cultural differences that exist".

In attempting to articulate the significance of the convergence of masculinities and management, I am aware that we could easily fall prey to globalizing notions in the same way as management is often universalized. Indeed, any attempt at an alternative epistemology and its critical interruption will always be illusory and temporary, yet arguably essential continuously to highlight the gender inequalities in the workplace.

Multiple masculinities/multiple managers

Multiple masculinities (Hearn 1987, Brittan 1989, Kerfoot and Knights 1993, Collinson and Hearn 1994, Kvande and Rasmussen 1994), and the notion of "plurality of masculinities" (Kerfoot and Knights 1993), are attempts to find a meaningful epistemology for the complexity of the male gender experience both in public and private spaces. This multilayered construction of the masculine subject which engages men as men, men as boys and men as women, while not always visible, is produced through "signifying practices" (Foucault 1980). If one accepts that masculinity itself is a site of deconstruction (Braidotti 1994), and is particularly demonstrable in contemporary managerial practices where the public sphere of management interactions are shadowed with the private "self" of the subject, then it is possible to unravel some of the complexities of men (women) as managers. Thus are particular identities, behaviours and attitudes reflecting themselves in multiple ways: "authoritarianism, paternalism, entrepreneurialism, informalism and careerism" (Collinson and Hearn 1994: 13).

Multiple masculinities at the management site could also be understood in terms of men's relationship with each other and with the "other": women, ethnic minorities and the dis-abled. Theunissen (1984: x) argues that "there is a strong tradition in Western thought – stretching back to Hegel, Schelling, and beyond – according to which the linkage between I and Other is not a relation of exclusivity but one of mutual dependence". Cixous (1986/1992: 147) also reminds us that that "there is no invention possible . . . without there being in the inventing subject an abudance of the other". Spivak (1988), in a feminist, Marxist, deconstructivist, "third world voice", reminds us of the "epistemic violence of the imperialist project" which positions the "other" as an historically mutated subject (see Parry 1987). Said (1978: 1–2) also contends that "the Orient has helped to define Europe (or the West) as its contrasting image, idea, personality, experience . . . supporting institutions, vocabulary, scholarship, imagery, doctrines . . .".

However, the thesis that men and masculinities are constituted through their relationship with the many and various "others" can be problematic, since the "other", epistemologically and conceptually, like masculinities, is complex and not fully examined especially at work and in organizational discourses. Since the "other" is not privileged but remains marginal and multiple, it gives rise to "the manager as problematic". In other words, the theory and practice of man(aging) and man(agement) is perceived to be "real", historical and profound, as opposed to the affective, irrational and vulnerable "self" which occupies the "other" space in the workplace. Seidler (1994: 19) suggests that "with the identification of masculinity with reason, men become the protectors of and the gatekeepers for this dominant vision of modernity". This has profound implications in the face-to-face relationships of men (and women) through management and managerial practices, especially with the "other", where masculine projections of "otherness" may be displayed and displaced in multiple ways, often resulting in much anxiety and work-related stress disorders. These issues are developed later in the chapter.

The "other" then becomes the catalyst for masculinity to demonstrate its multiplicity, versatility and its ability to (re)create itself in a state of continuous articulation, moving in and out of historical, cultural and social time and space. It does this by changing the borders and borderlines of sexual and gender identities, and eventually by transforming itself into the "other" if necessary. And here I am not just alluding to the ability of men (women) managers to speak for the "other" or in the voice of the "other", but to experience a cultural and political metamorphosis of the oppressed "other". These managers are able to demonstrate a degree of empathy with the "other" which can only be achieved with the ranks of the disadvantaged and marginalized "other". What was once an impossibility in terms of emotional identification of the "other" has now been transgressed by the stereotypically cold, unemotional and rational manager. There seems to be a trend amongst the "new man"-agers to engage in this kind of pastoral and humanistic role.

Clearly, it seems that contemporary managerial practices, by adopting strategies such as psychological counselling and therapeutic supervision, are placing the "welfare of the individual" within the context of the organization. Another strategy yet is added to this multiple repertoire of inter- and intrapersonal skills: some managers are engaging in so-called "community consciousness raising", i.e. engaging at a personal level in the cultural, geopolitical and socioeconomic environments of the "other" as strategies of multiple man-agement styles. Moreover, although the evidence is anecdotal, it seems that some managers have now taken up another new hobby, "reading" metaphysical poetry, as a way of enhancing their multiple role in the organization.

Managerial/masculine masks

Torrington (1991: 1, 235), suggests that the "most significant events in organisations hinge on managers' competence in working face-to-face . . . in a range of interactive episodes with a variety of other people". It is through this physical, emotional and psychological "face-to-face" relating that management tends to produce and reproduce the organization's culture and ethos, as well as its pathology. However, the differing styles of men (women) in management suggest that they bring to it a very personal dimension beyond any stereotype management profile, but one that is embedded in the individual man-ager's social, cultural, historical and political make-up. Within a given moment and movement in an organization's life, a manager's behaviour may reflect the complex and sometimes confused way in which human psychosocial development is constituted and comprehended. According to Rosenbaum and Garfield (1996: 294):

> Representations of self and other may be displaced or shunted to the level of fantasy, and if these are equally chaotic then the displacement will continue through to physiological symptoms and moods in affective–perceptual dimension.

These forms of behaviour could also be displayed in the symbiotic personas of management "tribes", where each individual of the management team takes on a different but complementary role. For example, where a middle manager relates aggressively and demands increased productivity in an environment of diminishing resources, the senior manager's behaviour with the same staff shifts to the other end of the interpersonal spectrum – the staff are offered empathy, consideration, and offers of material and psychological support.

Such performances of changing patterns of behaviour or "theatre of masks" are becoming the norm not only at the managerial level but also at the organizational level. An example of this is the EAP (Employee Assisted Programme) that is being instituted across both the public and private sectors for management and workers alike (Wise 1988, Feltham 1997). In this programme, employees are offered counselling and therapy for stress-related concerns. The source of the distress is focused on the domestic and family environments rather than within the organization, where the real cause of these disturbances often lies. Invariably, there is a tension between the values and philosophy of the organization, the counsellor – who is paid by the organization – and the employee (Bond 1992, McLeod 1993). Clearly, this seems to be what the modern managerial practices are advocating; "compassion with a hard edge". Such perverse qualifiers demonstrate, time and time again, the ability of "new man"-agers to constitute and reconstitute themselves in relation to the "other" without exploring its contradictions.

The "other" – women, ethnic minorities, the dis-abled, and gay and other subordinate men – quite often experience these multiple displays of management as projections which they may internalize or ward off. As hegemonic masculinities, they are displaced as "otherness" – sexism, discrimination, aggression and harassment – leading to "acts" of psychological and physical abuse and violence. For example, anger may have a distinct role in supervisor–subordinate relations (Glomb and Hulin 1997: 284), as an information function (De Rivera 1977) or as a policing function (Tavris 1982). Anger, which has received very little attention in organizational literature (Begley 1994: 503), is reported to be a major factor that produces abusive bosses (Dumaine 1993, cited by Begley). Begley also notes that multiple forms of anger exist in the workplace, some of which may be healthier than others. Sexual harassment also continues to be a problem that plagues organizations (Gutek 1985, Pryor and McKinney 1995, Pierce and Aguinis 1997).

There are other masks – the "new man" ager, the liberated man-ager, the anima[2] manager and so on – which may be dis-played. The actors in this theatre are seen as a never ending masquerade, a parody, a carnival of masculinities acting out at the intersubjective level the full range of emotions and behaviours. A repetition of different and diverse aspects of the masculine/managerial self is dis-played and at the same time disguised through the metaphor of the mask. The managerial scene becomes a centre point, a common ground for the display of the repertoire of the globalized entrepreneurial philosophy. This metaphor of the mask creates a temporary illusion of a mutual and symbiotic interaction of the socio-economically constructed subject. The masculine masquerade in turn renders the "other" as invisible to the candidature of management and managerial discourses.

Some man-agers have responded to these challenges by learning to articulate in the "voice" of the "other" and adapt feminist contexts in an empathetic way to masculine discourses. In other words, they have adapted their behaviours to do the right thing with political correctness. It is easier for men to speak in the terms of the "other" than to explore their feelings as men, because they have historically been speaking for the "other" in a "supposedly neutral and impartial language of reason" (Seidler 1989: 3). The versatility of masculinity to masquerade as the "new man" or the unbecoming man in equal opportunity dress demonstrates the ability of masculinity to shift in and out of its borders and to change its borderlines to meet the requirements of the "other", creating the illusion that the organization is asexual, non-racial, classless and so on. Hearn (1998: 3) reminds us that:

... the power of sexuality in organisations is furthered by the frequent construction of organisations as asexual. In some, often male dominated, discourses, a situation or person can paradoxically become more sexual or more sexualised in the presence of asexual signifiers or asexual contexts.

The binary arrangement of "I" and the "other" is subverted by masculinities in which the "Man"ichean Mask[3] is dis-played and dis-placed at the same time.

In attempting to decipher the idea of "dis-placement through the mask", masculinities are seen as a series of repressed parts of the "self", dis-placed (projected) on to the "other" in order to become "known" (assimilated into consciousness). These projected parts are themselves fragmented and incomplete, and their displacement is constantly being repeated towards an imaginary unity of wholeness. Repetition and displacement do not exist in separate domains. They are interlinked and coexist. For example, we now hear of the compassionate, caring and empathetic (masks of) "man"-agerial practices undertaken by the "new man"-ager who can produce certificates of achievement in counselling and equal opportunities training. A person-centred approach is engraved not only in the public text-ualization of mission statements, but "new man"-agers are "on the walk about", with an enhanced "physical" presence in the workplace. This supervisory strategy by managers, using private spaces to display their affective mask as a shared human experience in a caring climate, is on the increase. Very personal and private stories are exchanged in these spaces.

The managerial/masculine mask is an interface in a dynamic elliptical form, which appears to be constantly shifting, changing and man-ifesting a modernist metamorphosis, a necessary transformation. For, in the process, it releases the repression of guilt for having "power" over the "other". Men (women) managers can now legitimately express their affective masks through the use of particular vocabularies of the "feminine". For Lechte (1996: 19):

> ... the repressed, which can never appear directly in language (for language is symbolic, and the repressed is real), always takes on a mask-like quality. The mask as a virtual object, is also always displaced. The repressed, unable to appear directly in symbolic form, therefore becomes a mask.

This repetition then displaces its self on to the "other". However, since its displacement is partial and repeats itself constantly, in a masturbatory fashion, like masks upon masks, superimposed one on top of another, it could never find any real form to assimilate the "loss" and therefore remains a mask. Masculinities clearly, then, appears to be the signifier and the signified at the same time as the symbolic mask facing the "other". The "new man"-agement cycle continues through hi(s)tory – in repression, repetition, displacement, discovery – in a never ending story of an unfinished "man"-u-script.

Autobiographical notes

The (re)entry into the texts of masculinity/managerial discourses could only be partial and fragmented, splitting the gendered text through insertions, hyphens and inverted commas or through other forms of grammatical punctuation, thus creating new pauses and neologisms which challenge masculine epistemologies and the "Law of the Father" (Lacan 1977). The use of a particular set of vocabularies, the Law of the (m)Other, as it were, re-textualizes the voices of women, blacks, dis-abled, gay and lesbians as an authentic discourse of gender politics on its own term(minologie)s, attempting to reject logocentric assumptions of rationality which reinforce the "female malady" (Showalter 1985) as normal. So, like the feminist, I have adopted in this chapter a particular set of vocabularies including multiple parentheses and hyphenations prompted in a timely fashion by singular pauses, not to seek a unity of wholeness of the subject but to find a new form(ulation) in an attempt to under-stand the fragmented, dis-placed and dis-guised faces of masculinity. I do this with a cautionary note that some of the so-called subversive vocabularies[4] of the "other" are themselves "robes of masculinities" in disguise.

The unmasking, then, in relation to feminism and feminities, in relation to gay and other subordinate men and to the subordinate "other" – in terms of "race", dis-ability and class – has constantly reminded me of the phallocentric ideas which dominate such an analysis of masculinities. For, in so doing, it has constructed masculinities as a dialectic between masculine strategies for creativeness and its allied and opposite number, the agency of aggression. I felt that this was an important analysis to undertake in trying to understand the various masculine masks that I experienced in management, particularly by those who masqueraded as "the boss" (my experiences in apartheid South Africa remind me that "boss" meant Bureau of State Security, from which I escaped in good time, but many did not), and their masks in relation to the "other". Another reason to engage in this exploration is my failure to make sense of the sophisticated strategy of the so-called new man-agers making their claim to modernity as the "new man" or as the unbecoming man in equal opportunities dress. These modernist men at the same time engage in the absolute negative masculinity, the agency of aggression, sometimes in violent ways.

I was also concerned to understand myself and the "other" colleagues, black like myself, who had internalized this masculine agency and were behaving in the stereotypical way of "being better than the best"; that is, to be more aggressive than the white male manager. This latter "projective identification" with the aggressor seems to be growing amongst many ethnic minority colleagues in management. One senior black education advisor was informed by black (and some white) women teachers that the few black (and some white) female managers in the department have dis-played aggressive forms of behaviour towards them in and out of manage-ment situations (personal communication). The representative figure of this perversion may also be understood in Kleinian (1985) psychoanalytical terms, as a projection of the internalized "bad object". In other words, some of these black managers, having internalized the negative stereotype of Otherness, identify with the white male aggressor by dis-playing and dis-placing the "Man"ichean Mask.

I am left wondering whether the complexities and contradictions of the masculinized management condition have differential effects on risk for health, particularly for the "other". Understood in relation to the job-strain theory (Karasek and Theorell 1990), "chronic exposure to high levels of job demands is associated with increased risk of health problems, especially in the absence of job control" (Barnett and Brennan 1997: 254). On the other hand, Lowe and Northcott (1988) suggest that gender has little effect on the relationship between job stressors and psychological distress. "There has been little conscious conceptual thinking . . . when dealing with the effects of both organisational hierarchy and racial dynamics within an organisation" (Alderfer and Tucker 1996: 45). Landu (1995) also notes that there are very few studies that have considered the interaction of "race" and gender in management. For example, Pettigrew and Martin (1987) talk about "triple jeopardy": negative racial stereotyping; the solo role, being the only black person in the group; and the token role, attaining a position through a particular affirmative action.

To return to my narrative at the place of the "other", my appointment as the Programme Area Manager of Access to Higher Education and later as the Assistant Director–Research and Development was surrounded by the marginality of "middleness" in communication with colleagues. As the only black middle manager – indeed, the only black senior member at the time – I was reminded of playing out the metaphor of Fanon's (1967) "Black Skin, White Masks". It seems that I was acting out the "desires" and "wishes" of the all male senior management project(ion)s and that meaning was only derived as Fanon (1967: 134–5) argued:

> . . . it is not I who make a meaning for myself, but it is the meaning that is already there, pre-existing, waiting for me . . . waiting for that turn of history. The dialectic that brings necessity into the foundation of my freedom drives me out of myself.

This made me realize that my subjectivity and that of the other two black colleagues (in the college) who were in my section had dis(embodied) ourselves through this particular management project(ions). The challenge, as feminism so clearly points out, was a rewriting of my male text, subtext and context. One way in which this may be achieved in Biko's (1978: 30) words was "to seek a sense of positivity and a oneness of community" in a "frank talking" way (see Moodley 1998).

I started on a process of beginning to de-idealize aspects of my masculinity, at the same time remembering Strathern's (1995: 54) words:

> . . . idealised masculinity is not necessarily just about men; it is not necessarily just about relations between the sexes either.

Clearly, for me it was about attempting to understand the fear of conventional "self", male, fragmentation that preceeds this kind of exploration/transformation. I began to resent and resist the mannerisms and "strategic plans" of the male colleagues in their roles as new managers. Kerfoot and Whitehead's (1998) research established that "the discourse of new managerialism in FE is constant with, and constitutive of, a form of masculinity that achieves validation through control and power of others". In her research of new management in FE, Leonard (1998: 78) reports that "not only was the management style viewed as unquestioningly masculine, but the shift reflected a patriarchal exercise to reconfirm men's rightful location in the upper sections of the power structure" (see also Whitehead 1999). The only escape I had from the realism of this structure was to enter my own subjectivity and practice: teaching non-traditional adults. From this point I began a journey of becoming a "profeminist man" while at the same time taking into account the critique of black womanists. In fact, it was this "metaphysics of presence" that at times caused my management mask to slip, exposing the ambivalence of my masculinity.

When the mask slips it seems that a form of re-ordering takes place, even if it is momentary. The ambivalent moment of difference when the mask slips allows for a shift in the traditional managerial persona and the ambiguity of masculinities. For example, as a result of unconscious guilt feelings relating to their roles as "powerful" leaders and decision-makers, some men managers were finding release in a number of ways. One transformed his vocabulary and communication into "race" and feminist PC (political correctness) speak, another demonstrated feelings more openly, and yet another engaged with women and blacks in a supportive "trusteeship" way. Relating in this way, masculinities sometimes seemed to lose the dimension of power and simply signify plurality or diversity (Brod 1994: 86). In talking of "men", "masculinity" and "masculinities", it is particularly important to continually contextualize the discussion in power and power relations (Hearn and Collinson 1994: 97), especially since men have come to see power as a capacity to impose control on others . . . [the] domination of men over women (Kaufman 1994: 145–6).

While these men managers found release outside themselves, there were some who suppressed and internalized their feelings. It seems that their physical bodies engaged in a search for some meaningful understanding to the received notions of what it was to be a male in management in the changing climate of further education. This search for an equilibrium of "self", based on logical assumptions of everything being "straight"-forward and not at the "edge of chaos", is man-ifested through men's psychomatic systems. One senior manager's body appeared to act as a conduit for the "collective unconscious" of the management team. In attempting to find meaning of the slipping of his masks, he underwent major heart surgery within three months of having one of his kidneys removed. And this was not the end of the internalization: just before he retired, he was being examined for "spots" on his lungs. It seems that this mask slipping embodies the psychopathologies that are not just confined to the "brain/mind" but affect the "other" organs; for example, the stomach, heart, lungs and skin become sites for transformation – an acting-out (in) of the "physicalization of the body" (Smith 1985).

Another manager who through reorganization had lost his "section chair", literally as well, since he was requested to move office, and needed surgery to remove "a spot, a lump, a small blip" (personal communication) from his (gastro-intestinal system) body. The kneecaps (muscular skeletal structure) became the focus of another manager and the genito-urinary tract, another. Since the body is always imagined and constitutive of the sociohistorical and religiocultural specificity of masculinity, such psychosomatic conditions become all the more "real" when experienced in masculine organizations. Many man-agers, it seems, resort to surgery, making sure of the removal of the affected part of the body in the hope that their managerial/masculine mask will remain intact. There are of course "complex reasons behind psychological ill health at work . . . [and] . . . between the psychology of the self and the psychology of the organisation" (Walsh 1996: 15). Fulcheri et al. (1995: 3) suggest that "managers are suffering extreme physiological symptoms from stress at work, such as disabling ulcers or coronary heart diseases, which force them to retire prematurely from active work" (see also Cooper and Melhuish 1980, 1984).

The institution began to see these scenes of recovery or, rather, the myths of masculinity re-dramatized – "man" falls and is then resurrected, with a more aggress-ive behaviour for living (for work). For example, some of these men managers now talk of being "compassionate with a hard edge": pity and sympathy is not on offer, but empathy is extended to workers' communications because of their emotional and death-bed experiences. Indeed, this strategy is one that prevents the loss of masculinities, which could lead to death. In some cases the embracing of positive and negative masculinities may lead to management creativeness. This, of course, is supported by the traditional process of the old-boy "network of influence", in which the "gatekeeping" by dominant forms of masculinity establishes the network that maintains the status, careers and continuity of itself. In such a reciprocal relationship, where the agency of mentors, role models and the old-boy network are a form of brotherhood solidarity, "the senior men identified their successors and then enabled their careers by mentoring and patronage" (Heward et al. 1995: 151).

On leaving the organization, the particular senior manager discussed above "brought in", and offered "custody" of the organization, a retired, white, male "col-league" from the local education authority, where both had worked previously. Within such a "system of patrilineal, primogenital ordering" (Collier 1995), the ques-tion of sponsors and mentors for the "boys" have clearly proved to be effective at this particular institution. Masculinity itself became a performance of dominance (Conway-Long 1994), in which "the 'gatekeepers' are white men whose judgements are highly influential for reputations in the academic profession" (Heward et al. 1995: 152). The new incumbent, inexperienced in the management practices of further education, began to lead a multimillion-pound, major inner-city institution, serving a large multi-ethnic community. At the same time, the organization began to reflect the tensions and anxieties which resulted from the Thatcherite policies that had swept the country during the previous decade (see Ainley and Bailey 1997). At this institution and many others like it, we began to see particular styles of management putting professional ethics, workers' rights, trade union law and, in some cases, the infringement of civil and human rights under tension.

Some of the women managers whom I felt were "left of centre" at this institu-tion had (intentionally) mimicked some of these masculine behaviours in order to reach the "glass ceiling". Moi (1985: 135) sums up Irigaray's thoughts about women managers who find themselves in this impossible situation. She indicates that since women are caught in the specular logic of patriarchy, a woman can choose either to remain silent or to enact the specular representation of herself as a lesser male. The

226

latter option, the woman as mimic, is, according to Irigaray, a form of hysteria. The hysteric mimes her own sexuality in a masculine mode, since this is the only way in which she can rescue something of her own desire. Women who achieve senior rank usually resemble men in their personality and behaviour characteristics (Grant 1988, Rosner 1990). In some cases, where women have internalized the negative project(ion) of male desire (i.e. absolute aggression towards their own sex), they have shown forms of behaviour which appear as "raw" masculinities. This display is beyond the mimicry of "the hysteric" but is an enactment of a mis-conception of aggressive masculinities projected in the form of the feminine "animus mask",[5] sometimes with such emotional tension that the deep layers of "self" are exploded at the surface. Within the context of new management skills of empathetic face-to-face relating, this form of communication may be experienced by the "other" as something primitive and arising from a fossilized history – a protolinguistic mask. The college becomes the therapy room for such dysfunctional and pathologized women man-agers, who draw on deeply embedded internalized aggression and project it on to the unsuspecting "other".

Thus the dominant masculine drama was being played out to its fullest extent in this FE college. Over a period of 18 months, the entire senior management team – with one exception – took early retirement or found jobs elsewhere. My own position became untenable. My masculine/managerial masks were slipping, offering no space for the hybridity of the traditional schemas of management roles. I appealed to the "other" sociopolitical construct – "race" – which often provided strength in management trials and tribulations. To legislate from this form of identity (subjectivity) was to speak with a fractured voice, because the very presence of black managers in Eurocentric institutions is riddled with contradictions and paradoxes. For example, the experience of black men managers asserting blackness may often go hand-in-hand with asserting "male"-ness.[6] The black masculinist project in this instance may also be informed by the sociopolitical and ethnic cultural histories of black men before and after colonization, migration and Europeanization. In this, the black manager is required to occupy two spaces, two identities: articulating a form of masculinized "blackness" and a "not-black feminized" identity at the same time. Heward et al. (1995: 155), in their study of gender and race in the academic profession, found an "invisibility of members of minority ethnic groups in the academic profession . . . [particularly] . . . in senior posts". Thus, a black man-ager working in these schizoid positions may "act out" the "mask of madness", thereby reinforcing eighteenth-century perceptions of women (Showalter 1985) and blacks (Thomas and Sillen 1972, Gilman 1985) as inherently mad.

One way to avoid the ambivalence and ambiguity, I felt, was to take up the offer of voluntary severance, leaving the institution after eight creative and politically fulfilling years. At this time, the institution also lost the services of other middle managers and many staff, including a number of black staff. Was this the result of just the "old-boy network" myth manifesting itself to control modernity, or was it reflecting something deeper, in the way in which a group of men collectively – perhaps unconsciously – expressed their hegemony. Morgan (1992) argues that these particular sets of practices of masculinity maintain and reproduce patriarchal systems.

I am inclined to believe that these are just slipped masks of the subject intertwined in the dangerous hybrid space of aggression and identity.

Conclusion

A critical descent into the text-uality of gender and sexual identities in management discourses will not be "straight", deep or complete. Nor will it articulate an analysis that privileges particular individuals or groups who inhabit these spaces. Clearly, the limitations are not just confined to the temporality and fluidity of the "other" subordinate discourses – "race", class, dis-ability and sexuality – but are also problematized through the entry and re-entry into the (auto)biographies, histographies, ethnographies, sociographies and so on, of men (and women) in management and managerial discourses. The greatest constraint lies in the use of methodologies of the "Law of the Father". However, the pluralization of "valid" ontologies in recent times have led to greater transparency in the sharing of emotions, feelings and behaviours in the public domain of private narratives. This process, it seems, has made it possible for the exploration of alternative epistemologies to be constructed in examining masculinities and management. Therefore, any attempt to find a palimpsest to un-cover, re-cover or dis-cover the hidden text and sub-texts of the behaviours and actions of management will be fluid, elusive and ambiguous, in the same way in which multiple mask/ulinities are projected on to the "other".

Although the metaphor of the mask is an illusory spectacle – ambiguous and ambivalent – it does, however, engage us with the unrepresentable signifiers of masculinities. In other words, the masked "man"-ager enters the space and time of the "carnival" (Bakhtin 1984), where everything is turned upside down for the "therapeutic" dis-placement and re-placement of our multiple selves. Frosh (1989: 241–3) notes that the potential joy of multiplicity can be obscured by threat and terror:

> ... the terror of dissolution, the terror of disappearance and the threat of disintegration in the face of a fragmentary world ... Because of the fantasies of femininity and of ethnic otherness (particularly blackness) that are ideologically sanctioned in a society partly structured around oppositions of gender and race, these become the carriers of the threat to the safety of the psyche.

In management practices especially, the masquerading of multiple masculinities makes visible in the full gaze of the "other" the desires of masculine hegemony and hubris into which employees, employers and organizations are seduced. Those masculinities, which are always taken for granted, hidden, unexamined, sustained, reproduced and privileged in management practices, as a result of the disavowal of the "other", are unearthed to question the authenticity of the "man"-ager as the fountain head and "guru" of "all knowledge" pertaining to the private and public spheres.

228

Acknowledgements

I thank Stephen Whitehead, Deborah Kerfoot and Anissa Talahite for helpful comments on an earlier draft of this paper. I also thank Jim Fitzgerald for the stimulating discussions on masculinity and psychoanalysis.

Notes

1. Fitzgerald (1995), through a Jungian analysis, places the "father–son encounter" at the centre of the masculine construction. See also Connell (1994) for a discussion on the Freudian analysis of masculinity in the case study of the "Rat Man", the "Wolf Man" and the Oedipus complex.
2. "Anima" indicates the presence of femininity in masculinity and "animus" indicates the presence of masculinity in femininity: see Jung (1982). See also Connell (1994) for critical discussion of these terms.
3. The "Man"ichean Mask suggests a binary non-dialectical interface at which the symbolic, imaginary and the metaphoric fields/schemas of masculinity are interchangable with the "other".
4. In deciphering the language of the "other" and then claiming it for themselves, these theoretical drag queens don the trappings of femininity for a night on the town without so much as a glance back at the poor woman whose clothes they have stolen (Moore 1988: 185). This may be understood in the context of Lacanian Phallus where "the feminine is seen as full of subversive energy and excitement, but as having no agency and nothing to say . . . it slumbers, speaking only as something which is absent" (Frosh 1994: 71).
5. See note 2 above.
6. See Mac An Ghaill's (1994) study, illustrating the multiple determination of power in the interplay between a state institution, racism and the cultural formations of a black masculine identity.

References

Ainley, P. and Bailey, B. (1997) *The Business of Learning* London: Cassell

Alderfer, C. P. and Tucker, R.C. (1996) "A field experiment for studying race relations embedded in organizations", *Journal of Organizational Behavior*, **17**, pp. 43–57

Bakhtin, M.M. (1984) *Rabelais and His World* Bloomington, Ind.: Indiana University Press

Barnett, R.C. and Brennan, R.T. (1997) "Change in job conditions, change in psychological distress, and gender: a longitudinal study of dual-earner couples", *Journal of Organizational Behavior*, **18**, 3, pp. 253–74

Begley, T.M. (1994) "Expressed and suppressed anger as predictors of health complaints", *Journal of Organizational Behavior*, **15**, pp. 503–16

Bhabha, H.K. (1994) *The Location of Culture* London: Routledge

Biko, S. (1978) *I Write what I Like* Stubbs, A. (ed.) London: Heinemann

Bond, T. (1992) "Ethical issues in counselling in education", *British Journal of Guidance and Counselling*, **20**, pp. 51–63

Braidotti, R. (1994) "Of bugs and women: Irigaray and Deleuze on the Becoming-Woman", in Burke, C., Schor, N. and Whitford, M. (eds) *Engaging with Irigaray: Feminist Philosophy and Modern European Thought* New York: Columbia University Press

Brennan, T. (1992) *The Interpretation of the Flesh: Freud and Femininity* London: Routledge

Brittan, A. (1989) *Masculinity and Power* Oxford: Blackwell

Brod, H. (1987) *The Making of Masculinities: the New Men's Studies* Boston: Allen & Unwin

Brod, H. (1994) "Some thoughts on some histories of some masculinities: Jews and other others". See Brod and Kaufman (1994), pp. 82–95

Brod, H. and Kaufman, M. (eds) (1994) *Theorizing Masculinities* Thousand Oaks, Calif.: Sage

Chapman, R. and Rutherford, J. (eds) (1988) *Male Order: Unwrapping Masculinity* London: Lawrence & Wishart

Cixous, H. (1986/1992) "Sorties", in Easthope, A. and McGowan, K. (eds) *A Critical and Cultural Theory Reader* Buckingham: Open University Press, pp. 146–57

Cockburn, C. (1985) *Machinery of Dominance: Women, Men and Technical Know-how* London: Pluto Press

Collier, R. (1995) *Masculinity, Law and the Family* London: Routledge

Collinson, D.L. (1992) *Managing the Shopfloor: Subjectivity, Masculinity and the Workplace Culture* Berlin: de Gruyter

Collinson, D.L. and Hearn, J. (1994) "Naming men as men: implications for work, organization and management", *Journal of Gender, Work and Organization*, **1**, 1, pp. 2–22

Connell, R.W. (1987) *Gender and Power* Cambridge: Polity Press

Connell, R.W. (1994) "Psychoanalysis on masculinity". See Brod and Kaufman (1994), pp. 11–37

Conway-Long, D. (1994) "Ethnographies and masculinities". See Brod and Kaufman (1994), pp. 61–81

Cooper, C.L. and Melhuish, M.B. (1980) "Occupational stress and managers", *Journal of Occupational Medicine*, **22**, 9, pp. 588–92

Cooper, C.L. and Melhuish, M.B. (1984) "Executive, stress and health: differences between men and women", *Journal of Occupational Medicine*, **26**, 2, pp. 99–104

De Rivera, J. (1977) "A structural theory of emotions", *Psychological Issues*, **10**, Monograph 40 New York: International University Press

Dumaine, B. (1993) "America's toughest bosses", *Fortune*, October, **18**, 18+

Fanon, F. (1967) *Black Skins, White Masks* Trans. C.L. Markmann New York: Grove Press

Feltham, C. (1997) *The Gains of Listening: Perspectives on Counselling at Work* Buckingham: Open University Press

Ferguson, K.E. (1993) *The Man Question: Visions of Subjectivity in Feminist Theory* Berkeley: University of California Press

Fitzgerald, J. (1995) *The Father's Shadow and the Source of the Masculine* London: Guild of Pastoral Psychology and Colmore Press

Fondas, N. (1997) "Feminization unveiled: management qualities in contemporary writings", *Academy of Management Review*, **22**, 1, pp. 257–82

Foucault, M. (1980) *Power/Knowledge* Gordon, C. (ed.) Brighton: Harvester

Frosh, S. (1989) "Psychoanalysis and racism", in Richards, B. (ed.) *Crises of the Self* London: Free Association Books

Frosh, S. (1994) *Sexual Difference: Masculinity and Psychoanalysis* London: Routledge

Fulcheri, M., Barzega, G., Maina, G., Novara, F. and Ravizza, L. (1995) "Stress and managerial work: organisational culture and technological changes: a clinical study", *Journal of Management Psychology*, **10**, 4, pp. 3–8

Gherardi, S. (1995) *Gender, Symbolism and Organizational Cultures* London: Sage

Gilman, S.L. (1985) *Difference and Pathology: Stereotypes of Sexuality, Race, and Madness* Ithaca, NY: Cornell University Press

Glomb, T.M. and Hulin, C.L. (1997) "Anger and gender effects in observed supervisor–subordinate dyadic interactions", *Organizational Behavior and Human Decision Process*, **72**, 3, pp. 281–307

Grant, J. (1988) "Women as managers: What can they offer organizations?", *Organizational Dynamics*, **16**, 3, pp. 56–63

Gutek, B.A. (1985) *Sex and the Workplace: the Impact of Sexual Behavior and Harassment on Women, Men and Organizations* San Francisco, Calif.: Jossey-Bass

Harris, I.M. (1995) *Messages Men Hear. Constructing Masculinities* London: Taylor & Francis

Hearn, J. (1987) *The Gender of Oppression: Men, Masculinity and the Critique of Marxism* Brighton: Harvester

Hearn, J. (1992) *Men in the Public Eye: the Construction and Deconstruction of Private Men and Public Patriarchies* London: Routledge

Hearn, J. (1998) "On ambiguity, contradiction and paradox in gendered organizations", *Journal of Gender, Work and Organization*, **5**, 1, pp. 1–4

Hearn, J. and Collinson, D.L. (1994) "Theorizing unities and differences between men and between masculinities". See Brod and Kaufman (1994), pp. 97–118

Hearn, J. and Parkin, W. (1987) *"Sex" at "Work": the Power and Paradox of Organization Sexuality* Brighton: Wheatsheaf

Herdt, G.H. (1982) *Rituals of Manhood: Initiation in Papua New Guinea* Berkeley: University of California Press

Heward, C., Taylor, P. and Vickers, R. (1995) "What is behind Saturn's Rings?: methodological problems in the investigation of gender and race in the academic profession", *British Educational Research Journal*, **21**, 2, pp. 149–63

Hofstede, G. (1996) "The cultural relativity of organizational practices and theories", in Billsberry, J. (ed.) *The Effective Manager, Perspectives and Illustrations* London: Sage/Open University Press

Issacs, D. and Poole, M. (1996) "Being a man and becoming a nurse: three men's stories", *Journal of Gender Studies*, **5**, 1, pp. 39–47

Jukes, A. (1993) *Why Men Hate Women* London: Free Association Books

Jung, C.G. (1982) *Aspects of the Feminine* Princeton, NJ: Princeton University Press

Kandiyoti, D. (1991) "Islam and patriarchy: a comparative perspective", in Keddie, N.R. and Baron, B. (eds) *Women in Middle Eastern History: Shifting Boundaries in Sex and Gender* New Haven: Yale University Press

Karasek, R.A. and Theorell, T. (1990) *Healthy Work: Stress, Productivity and the Reconstruction of Working Life* New York: Basic Books

Kaufman, M. (ed.) (1987) *Beyond Patriarchy: Essays by Men on Pleasure, Power, and Change* Toronto: Oxford University Press of Canada

Kaufman, M. (1994) "Men, feminism, and men's contradictory experiences of power". See Brod and Kaufman (1994), pp. 142–63

Kerfoot, D. and Knights, D. (1993) "Management, masculinity and manipulation: from paternalism to corporate strategy in financial services in Britain", *Journal of Management Studies*, **30**, 4, pp. 659–79

Kerfoot, D. and Whitehead, S. (1998) "'Boys own' stuff: masculinity and the management of further education", *The Sociological Review*, **46**, 3, pp. 436–57

Kimmel, M. (1986) "Introduction: toward men's studies", *American Behavioral Scientist*, **29**, 5, pp. 517–29

Kimmel, M. (1994) "Masculinity as homophobia: fear, shame, and silence in the construction of gender identity". See Brod and Kaufman (1994), pp. 119–41

Kimmel, M. and Messner, M. (eds) (1989) *Men's Lives* New York: Macmillan

Klein, M. (1985) *The Writings of Melanie Klein* (4 volumes) London: Hogarth Press and the Institute of Psychoanalysis

Knights, D. and Murray, D. (1994) *Managers Divided. Organizational Politics and Information Technology Management* Chichester: John Wiley

Kvande, E. and Rasmussen, B. (1994) "Men in male-dominated organisations and their encounter with women intruders", *Scandinavian Journal of Management*, **10**, 2, pp. 163–73

Lacan, J. (1977) *Ecrits* Trans. A. Sheridan London: Routledge

Landu, J. (1995) "The relationship of race and gender to managers' ratings of promotion potential", *Journal of Organizational Behavior*, **16**, pp. 391–400

Lechte, J. (1996) "Editor's introduction: to Deleuze's Repetition for itself", in *Writing and Psychoanalysis, A Reader* New York: Arnold

Leonard, P. (1998) "Gendering change? Management, masculinity and the dynamics of incorporation", *Gender and Education*, **10**, 1, pp. 71–84

Lowe, G.S. and Northcott, H.C. (1988) "The impact of working conditions, social roles, and personal characteristics on gender differences in distress", *Work and Organization*, **15**, pp. 55–77

Mac An Ghaill, M. (1994) "The making of black English masculinities". See Brod and Kaufman (1994), pp. 183–99

McLeod, J. (1993) *An Introduction to Counselling* Buckingham: Open University Press

Middleton, P. (1992) *The Inward Gaze: Masculinity and Subjectivity in Modern Culture* London: Routledge

Moi, T. (1985) *Sexual/Textual Politics* London: Methuen

Moodley, R. (1998) "'I say what I like': frank talk(ing) in counselling and psychotherapy", *British Journal of Guidance and Counselling*, **26**, 4, pp. 495–508

Moore, S. (1988) "Getting a bit of the other: the pimps of postmodernism", in Chapman, R. and Rutherford, T. (eds) *Male Order* London: Lawrence & Wishart

Morgan, D. (1992) *Discovering Men: Sociology and Masculinities* London: Routledge

Morrison, E.W. and Robinson, S.L. (1997) "When employees feel betrayed: a model of how psychological contract violation develops", *Academy of Management Review*, **22**, 1, pp. 226–56

Nicholson, N. and West, M. (1996) "Men and women in transition", in Billsberry, J. (ed.) *The Effective Manager: Perspectives and Illustrations* London: Sage and Open University Press

Ozga, J. (ed.) (1993) *Women in Educational Management* Buckingham: Open University Press

Parry, B. (1987) "Problems in current theories of colonial discourse", *Oxford Literary Review*, **9**, 1&2

Pettigrew, T.F. and Martin, J. (1987) "Shaping the organizational context for black American inclusion", *Journal of Social Issues*, **43**, 1, pp. 41–78

Pierce, C.A. and Aguinis, H. (1997) "Bridging the gap between romantic relations and sexual harassment in organizations", *Journal of Organizational Behavior*, **18**, 3, pp. 197–200

Pryor, J.B. and McKinney, K. (eds) (1995) "Research advances in sexual harassment", *Basic and Applied Social Psychology* (special issue), **17**, 4

Ramazanoglu, C. (1992) "What can you do with a man? Feminism and the critical appraisal of masculinity", *Women's Studies International Forum*, **15**, 3, pp. 339–50

Rosenbaum, B. and Garfield, D. (1996) "Containers, mental space and psychodynamics", *British Journal of Medical Psychology*, **69**, pp. 281–97

Rosner, J.B. (1990) "Ways women lead", *Harvard Business Review*, **68**, 6, pp. 119–25

Said, E.W. (1978) *Orientalism* New York: Random House

Schein, E.H. (1965) *Organizational Psychology* Englewood Cliffs, NJ: Prentice Hall

Schein, V.E., Mueller, R., Lituchy, T. and Liu, J. (1996) "Think manager – think male: a global phenomenon", *Journal of Organizational Behavior*, **17**, 1, pp. 33–41

Seidler, V.J. (1989) *Rediscovering Masculinity: Reason, Language and Sexuality* London: Routledge

Seidler, V.J. (1994) *Unreasonable Men: Masculinity and Social Theory* London: Routledge

Showalter, E. (1985) *The Female Malady: Women, Madness, and English Culture, 1830–1980* London: Virago

Smith, E.W.L. (1985) *The Body in Psychotherapy* Jefferson, USA: McFarland

Spivak, G.C. (1988) "Can the subaltern speak?", in Nelson, C. and Grossberg, L. (eds) *Marxism and the Interpretation of Culture* London: Macmillan

Strathern, M. (1995) "Gender and identity in the New Guinea Highlands", in Faubion, J.D. (ed.) *Rethinking the Subject: an Anthology of Contemporary European Social Thought* Boulder, Col.: Westview Press

Tavris, C. (1982) *Anger: The Misunderstood Emotion* New York: Simon & Schuster

Theunissen, M. (1984) *The Other: Studies in the Social Ontology of Husserl, Heidegger, Sartre, and Buber* Berlin: Der Andere, trans. C. Macann (1977), Massachusetts Institute of Technology

Thomas, A. and Sillen, S. (1972) *Racism and Psychiatry* New York: Brunner/Mazel

Torrington, D. (1991) *Management – Face to Face* Hemel Hempstead: Prentice Hall

Walsh, S. (1996) "Adapting cognitive analytic therapy to make sense of psychologically harmful work environments", *British Journal of Medical Psychology*, **69**, pp. 3–20

Weeks, J. (1985) *Sexuality and its Discontents: Meanings, Myths & Modern Sexualities* London: Routledge & Kegan Paul

Whitehead, S. (1999) "From paternalism to entrepreneuralism: the experience of men managers in UK postcompulsory education", *Discourse: Studies in the Cultural Politics of Education*, **20**, 1

Wise, E.A. (1988) "Issues in psychotherapy with EAP clients", *Psychotherapy*, **25**, pp. 415–19

Index